Limpopo's Legacy

Related James Currey titles on South & Southern Africa

*South Africa. The Present as History: From Mrs Ples to Mandela &
Marikana*
John S. Saul & Patrick Bond

Liberation Movements in Power: Party & State in Southern Africa
Roger Southall

The New Black Middle Class in South Africa
Roger Southall

Mandela's Kinsmen: Nationalist Elites & Apartheid's First Bantustan
Timothy Gibbs

Women, Migration & the Cashew Economy in Southern Mozambique
Jeanne Marie Penvenne

*Remaking Mutirikwi: Landscape, Water & Belonging in Southern
Zimbabwe*
Joost Fontein

Writing Revolt: An Engagement with African Nationalism, 1957–67
Terence Ranger

Colonialism & Violence in Zimbabwe: A History of Suffering
Heike I. Schmidt

The Road to Soweto: Resistance & the Uprising of 16 June 1976
Julian Brown

*Markets on the Margins: Mineworkers, Job Creation & Enterprise
Development*
Kate Philip

*The War Within: New Perspectives on the Civil War in Mozambique,
1976–1992*
Eric Morier-Genoud, Michel Cahen & Domingos M. do Rosário (eds)

Township Violence & the End of Apartheid: War on the Reef
Gary Kynoch

Limpopo's Legacy

Student Politics &
Democracy in South Africa

Anne Heffernan

WITS UNIVERSITY PRESS

JAMES CURREY

James Currey
is an imprint of Boydell & Brewer Ltd
PO Box 9
Woodbridge, Suffolk IP12 3DF (GB)
www.jamescurrey.com
and of
Boydell & Brewer Inc.
668 Mt Hope Avenue
Rochester, NY 14620-2731 (US)
www.boydellandbrewer.com

Published in paperback in Southern Africa in 2019
(South Africa, Namibia, Lesotho, Zimbabwe & Swaziland)
by Wits University Press
1 Jan Smuts Avenue
Braamfontein
Johannesburg 2017
South Africa

British Library Cataloguing in Publication Data
A catalogue record for this book is available on request from the British Library
ISBN 978-1-84701-217-3 (James Currey cloth edition)
ISBN 978-1-77614-325-2 (Wits University Press)

The publisher has no responsibility for the continued existence or accuracy of
URLs for external or third-party internet websites referred to in this book, and
does not guarantee that any content on such websites is, or will remain, accurate or
appropriate

This book is printed on acid-free paper

Typeset in 10.5/12.5 Sabon with Myriad
by doubledagger.co.uk

Printed and bound in Great Britain by
TJ International Ltd, Padstow, Cornwall

For Mom and Dad, who always believed this was possible.

And for the generations of student protesters in South Africa, past and present, who have shaped history by reimagining the future.

Contents

Acknowledgements

All creative endeavours are collaborative, and perhaps this is especially true of historical monographs, which rely on the contributions of so many people. This book has been the work of many years, across countries and institutions; it bears the input of family, friends, colleagues, and, often, the kindness of strangers. It is beyond my capacity to list everyone here who contributed to it, in ways large and small. But there are those without whom it would not have been possible at all, who I must thank.

My family and friends in the United States believed this was possible even before I did. Their support and encouragement during what must have seemed an unending process has been unwavering. To the McGurns and Caves; the Jennings, Alessandros, Caraglianos, Boegels and Pizzos; the Heffernans and Cusacks; to Glynis McCorkle, the Lofaros, and the Porters: your love and support has gotten me here. Before I put pen to paper, Krisztina Schoeb, Nikki Barbeau, and Aliza Mamber quite literally gave me the words. The McDonough family generously gave me writing space when I was between countries and homes. Mom and Dad, thank you for giving me everything else.

This project began in 2010, when I arrived at Oxford University to begin my doctorate. My supervisor William Beinart guided it from its earliest stages – when all I knew was that I wanted to write about the history of Limpopo – and the finished product owes a great debt to his guidance. Along with William, Colin Bundy played a key role in deepening my knowledge of South Africa's past, and the late Jan-Georg Deutsch always prompted me to think beyond Limpopo's and South Africa's borders, and beyond my own comfort zone. From them I learned the skills of being both a scholar and a mentor. The influences of other scholars are also present here: Tim Scarnecchia, who introduced me to the study of Southern African history as an undergraduate; the late Terence Ranger, whose rigorous tutorials during my masters degree made a graduate student out of me; Nic Cheeseman, whose pragmatic advice on publishing has informed almost all of my work; Clive Glaser, Tshepo Moloi, and Dan Magaziner, whose work on student politics has informed my thinking about South Africa in the mid-twentieth century; and Peter Delius, Isaak Niehaus, and Sekibakiba Lekgoathi whose deep knowledge of Limpopo was my first introduction to the province.

While in Oxford I also benefited from the support of a cohort of friends, whose stimulation and encouragement kept me going when my energy flagged or the blank page overwhelmed: Khumisho Moguerane, Emma Lochery, Oliver Murphy, Liz Ramey, Michelle Sikes, Jason Robinson, Rouven Kunstmann, Zoe Marks, Julianne and Toni Weis, Justin Pearce, Jenny Molloy, Ben Winter, Hannah Christensen, Jenny Holden, Soohyun Lee, Amoghavarsha Mahadevegowda, Usha Kanagaratnam, Barbara Salas, Helen Pickford, Amy McLennan, and Florence Graham, thank you for cups of tea, for walks in the parks, for Wednesday afternoon seminars, and for long the evenings in the pub. So much of the thinking work of this project happened in those spaces. On the days when I didn't believe this was possible, you commiserated, and then persuaded me that it was. This wonderful group was assembled from my various Oxford communities: the History Faculty, the African Studies Centre, Jesus College, and the Sisters of the Sacred Heart student hostel at 11 Norham Gardens. These provided both intellectual and pastoral homes for the duration of my doctorate.

If Oxford is where the 'brain' of this project developed, its heart and its soul are situated firmly in South Africa. The research upon which this text is based would not have been possible without the tremendous generosity of the Ahmed family of Polokwane. Sattar, Shireen, Nazreen, and Amina – thank you for opening your family, your home, and your lives to me. You have made Polokwane my home, too.

In Johannesburg, the History Workshop at the University of the Witwatersrand provided me the space to take a doctoral thesis and turn it into a monograph. My colleagues there contributed so much to my knowledge of South and Southern African history and politics. The influences of Noor Nieftagodien, Arianna Lissoni, Tshepo Moloi, Julian Brown, and the late Phil Bonner enriched this book substantially, and I cannot imagine making it through the writing process without regular visits for advice to the offices of Franziska Rueedi, Faeeza Ballim, Zahn Gowar, and Antonette Gouws. Also at Wits, the Historical Papers Research Archive was a boundless source of inspiration and information. Gabi Mohale and Zofia Sulej made each of my visits to the archive there not only productive, but uplifting. Along with these friends, colleagues, and comrades, the friendship and support of so many in Joburg helped to make that enormous, exhausting, and exhilarating city mine: Joel Quirk and Stacey Sommerdyk; Khumisho Moguerane; Franziska Rueedi, Andile and Jama Magengelele; Michelle Hay; David Williams;

Matt Evans; Liz Fouksman and Andrew Saxe; Ryan Brown and Dhashen Moodley; Nicole Beardsworth and Micah Reddy; Nyonde Ntswana; Dineo Skosana; Sarah Godsell; Stuart Meyer and Hennie du Toit; and Faeeza and the entire Ballim-Ali family, thank you.

As anyone who has faced a blank page will know, writing can be a fraught process. To overcome the final hurdles of writing this manuscript, I left the hustle and bustle of Johannesburg for the mountain retreat of Clarens. Thank you to Karel Meyer and his team at Patcham Place B&B and to the whole crew at Highland Coffee, for providing good comfort, company, and caffeine during these weeks. And thank you to Noor and colleagues at the History Workshop for accommodating this time away from Wits.

In the transition from manuscript to book, Jaqueline Mitchell and her team at James Currey have been as supportive as I could hope, and the text has benefited greatly from the feedback of Colin Bundy, and two other anonymous readers for the press. Roshan Cader and colleagues at Wits Press are making preparations for the South African edition as I write these acknowledgements; I know it could not be in better hands there. I also owe special thanks to Dr Frances Jowell, for allowing the telex that is pictured on the UK cover to be reproduced from her mother's archive.

Aspects of this research have been funded by Jesus College, Oxford; the Beit Fund; the Andrew W. Mellon Foundation; and the University Research Committee of the University of the Witwatersrand. I am grateful for their financial support.

Finally, and most importantly, this project would never have come into being were it not for those whose stories are included in its pages. When William Beinart advised me to read about Turfloop and Onkgopotse Tiro in the early weeks of my PhD, he opened the door to a years-long fascination with the history of young people in northern South Africa. Generations of students from Limpopo have influenced – and continue to influence – political and social change in their communities, and in South Africa as a whole. Their legacies have sometimes been overshadowed by events in urban centres, but I hope this text goes some way to highlighting their importance for South Africa's history in the mid/late twentieth century. I must extend my profound gratitude to everyone who generously allowed me to interview them for this project. You brought this history alive for me, and I hope I have done justice to it here. Any mistakes that remain are, of course, my own.

Knoxville, Tennessee
July 2018

Abbreviations and Acronyms

AFM	Apostolic Faith Mission
ANC	African National Congress
ANCYL	African National Congress Youth League
APLA	Azanian People's Liberation Army
APLF	Azanian People's Liberation Front
ASM	African Students' Movement
AZAPO	Azanian People's Organization
AZASM	Azanian Students' Movement
AZASO	Azanian Students' Organization
BASA	Black Academic Staff Association (of the University of the North)
BCM	Black Consciousness Movement
BCMA	Black Consciousness Movement of Azania
BCMSA	Black Consciousness Movement of South Africa
BCP	Black Community Programmes
BLS	(University Colleges of) Botswana, Lesotho, and Swaziland
BOSS	Bureau of State Security
BPC	Black People's Convention
COPE	Congress of the People
COSAS	Congress of South African Students
COSATU	Congress of South African Trade Unions
CRIC	Community Resource Information Centre
EFF	Economic Freedom Fighters
FedSem	Federal Theological Seminary

FMF	*Frente de Libertação de Moçambique* (Mozambique Liberation Front)
FRELIMO	FeesMustFall
GSC	General Students Council (of SASO)
ICT	Inkatha Freedom Party
IFP	Institute of Contextual Theology
IUEF	International University Exchange Fund
MAYCO	Mankweng Youth Congress
MCA	Mankweng Civic Association
MDM	Mass Democratic Movement
MK	*Umkhonto we Sizwe* (The Spear of the Nation)
NEC	National Executive Council
NEUSA	National Education Union of South Africa
NGK	*Nederduitse Gereformeerde Kerk* (Dutch Reformed Church)
NUM	National Union of Mineworkers
NUSAS	National Union of South African Students
NYO	National Youth Organisation (sometimes also abbreviated as Nayo)
PAC	Pan Africanist Congress
PEYCO	Port Elizabeth Youth Congress
PWV	Pretoria–Witwatersrand–Vereeniging
REC	Regional Executive Council
RMF	RhodesMustFall
SACC	South African Council of Churches
SACP	South African Communist Party
SACTU	South African Congress of Trade Unions
SADF	South African Defence Force
SAP	South African Police
SASM	South African Students' Movement
SASO	South African Students' Organization
SANSCO	South African National Students' Congress
SASCO	South African Students' Congress

SAYCO	South African Youth Congress
SCA	Students' Christian Association
SCM	Students' Christian Movement
SEYO	Sekhukhune Youth Organization
SOYO	Soweto Youth Organization
SPA	Soweto Parents' Association
SRC	Students' Representative Council
SSRC	Soweto Students' Representative Council
STAC	Soweto Teachers' Action Committee
UBC	Urban Bantu Council
UCM	University Christian Movement
UDF	United Democratic Front
UNICON	University College of the North (uncommon abbreviation)
UNIN	University of the North (uncommon abbreviation)
UNISA	University of South Africa
WASA	Writers' Association of South Africa
ZCC	Zion Christian Church

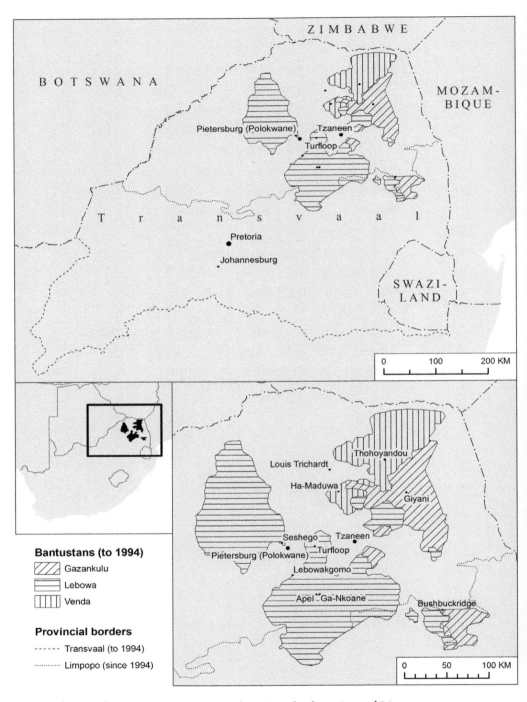

The north-eastern Bantustans showing the location of Limpopo

Introduction

The news broke first on Twitter: Just before six o'clock in the morning, on 28 September 2016, the University of Limpopo announced it was closing its gates in the face of student protests. All students were required to vacate their residences and to leave campus by five o'clock that afternoon, giving them just eleven hours to make plans for transport home – for some, in other provinces and even neighbouring countries – or to make alternative arrangements. By the afternoon a handful of journalists were snapping pictures of students lugging duffel bags and dragging suitcases down the roads of Mankweng township, making their way to taxi ranks that would take them on towards destinations as far afield in South Africa as the Eastern Cape, or across the northern border shared with Zimbabwe and Botswana. For many who could not afford the unexpected cost of the trip home the only shelter to be found was in the churches of Mankweng, which opened their doors to the students who had been displaced.

The university administration made the decision to indefinitely suspend all academic activities on the campus – colloquially known as Turfloop – to protect 'the safety and security of our students, staff, and University property'.[1] They did so in the context of national university protests during the second wave of FeesMustFall.

Slightly more than a week before Turfloop sent all of its students packing, an announcement about the future of funding universities in the country was met with an outpouring of protest across campuses. The plan, announced by the Minister of Higher Education Blade Nzimande, was, in fact, a direct response to weeks of protest and a national shutdown of South African universities in late 2015. In October of that year, students at the University of the Witwatersrand shut down their campus in protest at the rising cost of university fees; quickly the movement gained a hashtag: #FeesMustFall, and a national following. It also

[1] N.M. Mokgalong, 'Notice to All Students: Indefinite Suspension of All Academic Activities', tweeted from the official university twitter account, @ULvarsity 5:55am, 28 September 2016.

evolved beyond the issue of reducing fees to include calls for decolonizing South Africa's universities, and, eventually, a movement for free education. In a matter of days the students had pushed the issue beyond their individual universities, to the heart of government itself. On 23 October 2015 then President Jacob Zuma announced a 0% increase in fees for the 2016 academic year, effectively freezing fees at the 2015 rate. He also declared that the government would convene a commission to investigate existing fee structures and the possibility of implementing free education. Students across the country had won a major victory.

The form and substance of their struggle would inform important aspects of South African politics in the coming years, reaching the highest echelons of power. The work of the Commission of Inquiry into the Feasibility of making High Education and Training fee-free in South Africa (or the Heher Commission, as it is called for the judge who chaired it), took nearly two years to release its findings. It concluded that fee-free higher education in South Africa was neither feasible nor sustainable. The Heher Commission delivered its report to President Zuma in August 2017, and the office of the presidency released the findings to the public in November of that year.[2] But despite the commission's contention that fee-free university education was not sustainable,[3] a month after the public release of the report at the opening of the ANC's December 2017 National Conference in Soweto, President Zuma announced that higher education would be made fee-free for all students from families earning less than R350,000 per year, beginning in 2018.[4] Zuma's disregard of his own commission of inquiry's recommendation speaks to the political currency that the FeesMustFall movement had generated since late 2015. In the wake of the report's release, student wings of major opposition parties – the Economic Freedom Fighters and the Democratic

---

[2] Statement of the Presidency on the release of the Report of Commission of Inquiry into the Feasibility of making High Education and Training Fee-free in South Africa, 13 November 2017. [http://www.thepresidency.gov.za/press-statements/release-report-commission-inquiry-feasibility-making-high-education-and-training] Accessed 13 March 2018.

[3] The report did, however, advocate for fee-free structures to be put in place at TVET (Technical and Vocational Education and Training) Colleges. Bianca Capazorio, 'Heher Commission recommends all TVET students receive free education', *Times Live*, 13 November 2017. [https://www.timeslive.co.za/news/south-africa/2017-11-13-tvet-colleges-should-be-fee-free-heher-proposal/] Accessed 13 March 2018.

[4] 'Zuma announces free higher education for over 90% of students', 16 December 2017. [https://www.enca.com/south-africa/south-africa-to-increase-spending-on-higher-education-zuma] Accessed 13 March 2018.

Alliance – along with the ANC-aligned South African Students' Congress (SASCO) all rejected the Heher Commission's recommendations.[5]

When Nzimande announced the new funding plan for 2017 in mid-September 2016, the Heher Commission had not yet completed its work, and his announcement that universities would be able to determine their own fee increases, as long as they remained below 8% of current levels, was roundly rejected by students. They were not appeased by the fact that the new increases would only apply to those whose family income amounted to more than R600,000 annually, in an attempt to protect poor students and the so-called 'missing middle'[6] from the increase. Almost as soon as the words were out of Nzimande's mouth, the Wits campus reverberated with calls for another shutdown, and the speech sparked another round of nationwide campus protests.

The University of Limpopo was closed for a mid-term break during the week that Nzimande's announcement was made. As students at other universities resumed protests, all was quiet at Turfloop during the week of 19 September. When students returned to campus on Monday 26 September, however, they 'promptly joined' in the nationwide protests.[7] Over the course of that Monday and Tuesday, the campus was embroiled in running battles between students and security personnel – both with police from the nearby police station in Mankweng and with campus security. Six students were arrested on charges of public violence, for allegedly damaging university property and attempting to burn down a building.[8] On Tuesday, 27 September, the electricity to campus was cut off, including to the residences where students stayed. Some student leaders accused the administration of compromising student safety in

[5] 'Students react to fees commission report', 14 November 2017. [https://www.enca.com/south-africa/catch-it-live-sasco-reacts-to-fees-commission-report] Accessed 13 March 2018.

[6] The 'missing middle' became a popular term during debates over how to facilitate access to higher education in 2015–16. It refers to students who are not eligible for the government-funded National Student Financial Assistance Scheme (NSFAS), because their families earn above the threshold for the scheme's means-testing, but do not have the means to self-fund their education. The threshold for NSFAS eligibility varies, but as of early 2017 it was around R160,000 annually. [https://www.thedailyvox.co.za/everything-you-need-to-know-about-nsfas/] Accessed 21 July 2017.

[7] 'University of Limpopo shut down indefinitely', *Wits Vuvuzela*, 28 September 2016. [http://witsvuvuzela.com/2016/09/28/university-of-limpopo-shut-down-indefinitely/] Accessed 20 July 2017.

[8] K. Brandt, 'UL students continue to protest until demands met', *Eyewitness News*, 27 September 2016. [http://ewn.co.za/2016/09/28/University-of-Limpopo-students-to-continue-protests-until-demands-met] Accessed 20 July 2017.

an attempt to disrupt protests, and one student reported an alleged rape during the black-out. The university administration countered that the power cut had not been their decision, but was the result of a fault at Eskom, the state-owned national utility provider.[9] Protests continued into Tuesday evening. By early the next morning university administrators had made the decision to discontinue the academic programme and shut the campus, sending students home only days after they had returned from the mid-term break.

The scene – of protesting students battling police officers, and being displaced from campus with little notice – was strikingly familiar at Turfloop. Nearly forty-five years earlier, when the relatively small, isolated university was intended to train the civil servants of nearby Bantustans, a campus-wide protest over the inequities of Bantu Education led to the shutdown of the university and expulsion of all 1200 students. That incident, in April 1972, put Turfloop on the national map as a center of anti-apartheid student resistance, and is discussed in detail in Chapter 1. Two years later, almost forty-two years to the day before the 2016 wave of FeesMustFall erupted at Turfloop, another cohort of student activists led a pro-FRELIMO rally on the university sports pitch in September 1974. Their celebration of Mozambique's newly won independence ended in violent clashes with the police, and the arrest of several students – including future state president Cyril Ramaphosa. Those events are analyzed in Chapter 2.

Turfloop, in its iterations as the University College of the North, the University of the North, and the University of Limpopo, is central to a great deal of the history this book explores, and the argument it makes about the regional impact of South Africa's rural north on national political ideologies. The development of new forms of political thinking and activism among students at the university – and their connection to networks and groups far beyond its gates – form the crux of the story told in Chapters 1, 2, and 3. During the 1960s and the early 1970s Turfloop became a hotspot of political activism in the Northern Transvaal, but it was also an important node in networks of student and youth anti-apartheid activism that connected the entire country. The expansion and development of those politics and networks beyond the university is discussed in Chapters 4, 5, and 6, in which I link urban townships and rural villages in a history of connected and interdependent student and youth activism. Chapter 7 addresses this legacy, and the remnants of these networks and important nodes, like Turfloop, in the post-apartheid era.

---

[9] 'University of Limpopo shut down indefinitely', *Wits Vuvuzela*, 28 September 2016.

The argument and structure of this book

This book traces several strands of ideological history over the latter half and end of South Africa's apartheid era. It argues that regional and local experiences played a critical role in the transmission and transformation of the political ideas and practices of generations of youth and student activists, and that these have been broadly neglected in favour of a scholarship that focuses on urban politics. Through its focus on the Northern Transvaal (contemporary Limpopo Province), it considers the way that rural and peripheral histories have been marginalized in the national story of struggle, despite the prominent roles that local activists, institutions, and communities played in developing the ideas that went to the heart of national movements. It tells a history that cuts across movements, ideologies, and geographic spaces, and sometimes blurs the politically constructed boundaries between these by tracing the intersecting histories of generations of activists who were rooted in Limpopo, either by birth, family, or education.

The book is structured in three sections, each of which considers the political development of local institutions and activists, and their interactions with regional and national entities. It looks first at the genesis and growth of anti-apartheid politics on the campus of the University of the North, or Turfloop. The first three chapters deal with the increasing radicalization and national impact of politics on that campus during the 1960s and 1970s. In particular this section adds a new dimension to the growing scholarship on the history of Black Consciousness, by offering a deeply local perspective of its development on campus.

Chapters 4 and 5 adopt a wider lens than the previous section and consider the organizational decline of Black Consciousness and the reemergence of multi-racial Charterism at the regional and local levels. This section moves beyond the university student organization at Turfloop, and looks at the expansion of anti-apartheid activism in secondary schools and among non-student youth. Chapter 5, in particular, considers the changing ways in which violence came to be a form of political tool and expression. It includes analysis of the wave of witch-hunts that swept the northern Transvaal in the late 1980s in this context, and argues that these were both social and political acts.

Chapters 6 and 7 examine the ways that youth and student organizations positioned themselves during the final years of apartheid and the early years of democracy – in relation to one another, in relation to various liberation movements, and finally in relation to the state itself. By following the biography of two of Limpopo's most famous political youth leaders – Peter Mokaba and Julius Malema – these chapters pull

together many of the ideological and organizational developments that
the previous sections discuss. Mokaba and Malema are perhaps Limpopo's most famous young politicians, and both were well known for
their firebrand style. But as preceding chapters argue, the province has a
deep history of radical student and youth politics that transcended both
movements and generations.

Limpopo – a place of physical and political frontiers

Limpopo is democratic South Africa's northernmost province, lying
between the urban conglomeration of Gauteng to the south, which
includes both Johannesburg and Pretoria, and the northern borders
shared with Mozambique, Zimbabwe, and Botswana. It is predominantly rural; though the capital city of Polokwane is the country's tenth
largest municipality, and is home to more than 600,000 residents, the
overall population density of the province is only approximately forty-
four people per square kilometre, in contrast to neighbouring Gauteng,
where it is 675 people per square kilometre. Limpopo is also overwhelmingly poor. During South Africa's 2010 census, nearly two-thirds
of Limpopo's residents were defined as 'dependents' (of non-working
age – either below 15 or above 65 – and supported predominantly by
state grants), and for those of working age, more than 38% were unemployed. For youth, defined by StatsSA as aged 15–24, this number was
drastically higher – hovering just below 50%.[10]

These contemporary statistics are heavily informed by the past.
During the nineteenth and early twentieth centuries, under the Afri-
kaaner *Zuid-Afrikaansche Republick* (ZAR) and the subsequent Union
of South Africa, the area that is today Limpopo was the northern part
of the area called Transvaal – during its iteration as an independent
republic, and then as one of South Africa's four provinces. Before the
arrival of the Voortrekkers and their conquest and establishment of the
ZAR, the area was home to the Pedi polity under the rule of Paramount
Chief Sekwati and then his son Sekhunkhune. This history, of negotiation, conflict, and conquest is best chronicled in Peter Delius' *The
Land Belongs to Us: The Pedi polity, the Boers, and the British in the*

---

[10] StatsSA, Analysis of Limpopo by municipality, relying on 2010 census data.
[http://www.statssa.gov.za/?page_id=964] Accessed 1 August 2017. See also J.
Lestrade-Jefferis, 'The South African Labour Market: Selected time-based social
and international comparisons' (Pretoria: Statistics South Africa, 2002).

nineteenth century Transvaal.[11] *The Land Belongs to Us* and Delius'
later volume, *A Lion Amongst the Cattle: Reconstruction and resistance
in the Northern Transvaal,* offer the most extensive political history of
this part of South Africa, from the early nineteenth to the late twentieth
century.

After their election in 1948, the National Party began to develop and
implement apartheid's racist spatial segregation across South Africa.
Rural areas, already shaped in their racial composition by the Natives
Land Act of 1913[12] and subsequent legislation, became a key site of
'grand apartheid' planning. Apartheid was fundamentally concerned
with controlling African mobility in South Africa. Building on earlier
legislation like the Natives Land Act and onerous pass laws, National
Party apparatchiks endeavoured to extend and expand the racial segregation of previous eras. Their goal was to wholly separate white South
Africans from black, Indian, and coloured ones. Homelands, or Bantustans, were the envisioned pinnacle of achieving this control; apartheid
planners aimed to eventually transform existing native reserves into
self-governing territories that were organized by ethnic group. Ideally,
in the minds of the planners, all black South Africans would now have
citizenship in a particular homeland, based on his or her ethnicity. Their
right to travel or work in 'white' South Africa would be carefully controlled by pass. The legal groundwork for this plan was laid in 1959
with the passage of the Promotion of Bantu Self-Government Act. As
Saul Dubow has noted, the idea of Bantustans was couched in terms
of nation-building for each ethnic group concerned, and allowed the
South African government to attempt to 'wrong-foot its external critics by mimicking decolonization elsewhere in Africa'.[13] Initial planning
provided for eight ethnic homelands, and this later expanded to ten.

Three of these new Bantustans were carved out of the farmlands,
reserves, villages, and towns of the Northern Transvaal. Lebowa was the
largest of the three. Delineated for the BaPedi/Northern Sotho people,
it stretched, in several non-contiguous pieces of territory, from north to

---

[11] P. Delius, *The Land Belongs to Us: The Pedi polity, the Boers, and the British in
the nineteenth century Transvaal* (Johannesburg, 1983).

[12] The Natives Land Act (No. 27) of 1913 restricted black Africans to owning land
on reserves that made up approximately 7% of South Africa's land, leaving 93%
of the land under white control. It resulted in forced removals and dispossessed
Africans from land they had – in some cases – lived on for generations. This
spatial segregation and land alienation was reinforced by subsequent legislation,
including the Urban Areas Act (1923), Natives and Land Trust Act (1936) and
the Group Areas Act (1950).

[13] S. Dubow, *Apartheid, 1948–1994* (Oxford, 2014), p. 106.

south across the center of what is now Limpopo Province. It covered more than three times the area and had two to three times the population of its smaller neighbours, Gazankulu (for the VaTsonga/Shangaan) and Venda (for the VhaVenda). These both bordered the Kruger National Park on Limpopo's north-eastern edge. They shared a substantial border with one another, and with small Lebowan exclaves.

Each of these has a distinct political history. Delius' aforementioned books chronicle the history of Sekhukhuneland, which constituted a large part of southern Lebowa. Ineke van Kessel and Sekibakiba Lekgoathi have each written extensively about political organization in this area under the United Democratic Front during the 1980s, and in Lekgoathi's case, during the formation of homelands.[14] Barbara Oomen has traced the history of chiefly power in the area in relation to traditional authority in post-apartheid South Africa.[15] Scholarship on the area occupied by the two smaller homelands has been predominantly anthropological. Fraser MacNeill's *AIDS, Politics, and Music in South Africa* offers a rich, nuanced view of contemporary life – and biomedical understanding during the AIDS crisis – in the former homeland of Venda. MacNeill does an admirable job of historically grounding this story, particularly in his treatment of contestation over the succession of the Venda king. Isak Niehaus has taken a historical-ethnographic approach to analyzing the phenomena of witchcraft and occult beliefs in Bushbuckridge municipality, once a part of the Gazankulu homeland. But the history of these areas – though not incidental – is not at the core of either Niehaus' or MacNeill's scholarly concerns; their arguments lie fundamentally in the present. Alan Kirkaldy, Lize Kriel, and more recently, Michelle Hay, have written deep histories about these areas. Kirkaldy and Kriel's work on the history of religion and missionaries among the VhaVenda in the late nineteenth century details a contested local history on both ethnic and gendered lines nearly a century before the creation of the Venda homeland.[16] Hay has written of the protracted struggle for land rights

---

[14] I. van Kessel, *'Beyond our wildest dreams': The United Democratic Front and the transformation of South Africa* (Charlottesville, VA, 2000), pp. 75–150; S. Lekgoathi, 'Teacher Militancy and the Rural Northern Transvaal Community of Zebediela, 1986–1994', *South African Historical Journal*, 58(1) (2007), 226–52; S. Lekgoathi, 'Chiefs, Migrants, and North Ndebele Ethnicity in the Context of Surrounding Homeland Politics, 1965–1978', *African Studies*, 62(1) (2003), 53–77.

[15] B. Oomen, *Chiefs in South Africa: Law, power and culture in the post-apartheid era* (Oxford, 2005), pp. 123–62.

[16] A. Kirkaldy and L. Kriel, 'Converts and Conservatives: Missionary representations of African rulers in the Northern Transvaal, c. 1870–1900', *Le Fait*

and access over the course of the twentieth century by communities in present-day Letaba district, once part of the Gazankulu homeland.[17]

These assorted histories and ethnographies cover a range of periods, and a variety of places and communities. They each offer rich local detail, and some provide deep historical context, but none considers the region of the northern Transvaal as a whole, or the particular interactions – at a regional level – between the government and authority structures of Venda, Gazankulu, and Lebowa. This book argues that the interaction of these three governments with the South African government in Pretoria, and occasionally with each other, shaped conditions for young people in their territories in ways that affected political ideas and activism at the national level. The confluence of frequently impoverished and oppressive local circumstances with national liberation movements often confronted collaborative policing efforts, which aimed to repress resistance to apartheid. This was particularly true for events at Turfloop during the 1970s and 1980s, where students from around the country gathered and exchanged political ideas and developed forms of action. The university was responsible for educating students from all three Bantustans, as well as urban townships and other rural areas, but it was physically based in Lebowa and subject to policing both by local Lebowa police and by the South African police, and eventually the South African Defence Force. This particular confluence of national and local political interests and security forces are a recurrent theme throughout this book.

The regional history that is explored here is important because it has not been told collectively, and this raises new ways of thinking about both the local and the regional in the formation of anti-apartheid ideology. It contributes to the regional literature described above, and to the growing scholarship on Black Consciousness, and student politics in South African history. But it is also important because it makes a broader argument for the importance of geographically peripheral spaces in influencing national political trends that can be applied and tested beyond South Africa.

Missionaires, 18 (2006), 109–44; L. Kriel and A. Kirkaldy, '"Praying is the work of men, not the work of women": The response of Bahananwa and Vhavenda women to conversion in late nineteenth-century Lutheran missionary territories', *South African Historical Journal*, 61(2) (2009), 316–35.

[17] M. Hay, 'A Tangled Past: Land settlement, removals, and restitution in Letaba District, 1900–2013', *Journal of Southern African Studies*, 40(4) (2014), 745–60.

The Global Sixties – Student activism from south to north

The period in which this text begins its analysis – the late 1960s – is famed for the cultural revolutions that swept America and Europe. 'Paris 1968' has become a watchword for the flourishing of revolutionary ideas during this period, while referring specifically to events in May of that year when French students and workers joined forces in a multi-faceted protest against fascism, imperialism, and hierarchies of all sorts, and for freedom of political, cultural, creative, and sexual expression, as well as a strike for better working conditions and higher wages. Paris in 1968 followed student demonstrations in the United States against the Vietnam War and in support of civil rights and women's liberation, and the *68er-Bewegung* students' movement in West Germany against aggressive policing and a conservative state. It was in turn followed by the Italian worker's movement in late 1969 – known as *maggio strisciante* or 'the drawn out May', recalling the Parisian influence.[18]

Europe and the United States have dominated scholarship and broader discourse about this period,[19] but new scholarship is extending the analysis of the 'global sixties' to the global south. Andrew Ivaska has written compellingly of the emergence of Dar es Salaam as 'a key nodal point for transnational activism' during the 1960s, when it was a haven for exiles from white settler regimes in Southern Africa as well as for over a thousand African American activists who were 'fleeing FBI harrassment'.[20] Ivaska tells an explicitly transnational history, positioning Dar es Salaam as a hub for international activists who were moving between and across national spaces. But some events in the 1960s were globally linked, despite being nationally bounded. In 1968 the eyes of the world were on Mexico City as it became the first city in Latin America to host the Olympic Games. But just ten days before the opening ceremony, on 2 October 1968 Mexican police and soldiers fired on a student meeting in the public square of Tlatelolco, killing an untold number of

---

[18] M. Seidman, *The Imaginary Revolution: Parisian students and workers in 1968* (New York, 2004), p. 9.

[19] In addition to Seidman, for the Parisian revolution and its enduring impact on French contemporary history, see K. Ross, *May '68 and Its Afterlives* (Chicago, 2002), and C. Reynolds, *Memories of May '68: France's convenient consensus* (Cardiff, 2011). For a cross-cutting analysis of cultural and political protests across Western Europe and North America, see G.R. Horn, *Rebellion in Western Europe and North America, 1956–1976* (Oxford, 2007).

[20] A. Ivaska, 'Movement Youth in a Global Sixties Hub: The everyday lives of transnational activists in postcolonial Dar es Salaam' in *Transnational Histories of Youth in the Twentieth Century*, ed. R.I. Jobs and D.M. Pomfret (Basingstoke, 2015), pp. 188, 189

students and bystanders. Brewster and Brewster have detailed how the Mexican student movement arose from local and national proximate causes, but came to global prominence owing to its connection to the Olympic Games.[21]

Bahru Zewde's *The Quest for Socialist Utopia: The Ethiopian Student Movement, c. 1960–1974* does an exemplary job of situating that student movement among the global panopoly of student protests in the 1960s and 1970s, including South Africa's Soweto Uprising.[22] Zewde spends a chapter setting the global stage on which the Ethiopian Students Movement emerged, and he argues that its growth was influenced by national, continental and global factors. Zewde is somewhat unusual in including South Africa in his historiography of student politics of the mid-twentieth century; Soweto 1976, indisputably South Africa's most prominent moment of student organization, occurred nearly a decade after 1968, often taken as the global zenith of student protests. Even the South African historiography has traditionally considered the 1960s as a period of political 'quiescence' domestically or at best regrouping in the wake of harsh state repression.[23]

This book situates the rise of new political ideas among South African students earlier – in the late 1960s, sometimes in conversation with (or even appropriation of) global student and anticolonial discourses. It also, in contrast to most of the literature on student politics elsewhere – which, from Mexico City to Paris to Dar es Salaam, is predominantly urban in its focus – endeavours to highlight the contribution that rural local and regional politics made to the development of the new political ideas and forms of action that went on to inform national movements.

South African students and youth, from Sekhukhuneland to Soweto

This book addresses the variety of ways young people in Limpopo have engaged in formal politics, both in opposition to the apartheid state, and later in association with the ANC in government. My analysis extends across organizations, ideologies, geographic boundaries, and historical periods, but the theme that unites it is its focus on young political actors. I

---

[21] K. Brewster and C. Brewster, 'The Mexican Student Movement of 1968: An Olympic perspective', *The International Journal of the History of Sport*, 26(6) (May 2009), 814–39.

[22] B. Zwede, *The Quest for Socialist Utopia: The Ethiopian student movement, c. 1960–1974* (Oxford, 2014).

[23] One recent exception to this trend is Julian Brown's *The Road to Soweto: Resistance and the Uprising of 16 June 1976* (Oxford, 2016), which is discussed further in the next section of this introduction.

argue that young people have driven political change and development in the Northern Transvaal and Limpopo since the late 1960s. They have consistently been at the forefront of new forms of political protest and expression, and have been responsible for influencing the spread of such expression within and outside the province.

The University of the North at Turfloop played a critical role in the political conscientization of generations of these young political activists. From the late 1960s to the late 1970s it was the crucible of all major political activism in the Northern Transvaal. This indicates the prominence of student activism at a time of relative political quiescence among other social and generational groups in the province. In Chapter 1, I explore the genesis of this activism: campus groups like the University Christian Movement (UCM) exposed students at Turfloop to a form of politicized Christianity that inspired small pockets of radical activism in the student body. By the time the South African Students' Organisation (SASO) launched in 1969, the UCM had laid building blocks for greater political mobilization on campus, and SASO was able to capitalize on their legacy. It employed a technique of mass-affiliation through the Students' Representative Council that effectively expanded political action on campus to the entire student body. In Chapter 1, I argue that both UCM and SASO played critical and interlinking roles in politicizing students at Turfloop during the period from 1967 to 1972, but the rapidity with which their messages were adopted was also due to specific local circumstances. The peculiar hypocrisy under which Turfloop and the other so-called 'bush' colleges, designated as black institutions but run largely by whites, operated inspired outspoken protest from students like Onkgopotse Tiro in his 1972 graduation address. The combination of immediate concerns – like lack of access to books and basic resources – and ideological awakening through UCM and SASO programmes like Black Theology and Black Consciousness was a powerful mix. By 1972 politics was no longer the purview of a few students. When Tiro was expelled in April of that year, the entire Turfloop student body protested, and was supported in their action by the black academic staff, even touching off class boycotts at other universities around South Africa.

In these early days, youth protest in the Northern Transvaal was dominated by activism among university students. This was, in part, an effect of Turfloop's importance as a centre for activism, but it also reflected political trends at the time when a new generation of South Africans were rethinking and remaking ideas about liberation. The development of Black Consciousness ideology in the early 1970s was in part a remaking of Africanism, Anton Lembede's nationalist philosophy that rejected multiracialism; it shared and expanded an emphasis on psychological liberation with Africanism, and it was also a deeply intellectual project.[24] The roots of this project at Turfloop and other black universities are discussed in Chapters 1 and 2, building on previous histories of the Black Consciousness Movement by closely examining a local context that influenced the development of the movement as a whole. Black Consciousness thrived on university campuses and in schools because it appealed to the intellectual curiosity that education aims to foster.

This aspect of the text contributes to a substantial and growing body of literature on the history and philosophy of Black Consciousness. Almost as soon as it emerged on South African campuses in the late 1960s and early 1970s, Black Consciousness became the subject of scholarly interest. Two years after Black Consciousness organizations were banned, Gail Gerhart's *Black Power in South Africa: The evolution of an ideology* situated the rise of the movement in the lineage of Africanist and Pan-Africanist thought, linking it to the ideology of the Pan-Africanist Congress. More recently Magaziner's *The Law and the Prophets*[25] has provided a rich intellectual history of Black Consciousness, particularly as it developed through the university-based structures of SASO. Magaziner situates Black Consciousness both between and beyond the political differences of other liberation organizations like the PAC and ANC. New scholarship is also extending our geographic and temporal context for Black Consciousness. In his doctoral research, Toivo Asheeke explores Black Consciousness structures in exile beyond South Africa, and argues that a cohort of BC exiles pursued armed struggle under the auspices of the Azanian People's Liberation Front (APLF).[26] Recent contributions like Leslie Anne Hadfield's *Liberation and Development: Black Consciousness community programs in South Africa*[27] have expanded the scope of our understanding: Hadfield offers an in-depth history of the development projects that SASO-affiliate Black Community Programmes (BCP) undertook during the 1970s. She also argues that many of these projects have persisted well past the

---

[24] For the most developed argument on the ideological links between Black Consciousness and Africanism, see Gail Gerhart's *Black Power in South Africa: The evolution of an ideology* (Berkeley, CA, 1979).

[25] D. Magaziner, *The Law and the Prophets: Black Consciousness in South Africa, 1968–1977* (Athens, OH, 2010).

[26] T. Asheeke, 'Arming Black Consciousness: The turn to armed struggle and the formation of the Bokwe Group/Azanian Peoples' Liberation Front (APLF), April 1972–September 1976', under review at the *Journal of Southern African Studies* (2018).

[27] L.A. Hadfield, *Liberation and Development: Black Consciousness community programs in South Africa* (East Lansing, MI, 2016).

formal banning and ebb of Black Consciousness, even into the democratic era, thus extending the timeline in which historians must situate Black Consciousness and its influence. Hashi Kenneth Tafira also argues powerfully for the enduring impact of Black Consciousness in South African society, albeit from a different vantage point, situating Black Consciousness in a 'political lineage of Black Nationalism in Azania from early African nationalism [...] to BC in its contemporary forms'.[28] Similarly to Hadfield and Tafira, this text positions the work of student activists at the core of its analysis and argues for the influence of SASO's ideology and strategies after its banning in 1977, into the 1980s and beyond.

Students, then, are one critical category of the young political actors examined here, and university students are a subset of that: in the Northern Transvaal in the early 1970s, they were the vanguard of political protest. But political expression did not remain contained within universities for long. One of the primary goals of students like Onkgopotse Tiro and others politicized through SASO was to expand their influence beyond university campuses. The successes and failures of this project are analyzed in Chapter 2. The South African Students' Movement (SASM) was a major influence in schools, particularly in Soweto. Former university students from Turfloop liaised with this group (Tiro himself even served as an official advisor for SASM, linking it to SASO), and many got teaching jobs that allowed them to influence the political development of secondary school students in a classroom setting. By the middle of the 1970s SASM and some affiliated groups had established a presence in many key Soweto high schools, and in 1976 when the inflammatory issue of using Afrikaans as a teaching medium arose, Soweto's students took to the streets in their thousands. They had been politicized by the ideas and people flowing out of South Africa's black universities – particularly, as I argue in Chapter 2, those from Turfloop. My contribution here builds on the recent work of Julian Brown, whose *The Road to Soweto: Resistance and the Uprising of 16 June 1976*[29] traces the antecedents of the forms of protest that Soweto students used to both university campuses and labour unions in the early 1970s and mid–late 1960s. Aside from two institutional histories,[30] Brown's work offers the

---

[28] H.K. Tafira, *Black Nationalist Thought in South Africa: The persistence of an idea of liberation* (Basingstoke, 2016), p. 5.

[29] Brown, *The Road to Soweto*.

[30] See C. White, *From Despair to Hope: The Turfloop experience* (Sovenga, 1997) and C. Kanyane, *Turfloop, A Conscious Pariah: How University of the North*

most sustained engagement with the role of Turfloop in influencing these new forms of protest in the early 1970s.

Chapters 3 and 4 of this text deal with the incremental successes and failures of Black Consciousness, both locally at Turfloop and on the national stage. The movement for Africanization, which demanded black leadership at black universities, achieved its greatest success in 1976, when William Kgware was named the first black rector at the university – and indeed, the first in South African history. Despite this victory, establishing visible black leadership did not result in the political shifts both student and staff activists had hoped for at Turfloop. Kgware's appointment and beleaguered administration are the subject of Chapter 3.

Chapter 4 considers the structural and organizational challenges faced by the Black Consciousness Movement as it moved beyond the bounds of universities, gained national prominence, and thus attracted increased attention and suppression from the security police. It considers the role of former Turfloop students and staff on both sides of the ideological divide between Black Consciousness in its declining years, and the insurgent multiracialism of Charterism. Chapters 3 and 4 look particularly at the relationship between figures at and from Turfloop to school students in other parts of the country, during and after the 1976 Soweto Uprising.

Soweto 1976 has become a pivotal moment in South African history, when the core of student political action broadened from universities to include schools.[31] This shift meant that school students became another significant category of political actor in South Africa, in addition to their university counterparts. Brown has demonstrated the ways in which this happened through changing protest tactics, casting the Soweto schoolchildren as actors in a national story of evolving methods of activism. Earlier work by Jonathan Hyslop on the history of Bantu Education itself situates the uprising in a fifty-year struggle over education between

---

brought in the Age of Barack Obama beyond our wildest dreams (Trafford, 2010).

[31] There is a broad literature specifically on the Soweto Uprisings. In addition to Brown and Hyslop, see Baruch Hirson's *Year of Fire, Year of Ash: The Soweto schoolchildren's revolt that shook Apartheid* (London, 2016) for an early account of the impact of the event, and the structural factors that influenced it. For autobiographical accounts, see Sibongile Mkhabela's *Open Earth and Black Roses: Remembering 16 June 1976* (Johannesburg, 2001) and Sifiso M. Ndlovu's *The Soweto s: Counter-memories of June 1976* (Johannesburg, 1998).

students, parents, teachers, and the state.[32] Clive Glaser's *Bo-Tsotsi: The youth gangs of Soweto, 1935–1976* tells a deeper local history of youth politics in the township and the often confrontational and violent clashes between school students and youth gangs.[33] Drawing on Glaser, in Chapters 5 and 6 I examine the relationship and overlapping politics of students and non-student youth.

University and school students are closely related in many ways; their common identity as students gives them shared educational concerns. But they are also distinct: university students have particular patterns of movement between a base at home (wherever that might be) and their university. For those at Turfloop, particularly during the 1970s and 1980s, a large minority straddled centres of identity between home life in the townships of the Rand and university life in the Lebowa bush. The university also gathered students from a wide catchment area and differing backgrounds. The fact of this increased diversity meant that students at Turfloop were necessarily oriented more beyond the boundaries of their own institution than school students, and in an even more pronounced way than the third category of political actors this book addresses: non-student youth.

The 1980s marked important political shifts in South Africa: the multi-racial philosophy of Charterism espoused by the ANC reemerged as the dominant philosophy among those involved in the anti-apartheid movement, sidelining Black Consciousness. The birth of the United Democratic Front enabled civic organizations to become more overtly political, linking concrete experiences of oppression with political ideology on a much greater scale than had yet been accomplished. And the incursion of politics into schools at the village level, through the Congress of South African Students, led to the rapid expansion and localization of student politics throughout the country, particularly in the Northern Transvaal. This expansion also facilitated the incorporation of non-student youths into what had previously been almost exclusively student political networks. In the Northern Transvaal this sometimes bumpy process of incorporation – and the resulting shifts in political expression – happened in localized village youth congresses around the region. Groups like the Sekhukhune Youth Organisation, which I discuss in Chapter 5, originated in local COSAS branches, but became increasingly autonomous after that organization's banning in 1985, and shifted away from primarily student and school-related concerns

[32] J. Hyslop, *The Classroom Struggle: Policy and resistance in South Africa, 1940–1990* (Durban, 1999).
[33] C. Glaser, *Bo-Tsotsi: The youth gangs of Soweto, 1935–1976* (Oxford, 2000).

as more non-student youths were incorporated into their ranks. These young comrades – students and non-students alike – were bound by a generational consciousness, and by shared social and economic challenges. Consequently their political expressions shifted away from practical educational concerns to the social order; they began to adapt and subvert traditional practices like witch-finding and chiefly arbitration, but overlaid these actions with political, anti-apartheid rhetoric. Following work by Ineke van Kessel and Isak Niehaus, I argue in Chapter 5 that political violence became entangled in generational disputes, economic discontent, and close social relationships, resulting in subversions of an older social order and empowering youth during the chaotic states of emergency in 1985 and 1986. Despite this temporary social power, the groups wielding it – like SEYO – struggled to exert ideological control over their membership. The comingling of students and youth, and the deeply local orientation of youth congresses, brought about greater variety of political expression and had introduced new actors to the struggle, but it also introduced new levels of autonomy and local specificity to youth politics.

The South African Youth Congress (SAYCO), and then later the ANC Youth League, inherited these legacies. In Chapter 6 I discuss the emergence of SAYCO in 1987 as an umbrella organization for the many congresses that had been formed in the mid-1980s; it was explicitly protective of their autonomy, and in many cases even the names of the congresses did not change to reflect their affiliation to the new organization. Their composition continued to straddle both students and non-student youths, and SAYCO adopted the violent rhetoric of some of its constituents, if not necessarily their actions.

The distinctions between student politics and youth politics have remained contested into the post-apartheid period. At the founding of the ANC Youth League, in which SAYCO was instrumental, it was agreed that the explicitly student-oriented groups, the unbanned COSAS and SANSCO,[34] would remain independent from the League. This permitted them to pursue educationally specific agendas, while the Youth League focused primarily on non-educational issues. It was a tacit

---

[34] SANSCO, the South African National Students Conference, existed from 1986 (when it changed its name from the previous Azanian Students Congress (AZA-SO)) until 1990, when it merged with the National Union of South African Students (NUSAS) to become the South African Students Conference (SASCO), which remains a dominant force on South African campuses today. Saleem Badat addresses these changes in *Black Student Politics, Higher Education, and Apartheid: From SASO to SANSCO, 1968– 1990* (Pretoria, 1999), and they are further interrogated in Chapters 4, 5, and 6 of this book.

understanding that SASCO would operate on tertiary educational campuses, and that the Youth League would organize a similar demographic outside of educational institutions. But, in the mid-1990s, the Youth League began to contest Student Representative Council elections on the campuses of universities like Turfloop, causing tension between the two organizations. Mandla Seopela, a Turfloop student and the national president of SASCO in the early 2000s, described the situation:

> [T]he ANC Youth League in 1995/1996 in one of these gatherings took a resolution that it is now going to open branches in the universities of higher learning. So now it meant that now it is going to operate in the same space as SASCO. Because before then the feeling was that SASCO was the one organizing students, and the Youth League was organizing youth in general, students involved. When that resolution was taken, it meant that the Youth League was now going to contest space with SASCO. So that is why in most instances, I must indicate, there are those confrontational relations.[35]

Both SASCO and the ANC Youth League act as feeder organizations for the ANC itself. Their competition and sometimes outright confrontation, described by Seopela, arose from demographic overlap and territorialism, but it also indicates the fluidity of identities in the world of student and youth politics. Who counts where can be a challenge to disentangle; though students are sometimes in conflict or competition with youth, students also *are* youth, and their political agendas overlap and diverge in important ways. Capturing some of those convergences and divergences is one of the key aims of this book.

This positioning of young political actors in relation to the democratic state is the subject of Chapter 7, which considers the rise in prominence of the reconstituted ANC Youth League, and the emergence of Julius Malema as both a product of the deep history of youth political leadership in Limpopo, and as someone who elevated that style to a new national prominence.

This book analyzes regional influences on the ideologies that have underpinned South African student politics from the 1960s to the present. It considers the history of student organization in the Northern Transvaal, and the ways that students and youth in this relatively isolated area have influenced political change on a national scale, over generations. It does so by exploring the stories of several generations of key political actors – from Onkgopotse Tiro to Julius Malema – and

---

[35] Author's interview with Mandla Seopela, 17 September 2011, Melville, Johannesburg.

by analyzing critical spaces of political mobilization in the region, chief among these the university (first of the North, and eventually of Limpopo) at Turfloop.

1

Turfloop, Crucible of Change

1968 was a pivotal year for student protest around the world. As discussed in the previous chapter, from Paris to Mexico City, students embarked on protests that took them into direct and violent conflict with the state. That same year in South Africa, however, student politics took a surprising – and, to some, reactionary – turn. In apparent accordance with the apartheid ideology of the South African government, black South African university students broke ranks with their liberal white counterparts and formed their own racially exclusive student organization. The racialized split between the predominantly white National Union of South African Students (NUSAS) and the black South African Students' Organisation (SASO), is one of the key issues discussed in this chapter, as I explore the local context and causes of the break at the University of the North. It came nearly a decade after the official segregation of South Africa's universities, and the founding of ethnically exclusive 'University Colleges' for black, Indian, and coloured students.

On the cusp of the founding of SASO, the University College of the North, or Turfloop, in the rural Northern Transvaal, became an important centre for politically active black students. The university was less than a decade old, and had been situated on a farm miles from the nearest town. It incubated the new organization and contributed to the development of what would become SASO's core ideology, Black Consciousness, and to the related idea of Black Theology. Like SASO itself, these ideologies focused on an affirmation of what it was to be black in South Africa, and aimed to promote a positive reclamation of black identity. In the case of Black Theology, the scope of this was explicitly religious. At Turfloop and elsewhere, SASO worked through on-campus Christian groups to achieve deeper ideological diffusion and mobilization. Its strongest links were to the ecumenical and multi-racial University Christian Movement (UCM); the movements enjoyed a period of close collaboration until the 1972 dissolution of the UCM. This also marked an important moment in which SASO and its allies abandoned attempts to employ multiracialism as a strategy for political change.

During the late 1960s and early 1970s, Turfloop became a site for integrating many levels of protest. This was fostered by the closely inter-twined roles of Black Consciousness and Black Theology in SASO itself, and through politicized Christianity in student organizations like the UCM and the Students' Christian Movement. Daniel Magaziner empha-sizes the close religious links and influences among Black Consciousness leadership and ideologues in his intellectual history of that movement.[1] By considering the influence of these ideas on SASO's rank and file at one of its strongholds, this chapter situates Turfloop at the centre of black student politics, and religion at the centre of Turfloop's politics. Christi-anity preceded politics as an influence for most students at Turfloop, but the marriage of these two things in ideas like Black Theology gave SASO an unparalleled degree of influence at Turfloop and on campuses like it. The cumulative effect of all these pieces offered activists at Turfloop political legitimacy, and the scope to mobilize protests and resistance.

This chapter explores the process by which Turfloop went from sleepy farm to 'the hottest place in South Africa'[2] and a critical organizing point for student protests. It analyzes the role of particular groups in affecting mobilization on the local and national levels, and argues that the Univer-sity of the North, in spite of its geographical isolation, lack of resources, and academic limits, was a crucible of student political activism with roots in the late 1960s. The major vehicles for politicization were on-campus groups like SASO, and Christian affiliates like the University Christian Movement (UCM) and the Students' Christian Movement (SCM). The rhetoric of student and staff leaders at Turfloop successfully melded Black Consciousness ideology and anti-apartheid politics with a particular brand of Christian evangelism, and it was this amalgamation of ideas that gave the movement currency and scope for mobilization.

Founding the University College of the North

In 1959, the apartheid government extended the power and scope of its earlier Bantu Education Act (1953) by passing the Extension of Uni-versity Education Act and the University College of Fort Hare Transfer Act. These two pieces of legislation served to extended the policies of separate development to South Africa's universities and created five 'university colleges' (or, pejoratively, 'bush colleges'). These were segre-gated by race and ethnic group. They were conceived to be institutions

---

[1] D. Magaziner, *The Law and the Prophets: Black Consciousness in South Africa, 1968–1977* (Athens, OH, 2010).
[2] Ishmael Mkhabela, quoted in ibid., p. 150.

where African, Indian, and coloured students could separately pursue higher education. In the northern Transvaal, the University College of the North at Turfloop (later simply the University of the North) was, according to its founding act, designed to educate students from the Sotho, Tswana, Tsonga, and Venda 'national units'.[3] In this sense it was from the start more ethnically diverse than its fellow black universities, which were required only to admit students of a single ethnic background: the University College of Zululand at Ngoye was for Zulus, the University College of Fort Hare was for Xhosas, the University College of Durban-Westville (previously Salisbury Island) was for Indians, and the University College of the Western Cape was for coloureds.

Located 30 kilometres south-east of the largest regional town of Pietersburg, and later subsumed within the southern portion of the Lebowa Bantustan, sleepy Turfloop was an unlikely setting for political activism and protest. The campus of the University of the North was erected on a local farm called Turfloop, which gave the university its enduring nickname. It was intentionally isolated – built well away from the white town of Pietersburg, and even further from the busy African township of Seshego, on Pietersburg's north-west side. Rural farming areas and open veld bounded the university on its northern, eastern, and southern edges. The small township of Mankweng flanked the campus on the west, and provided shops, services, and housing for black staff and some students. This choice of location was no accident on the part of early University planners and administrators. Like Ngoye, in Zululand, which was developed at the same time and under similar circumstances, Turfloop was designed to be remote, and to focus students' energy and attentions on the local areas and homelands they inhabited.

Courses were designed to produce graduates who would build the Bantustan 'homelands' that apartheid envisioned. A 1958 commission, established to comment on the final Extension of University Education Act, recommended that the new university colleges should develop the culture and promote 'the general progress and welfare' of their respective ethnic groups. The architects of this system wanted these new colleges to produce the educated elite of the new quasi-states they were establishing: 'The students [of the university colleges] should be the pioneers in the whole process of civilizing the ethnic group concerned,'[4] the commission

---

[3] J.G.E. Wolfson, *Turmoil at Turfloop: A summary of the Reports of the Snyman and Jackson Commissions of Inquiry into the University of the North* (Johannesburg, 1976), p. 5.

[4] *Main Report of The Commission of Enquiry on the Separate University Education Bill, 1958*. pp. 14–15 (quoted in White, *From Despair to Hope*, p. 74).

declared. The University Colleges, then, were not only physically isolated from South Africa's urban centres, and ideologically focused on building black communities outside South Africa proper; they were designed to produce graduates who would support and embody apartheid's policies.

At its founding, the University College of the North was a tiny institution with only 87 students, but it grew quickly and by the end of the decade its enrolment had increased more than seven-fold.[5] By the early 1970s it was already larger than the much older University of Fort Hare, with nearly 1200 students to Fort Hare's approximately 900.[6] Turfloop's students were drawn from a wide geographical swathe of South Africa. They came from the Western, Northern, and Eastern Transvaal, as well as from the Orange Free State, and from five different homelands: Lebowa itself, Venda to the north, Gazankulu to the east, Bophuthatswana to the west, and, eventually, Qwa Qwa to the south. A significant portion of students also came from the country's urban townships – mostly from those surrounding Johannesburg and Pretoria. In his institutional history of Turfloop, Chris White has demonstrated that, while during the early 1960s numbers of rural and urban students remained relatively balanced (with slightly higher rural numbers), from 1968 the balance shifted, and during the 1970s and 1980s there was a 'constant increase in students from urban areas'.[7] Given such varied backgrounds, Turfloop students comprised a much more diverse group than had been envisioned by the framers of the Extension of University Education Act, and their affiliations were often divided between urban townships and rural homelands. Many of those who came out of township schools had family connections to rural areas, and some who were raised by nuclear families in places like Soweto were sent away to extended family in villages for primary or secondary schooling. Even from its inception, the constituents of the Turfloop student body bore little resemblance to the 'pioneers', with singular affiliations to homelands, that the University Colleges had hoped to produce.

The expansion of schooling under Bantu Education in the late 1950s and 1960s, which Jonathan Hyslop has argued was forged under the pressure of rapid urbanization that bordered on a crisis for the apartheid state,[8] prompted the massification of primary and secondary education in South Africa. Higher education, though still only available to a relative

---

[5] 'Turfloop: Growing the University of the North', *The Star*, 16 May 1968 [Historical Papers Research Archive, hereafter HPRA, AD1912/258.16].

[6] Massey, *Under Protest*, p. 210.

[7] White, *From Despair to Hope*, p. 83.

[8] Hyslop, *The Classroom Struggle*, p. 53.

few, also expanded exponentially with the establishment of Turfloop and its fellow bush colleges to supplement Fort Hare, the University Colleges of Botswana, Lesotho, and Swaziland (BLS), and the open universities like Cape Town and Natal, which had taken some black students during the first half of the twentieth century (until they were disallowed from doing so). This rapid expansion of the black university-going population had important implications for student politics on campuses. Daniel Massey has suggested that during the 1960s and 1970s Fort Hare's student body was riven by philosophical divides over liberalism and racialism, 'with students from the north generally supporting SASO and those from the south, having grown up in the liberal tradition, opposing it'.[9] These factions were known on campus as the abaKaringes (representing the SASO-supporters) and the abaThembus (who advocated liberal nonracialism). This divide also cleaved along class lines, with most of the abaKaringes being 'products of northern locations and townships, who arrived at Fort Hare mostly as a result of their own labour in factories and even in mines', while the abaThembus 'were from Eastern Cape families and were primarily the children of teachers, principals, and nurses'.[10] Massey, drawing on an interview with Barney Pityana, himself an alumnus of Fort Hare and of the SASO executive, positions this divide as a product of Fort Hare's deep roots in the liberal tradition; the abaThembus took pride in defending this legacy. Its later founding meant that Turfloop was not invested in an institutional history like Fort Hare's; but its students, coming increasingly from urban townships on the Rand and elsewhere in the Transvaal also likely resembled the backgrounds of the radical abaKaringes more than the liberal abaThembus. Onkgopotse Tiro himself had worked, among other jobs, on a manganese mine before matriculating at the university.

In the early years of its formation, Turfloop's staff also gave the lie to the premise of an African university for Africans: white academic staff outnumbered black by approximately three to one, and all senior positions were occupied by white academics and administrators. Turfloop's white staff had long been drawn from a particularly conservative section of Afrikaner society, and many, especially the most senior, were linked to the secretive Afrikaner group, the *Broederbond*.[11] White has argued

---

[9] Massey, *Under Protest*, p. 210.
[10] Ibid.
[11] Van Kessel, *Beyond Our Wildest Dreams*, p. 96; White, *From Despair to Hope*, pp. 115, 142; and M. Nkomo *et al.* (eds), *Within the Realm of Possibility: From disadvantage to development at the University of Fort Hare and the University of the North* (Cape Town, 2006), p. 25.

that the *Broederbond* exerted powerful control over various aspects of campus life during the 1960s and 1970s through its control of the powerful University Council, and influence over financial decisions.[12] This lack of autonomy and black leadership became a theme in protests on campus throughout the first two decades of the university's existence.

A 1969 *Rand Daily Mail* editorial articulated another important problem with the premise of all the University Colleges. They were faced with 'the difficult task of trying to educate people without arousing their expectations; of opening their eyes and minds to the world and yet trying to ensure that they still know their place [...]. Events at Fort Hare and Turfloop have shown that you cannot open minds and control them at the same time.'[13]

Indeed, as the *Rand Daily Mail* editorial alludes, the reality of life and politics at Turfloop was very different from what was imagined by the Commission of Inquiry in 1958. In spite of the conscious effort to tailor students at Turfloop and its fellow black universities into model apartheid citizens, by the early 1970s Turfloop had defied these roots and become a crucible for the student political activism that came to characterize that decade of South African history.

The University Christian Movement

In spite of its isolation, Turfloop was no stranger to national student politics as early as the late 1960s, and student engagement with on-campus politics began even earlier. At the time of its founding in 1960, Turfloop's Rector E.F. Potgieter instituted a system of prefects to represent and administer the student body.[14] These hand-picked students were responsible for patrolling the hostels and monitoring visitors on campus. This system, whereby some students were given powers of monitoring and punishment over others, quickly produced an outcry among the small student body. In response to student discontent, the Rector permitted the creation of an elected Student Representative Council; in June 1960 students convened a mass meeting and elected a committee to draft the new SRC's constitution. In early 1961, Turfloop's first SRC was elected with Gessler Muxe Nkondo as its president.[15] Nkondo would go on to

---

[12] White, *From Despair to Hope*, p. 142.

[13] 'Different "Freedom"', *The Rand Daily Mail*, 26 May 1969 [HPRA AD1912/258.16].

[14] White, *From Despair to Hope*, p. 90; Nkomo *et al.*, *Within the Realm of Possibility*, p. 69.

[15] Nkomo *et al.*, *Within the Realm of Possibility*, p. 69.

become a prominent and outspoken faculty member at the university during the tumultuous years of the early 1970s.

The SRC inherited the prefects' role of representing the needs of the student body to the University Rector and Senate, but not those of monitoring and enforcement. Prefects continued to serve in this capacity for more than two decades. The Turfloop SRC was born in response to what was perceived as an unfair and undemocratic system, and from its inception it worked to advocate for student concerns that were expressed on campus – the quality of food served in the canteen was a perennial issue – and increasingly for ways that the Turfloop student body intersected with the outside world. In an early example, the 1961 SRC intervened on behalf of one of their number, sports chair Cornelius Motumi, who was expelled for inviting the soccer team from the white University of the Witwatersrand to play a fixture at Turfloop without prior permission.[16] This was the first example of a Turfloop student publicly flouting apartheid restrictions on racial segregation. After SRC intervention Motumi's expulsion was repealed, but the incident set the tone by which many subsequent SRCs would abide: they sought to make and maintain linkages outside Turfloop. This sometimes brought them into conflict with the university administration, and later with the state itself.

This pattern was replicated in 1968, when the SRC led a push to formally affiliate with NUSAS, South Africa's multi-racial national union of students. The University Senate, reinforcing the tendency of the administration to prevent external contact with its student body, eventually banned the move.[17] Despite this, some other national student groups were allowed to be active on campus. From its inception in 1967, the University Christian Movement (UCM) was a powerful organization on a campus where Christianity was a major mobilizing force. In a 1972 interview with the *Pretoria News*, Professor William Kgware noted that at Turfloop 'there were more religious societies than any other students' organizations'.[18] In part this was because non-religious, more overtly political organizations were banned (as was the case with NUSAS), but it also indicates the importance of Christianity both for Turfloop administrators, who permitted religious activism while they actively worked to

[16] Ibid., p. 69.
[17] 'Students on tightrope: Quiet but "restive" at Turfloop', *The Star*, 14 September 1968 [HPRA AD1912/258.16].
[18] 'Black schools have lost church quality', *Pretoria News*, 22 May 1972 [HPRA AD1912/258.16].

prevent political activism, and for the students themselves, who participated in these religious groups.

Though it arrived quickly on campus at Turfloop and fellow 'bush'
colleges, UCM was founded by a cohort of white chaplains and launched
at Rhodes University in the Eastern Cape. One of its founders and its
first president, Basil Moore, was the Methodist chaplain at Rhodes in
1966 when, with the national Catholic students' chaplain Father Colin
Collins, he developed the idea to 'form a new non-racial and radically
ecumenical student Christian body'.[19] In each of these facets the UCM
introduced a new form of student society to South Africa's campuses;
until its launch major Christian student groups had been both sectarian
and racial in their divisions. At its founding, the UCM was supported
by five 'mainstream' churches: the Methodist, Catholic, Anglican, Presbyterian, and United Congregational churches. This coalition was fostered by founders Moore and Collins, who were active in the student
organizations of their own denominations, and it also owed a debt to
their concerted outreach to other churches in order to make UCM as
ecumenical as possible.

The new organization received tacit support and sometimes contributions of funds and space from the coalition of churches behind it, but
as it became increasingly radical in its politics it also sometimes came
into conflict with them. In particular, its relationship with the Catholic
Church came under strain as early as 1969. In spite of the fact that
UCM's General Secretary at the time, Collins, was a Catholic priest,
many local and national church leaders viewed the movement with
mistrust and suspicion of its political motives. Reverend Clemens van
Hoeck, the Bishop of Pietersburg at the time, sent Collins a letter in
March 1969, banning the UCM from affiliating with Catholic students
at Turfloop, and from using the church's nearby property, St Benedict's
Mission in Magoebaskloof, for any UCM activities.[20]

Though its genesis was in white institutions and leaders, the UCM
quickly embraced its non-racialist ideology at all levels of the organization. In addition to white leaders like Moore and Collins, black student activists became involved and moved into prominent positions. In
1968, three of its five regional directors were African, and by 1969 it
had elected its first African president, Justice Moloto. He held the post
for two years and was succeeded by an African woman, Winky Direko,
though Moloto stayed on in the role of General Secretary during her

---

[19] Author's correspondence with Rev. Basil Moore, 14 August 2012.
[20] Letter from Clemens van Hoeck, Abbot Bishop of Pietersburg, to Father Colin
B. Collins. Pietersburg, 7 March 1969 [HPRA AD1126/G2].

administration. These demographic shifts were also reflected in the composition of UCM's student body, and by the late 1960s it was already a black-majority organization. Basil Moore attributes this to its success on campuses like Turfloop, where SRCs had been banned from affiliating to NUSAS and other overtly political organizations, but where UCM still offered space where 'black students could meet to discuss issues relevant to them'.[21] Further, John de Gruchy has suggested that the UCM's focus on Black Theology and Black Consciousness had alienated some of its white student constituents.[22]

UCM's ideological scope also reached beyond that of many of its fellow Christian groups and went firmly into the realm of political action. This was partly a conscious aspect of its founding, and partly a result of it becoming the *de facto* forum for political expression on black campuses. Moore notes that for the delegates at that first conference, 'Certainly political issues were of far greater significance to the participants than the ecumenical issues.'[23] The organizers worked to link these two strands: UCM's ethos was one of an active approach to Christianity, encouraging members to participate in 'projects like work-camps, literacy campaigns and similar projects aimed at alleviating the seriousness of conditions that come as a result of poverty and general deprivation'.[24] For the UCM the link between this general deprivation and apartheid policies was stark. After returning from a UCM trip to the United States, Turfloop student Bob Kgware wrote disappointedly to Basil Moore of the racial segregation he encountered abroad:

> [A]t the great free 'Process '67' in the stimulating Black Power caucuses no white man dared to go there. Even outside the caucuses, you would be fortunate to discuss the 'Black Power' movement in the presence of both Blacks and Whites. Either the Blacks would be unwilling to enter such a discussion, [...] or the Whites would also not enter conversation with the same openness or vivaciousness shown in other fields or subjects.
>
> One then wonders what [...] effective interaction exists between those whites who are helping the blacks in their struggle, and the blacks themselves? One wonders whether that 'I know what's good for you' element would not prevail? So much for this. Just like home.[25]

---

[21] Author's correspondence with Rev. Basil Moore, 14 August 2012.
[22] J. De Gruchy, *The Church Struggle in South Africa*, 2nd edn (Cape Town, 1982), p. 155.
[23] Author's correspondence with Rev. Basil Moore, 14 August 2012.
[24] SASO memo, 3 November 1970 [HPRA AD1126/J].
[25] Letter from Bob Kgware to Basil Moore, 7 April 1968 [HPRA AD1126/F].

The entire Kgware family were active participants in the UCM branch at Turfloop, often to their own detriment, as it brought them into conflict with the university administration on more than one occasion. Bob's father, Professor William Kgware, formally withdrew his own membership of the UCM in 1968,[26] as the organization's increasingly political profile on campus caused tension in his role as a senior faculty member, although much of his family remained active in the organization – and in anti-apartheid politics – for long after that. His wife Winifred continued to act as a coordinator for the Turfloop UCM in the early 1970s when it was banned by university authorities and driven off-campus into Mankweng Township for its meetings. She eventually became the first president of the Black People's Convention (BPC), an offshoot of the South African Students' Organisation (SASO) and the Black Consciousness Movement that sought to mobilize people outside the student community. Their daughter Manana Kgware was very active in campus politics at Turfloop: she was a member of the UCM, of the SRC, and a founding member of the SASO branch at Turfloop. She remained active in that organization even after leaving Turfloop and moving to the Orange Free State to work as a teacher. Her brother Bob had been a prominent member of the UCM nationally, and was one of only three in the South African delegation that was sent to the UCM's conference in the United States.

In contrast to the rest of his family, Professor Kgware struggled with his role as a senior faculty member at Turfloop and his family's activism against apartheid oppression. Resigning his UCM membership to prevent conflict with the university administration was the first in a series of compromises, which, nearly a decade later, helped him to become Turfloop's first black rector.

A year after Professor Kgware's resignation, in the winter of 1969 UCM was formally banned from campus at Turfloop (and also at Fort Hare, the University of the Western Cape, and the University of Zululand).[27] However, UCM drew the suspicion and ire of university authorities well before its banning: in October 1968, Manana Kgware wrote to UCM executive member James Moulder in Johannesburg with the news that 'a list of dangerous students' had been drawn up by the university administration, and that the twenty names included her brother Bob and several other UCM members. Surprisingly, Manana

---

[26] Minutes of the Executive Meeting held in Johannesburg, 27–29 September 1968 [HPRA AD1126/A3].
[27] Letter from Fr Colin Collins to Barney Pityana, 25 August 1969 [HPRA AD1126/G2].

herself was not among these. In her own words: 'The most interesting thing is that I am not included, the reason of course is only one, being in the SRC executive, it is dangerous to take me to task. [The Rector] is aware that this SRC has the backing of the student body [...].'[28]

In light of later developments in student politics at Turfloop, Manana's assertion of the SRC as a safe place, or a refuge from the university authorities is remarkable. This marked a particular and fleeting moment in the life of student politics at the university: less than four years after Kgware's letter, an inflammatory graduation speech by Onkgopotse Tiro, himself a former SRC president, was to lead to his own permanent expulsion from the university, as well as to the expulsions of all members of the SRC who had invited him to speak. By this stage, association with the SRC was no longer a place of refuge; rather it located students on the frontlines of the political struggle on campus. A primary factor in this shift was the presence on campus of the South African Students' Organisation, which formed at Turfloop in 1969.

SASO's arrival at Turfloop was a pivotal moment for mass mobilization in student politics.

This new organization had close links to the older UCM; many of its founding members, including Steve Biko and Barney Pityana, had been UCM members themselves. Some of the initial plans for SASO were laid out at the 1968 UCM Conference in Stutterheim.[29] And at Turfloop some of the key UCM leaders transitioned into roles with SASO, Manana Kgware among them. But SASO's mobilization approach was broader than that employed by UCM. Whereas individual students made the decision (or not) to join UCM, SASO organized its affiliation through SRCs, so that by virtue of its mandate from the students an SRC could affiliate the entire student body to SASO.[30] SASO thus brought political activism into the mainstream of life at Turfloop. While the UCM remained firmly on the radical side of most campus organizations, SASO successfully situated itself and its politics at the centre of campus life. Its ability to do so owed a debt to the earlier mobilization and structure of the Turfloop branch of the UCM. Though the UCM was officially banned on campus by the time SASO was inaugurated in 1969, both groups shared overlapping ideology and leadership while Turfloop's UCM branch continued to remain active from its new base

---

[28] Letter from Manana Kgware to James Moulder, 4 October 1968 [HPRA AD1126/F].

[29] Interview with Harry Nengwekhulu by author (a), 19 October 2011.

[30] Interview with Pandelani Nefolovhodwe by author, 27 September 2011.

outside campus.[31] For the period of their co-existence (1969–72) the two organizations worked in close cooperation on projects that joined anti-apartheid politics with Christian activism.

For UCM, practising Christianity in active opposition to apartheid and racist policies culminated in the development of the Black Theology programme. It formally adopted this approach in 1971 with the explicit support of SASO, which later assumed responsibility for the project after the dissolution of UCM in 1972.[32] Black Theology sought to combat the apartheid regime's use of religion as a tool for the oppression of black South Africans. Like Black Consciousness, with which it is closely associated, it was directed within the black community itself to combat the effects of oppression experienced through existing theologies. The development of a Black Theology programme in 1971, in conjunction with SASO's new philosophy of Black Consciousness, was not an accident of timing. Louise Kretzschmar notes their 'interdependence and mutual influence',[33] and SASO declared the role of black theologians and black ministers to be 'intrinsically interwoven in the surge towards Black Consciousness and liberation'.[34] Though a project, and later a movement, in its own right, Black Theology owed much of its thinking to the philosophy of Black Consciousness, which was informed by the writings of men like Stokely Carmichael and the American Black Power Movement. Critics, ranging from the South African government to some disaffected SASO members, even accused SASO of importing its philosophy of Black Consciousness wholesale from black Americans, pointing to commonalities in both ideology and phrasing. Magaziner argues that these commonalities amounted to more than straightforward plagiarism,

---

[31] Notably, although the Turfloop branch moved off-campus after its 1969 banning by Acting Rector Professor Engelbrecht, it still faced challenges operating and holding meetings in Mankweng Township. On 1 June 1969 ten white students from the University of the Witwatersrand in Johannesburg were arrested at the Anglican Church in Mankweng while attending a religious service and UCM meeting. ('University Christian Movement Information for the Churches', undated memo, c. 1969 [HPRA AD1126/A]); affidavits of not-guilty declaration from Charles Murcott, Robin Benger, Anthony Bowers, Jill Bannatyne, Ann Ohlssen, Charles Simkins, Richard Schaerer, Jennifer Rodda, Renfrew Christie, and Antoinette Halberstadt, all dated 5 June 1969 [HPRA AD1126/G5].

[32] SASO Newsletter, August 1971, 'The Commission on Black Theology' [HPRA AD1126/J].

[33] L. Kretzschmar, *The Voice of Black Theology in South Africa* (Johannesburg, 1986), p. 60.

[34] SASO Newsletter, August 1971, 'The Commission on Black Theology' [HPRA AD1126/J].

however: 'Activists copied, but they also translated; they read words from one context and wrote them into their own.'[35]

Black Theology also had roots across the Atlantic, most particularly in the work of black American theologian James Cone. Cone's *Black Theology and Black Power* (1969) and *A Black Theology of Liberation* (1970) became seminal works for the founders of the Black Consciousness Movement and Black Theology in South Africa. During their trip to the United States in 1967, Basil Moore and Bob Kgware were exposed to Cone's writing and later met Cone himself.[36] In addition, his article 'Toward a Black Theology', published in a 1970 edition of the African American magazine *Ebony*, was photocopied and distributed in its entirety to delegates at the SASO 1971 General Students Council despite the fact that *Ebony* was a banned publication in South Africa at the time.[37] Cone's Black Theology posits Christianity as 'a religion of protest',[38] and he rails against the status quo in America that had, with both the tacit and sometimes open support of churchmen and women, colluded in the oppression of American blacks. Christ, he determines, was a far more revolutionary figure:

> Jesus had little toleration for the middle- or upper class religious snob whose attitude attempted to usurp the sovereignty of God and destroy the dignity of the poor. The Kingdom [of God] is for the poor and not the rich because the former has nothing to expect from the world while the latter's entire existence is grounded in his commitment to worldly things.[39]

Cone cautions against allowing this perception of the Kingdom of God to be 'merely an eschatological longing for an escape to a transcendent reality'.[40] He called for black Americans to recognize 'what Jürgen Moltmann calls "the political hermeneutics of the gospel".'[41] Moltmann contends that the Christian gospel, when properly interpreted, offers a 'categorical imperative to overthrow all conditions in which man is a

---

[35] Magaziner, *The Law and the Prophets*, p. 48.

[36] Moore, 'Learning from Black Theology', pp. 1–2; Moore asserts that he and Bob Kgware were exposed to *Black Theology and Black Power* on their 1967 trip, but the text was not published until 1969. However, they did meet Cone on their visit to the United States, and it is certainly possible that they were exposed to early versions of his thesis on black theology during their interactions.

[37] T. Sono, *Reflections on the Origins of Black Consciousness in South Africa* (Pretoria, 1993), pp. 48–9.

[38] J. Cone, *Black Theology and Black Power* (New York, 1969), p. 37.

[39] Ibid., p. 36.

[40] Ibid., p. 37.

[41] Ibid., p. 37.

being who labors and is heavily laden'.[42] To support his arguments Cone relies heavily on biblical quotes directly from the gospels, wherever possible drawing these from Jesus himself: 'The last shall be first and the first last' (Matthew 20:16), and 'The blind receive their sight, the lame walk, the lepers are cleansed, the deaf hear, the dead are raised up, the poor have the good news preached to them' (Luke 7: 26).

> This is not pious talk [Cone says], and one does not need a seminary degree to interpret the message. It is a message about the ghetto, and all other injustices done in the name of democracy and religion to further the social, political, and economic interests of the oppressor. In Christ, God enters human affairs and takes sides with the oppressed.[43]

In contrast to theorists (like Marx) who argued that religion acts primarily as a pacifying force to keep the poor and working class focused on a heavenly afterlife rather than addressing structural inequality in the present, Cone's theology demanded active resistance. He called for revolution in black America, which he described as 'a radical black encounter with the structure of white racism, with the full intention of destroying its menacing power'.[44] Such a revolution had to grapple with the issue of violence. Cone acknowledged the difficulties of addressing this from a theological viewpoint: the Jesus presented in the New Testament explicitly denounces violence and advocates forgiveness. But Cone cautions against reading such biblical passages too literally: 'We cannot solve ethical questions of the twentieth century by looking at what Jesus did in the first. Our choices are not the same as his.'[45] In the context of race in twentieth-century America he declares,

> [Christians] must ponder whether revolutionary violence is less or more deplorable than the violence perpetuated by the system. There are no absolute rules which can decide the answer with certainty. [...] But if the system is evil, then revolutionary violence is both justified and necessary.[46]

Writing in the late 1960s, at the height of the American civil rights movement, Cone declared that incremental political gains were not enough: 'It does not matter how many gains are made in civil rights. Progress is irrelevant. The face of the black revolutionary will always be there as long as white people persist in defining the boundary of black being.' In this he called for a shift in the way black people understood

---

[42] Jürgen Moltmann, quoted in ibid., p. 37.
[43] Ibid., p. 36.
[44] Ibid., p. 136.
[45] Ibid., p. 139.
[46] Ibid., p. 143.

and defined themselves, something that both Black Theology and Black Consciousness in South Africa embraced.

For Cone a true realization of Christian faith, then, was not patiently awaiting a heavenly afterlife. Rather it was the highly politicized pursuit of justice and freedom for the oppressed in *this* world. This call-to-arms of the faithful spoke directly to the student leaders of the fledging Black Consciousness and Black Theology movements in South Africa. Many were Christian believers themselves and had been raised in the churches, but were frustrated with the delayed justice that was promised in a heavenly reward. Cone's Black Theology, with its political appeals against injustice, revolutionary language, and heavy reliance on the New Testament gospels, became a cornerstone of their own version of Black Theology for the South African situation. SASO leadership even invited Cone to speak at one of their annual General Student Councils. Though he was denied a visa and unable to come, his interpretation of Black Theology was a central point of discussion at the council.[47]

The co-development of Black Theology and Black Consciousness, and the appeal of the highly political theology of men like Cone and Moltmann, are indicative of the close relationship between politics and religion in both the UCM and SASO's ideology. In 1971 UCM executive member (and SASO member) Sabelo Stanley Ntwasa led a Commission on Black Theology, which was initiated to evaluate the future and role of Black Theology as a project within the UCM. Ntwasa was an Anglican seminarian at the Federal Theological Seminary (FedSem) near Fort Hare who had been seconded to the UCM while on leave from his studies, particularly to study the concept of Black Theology.[48] He was also the nephew of banned Pan Africanist Congress (PAC) leader Robert Sobukwe.[49] His commission concluded that 'Theology as taught in schools conducted by the various education departments was aimed at brainwashing pupils. The commission also found that religious instruction was being used as a part of the [South African state's] propaganda machinery.'[50] The commission indicted white churches for supporting the status quo and furthering oppression by proposing token fixes like

---

[47] Author's interview with Harry Nengwekhulu (a).

[48] Magaziner, *The Law and the Prophets*, pp. 100–1; for more on the history of FedSem and its involvement in student protests, especially at Fort Hare, see Massey, *Under Protest*.

[49] X. Mangcu, 'South Africa: Neglected Ntwasa was a stalwart of Black Consciousness Movement', *Business Day*, 27 May 2004.

[50] SASO Newsletter, August 1971, 'The Commission on Black Theology' [HPRA AD1126/J].

'interracial fraternization as a solution to the problems of this country, whereas [the churches] are fully aware that the basic problem is that of land distribution, economic deprivation and consequently the disinheritance of the Black people'.[51] This marks an early articulation of the growing concern over multi-racialism within the UCM, which became a significant problem the following year. In support of the work of the commission, the SASO General Students Council (GSC) passed a resolution declaring,

> Black Theology asserts its validity and sees its existence in the words of Christ, who in declaring His mission said: 'He has sent me to bring good news to the poor, to proclaim liberty to the captives, and to the blind new sight, to set the downtrodden free, to proclaim the Lord's year of favour.' [Luke 4: 18–19] Black Theology, therefore, understands Christ's liberation not only from circumstances of internal bondage but also a liberation from circumstances of external enslavement.[52]

Such language makes it clear that Black Theology as an undertaking of both UCM and SASO had overtly political motives; its goal was to use Christianity to affect psychological and political change in South Africa, and its emphasis on black self-reliance aligned it with Africanism.

Black Theology itself did not mark a major theological shift for the UCM, however. As defined in a 1970 paper by Basil Moore, the organization was already committed to a politicized theology that was greatly informed by social circumstances. Moore declared outright that 'accepting the inferiority of black people is a social evil and hazard, a vitally important means of encouraging social change would be to counter the current South African trend in the education of blacks by infusing them with a sense of pride and dignity'.[53] Later that year the development of Black Consciousness ideology, and then Black Theology in 1971, fit neatly into this framework. Black Theology also found direct biblical roots for political action in the South African context, as the quote above from the gospel of Luke, about Christ liberating captives and setting the downtrodden free, indicates. This was a key aspect of their intellectual project. Victor Mafungo further articulated the connection between Christ and South African blacks in an article in the SASO Newsletter. Incorporating a strain of self-reliance that had echoes of Black Consciousness, he wrote that a neglect of Christ's own oppression was the 'missing link' in white-dominated Christian discourse, and

---

[51] Ibid.
[52] Ibid.
[53] B. Moore, 'A 1970 Theological Point of View of the UCM' (unpublished, 1970), p. 6 [HPRA AD1126/A].

that it was up to black theologians to fill that void and to link Christ to the struggles of twentieth-century black South Africans.[54]

From its inception the UCM had been an ecumenical organization, and as such it had difficulty forming a concrete theological basis beyond its commitment to social change, as embodied in Black Theology. It consciously avoided basing itself on a statement or confession of faith that would be restrictive or exclusive, and concerned itself instead with what its membership should be doing rather than what they should be believing.[55] This is yet another example of the UCM's deep roots in the pursuit of social justice, almost to the exclusion of any denominational doctrine or theology. This ecumenism was radical for its time; most religious youth groups in South Africa were bound not just by racial divisions, but by allegiance to a particular church or creed. By 1970 the challenges of this approach had become clear to some leaders of the movement, who recognized the challenge it posed to established churches, including some of the UCM's early supporters. Basil Moore wrote that though these groups might be threatened by the UCM's 'search for meaning through new experiences', this was a fundamental, yet common, misunderstanding of Christianity. 'Christ himself died on a political cross at the instigation of the "church" authorities, for neither could tolerate the idea of change inherent in the concept of "redemption".'[56]

Its ecumenism across many churches with primary affiliation to none and its unwavering commitment to fundamental change in the practice of South African Christianity finally contributed to the dissolution of the UCM in 1972. In the motion for that dissolution, the executive noted three primary barriers to the group's continued operation: the withdrawal of support by three of the five founding churches of the UCM; increasing state pressure against the organization, including harassment by Special Branch police and the banning of several UCM leaders; and a new advocacy of 'black/white polarization' among its mixed leadership, in contravention of the multi-racial foundations of the UCM itself.[57]

The first of these, the withdrawal of church support, was a significant but not sudden factor. The disintegration of support by the founding churches began well before the UCM's final dissolution. Among these five, the Roman Catholic Church had a tense relationship with the UCM from as early as 1969, as mentioned earlier in the conflict between Father

---

[54] V. Mafungo, 'Black Theology: A re-assessment of the Christ', SASO Newsletter, 1(4), September 1971, p. 7 [HPRA AD1126/J].
[55] Moore, 'A 1970 Theological Viewpoint of the UCM', p. 1 [HPRA AD1126/A].
[56] Ibid., p. 7 (emphasis original).
[57] Motion of Dissolution of the UCM, 1 April 1972 [HPRA AD1126/A1].

Collins and the Bishop of Pietersburg. Continued tensions between the
UCM and a growing segment of the Catholic Church, most particularly
those bishops of areas with universities in them,[58] finally led Father Collins to resign from the priesthood in early 1970. This decision placed
him firmly on the side of politicized religion and the push for social justice espoused by the UCM; his affiliation to its doctrine of social change
led him to formally break with the more conservative structures of the
Catholic Church. Steve Biko, founder of SASO and member of UCM,
congratulated him on this move.[59] Collins's decision was recognized by
activists like Biko as a political triumph, but it was also a mark of the
hardening lines between religion and politics. Organizations like the
UCM, and people like Collins, who blurred the scope of each of these,
were to face a great deal of pressure in the coming years. Following
Collins's break with the Catholic Church, and increasing pressure by
the state security apparatus on the UCM, by the time of its dissolution in 1972, the Methodist and Presbyterian Churches had formally
withdrawn their support from the UCM, and the Anglican Church had
begun to question the wisdom of their support, leaving only the United
Congregational Church of the original five founding churches in support
of the UCM.[60]

Authorities outside the founding churches extended this isolation, as
well. By August 1969 the UCM was banned by university administrators
from operating on four of the University College campuses, including
Turfloop.[61] The security police had begun to take a close interest in the
activities of the movement. Correspondence between Father Collins and
Father D. Medard van de Rostijne indicates that Special Branch paid
visits to the UCM headquarters in Johannesburg and to St Benedict's
Mission outside Tzaneen after some UCM students were temporarily
housed there.[62] This pressure eventually resulted in the government banning three members of the UCM executive, including two past presidents and the director of the Black Theology programme, in the spring
of 1972.[63]

---

[58] Letter from Fr Colin B. Collins to Rev. Clemens van Hoeck, Bishop of Pietersburg. 24 March 1969 [HPRA AD112/G2],
[59] Letter to Colin Collins from Steve Biko, undated, c. March 1970 [HPRA
AD1126/F].
[60] Motion of Dissolution of the UCM, 1 April 1972 [HPRA AD1126/A1].
[61] Letter to Barney Pityana from Colin Collins. 25 August 1969 [HPRA AD1126/
G2].
[62] Letter to D. Medard van de Rostijne from Colin Collins, 3 June 1969; letter to
Colin Collins from D. Medard van de Rostijne, 1 July 1969 [HPRA AD1126/F].
[63] Motion of Dissolution of the UCM, 1 April 1972 [HPRA AD1126/A1].

The dissolution of the movement was undertaken in the midst of these isolating pressures. It was initiated by the multi-racial executive commit-tee, including Colin Collins and then General Secretary Chris Mokodi-toa. This group resolved that, in spite of the multi-racial founding ethos of the University Christian Movement, 'our own projects show that we no longer believe that multi-racialism is a viable strategy to bring about change'.[64] These projects included a Literacy outreach programme in rural areas, a White Consciousness Project, and Black Theology.[65] The last was UCM's most enduring legacy.

The dissolution of the UCM also marks an important moment when SASO and its allies abandoned attempts to employ multiracialism as a strategy for political change. To some degree, since the development of Black Consciousness as an ideology in 1970, and even since SASO's formation in 1968, which was predicated on breaking with multi-racial groups like NUSAS, the writing had been on the wall. But it was the self-dismantling of the UCM, which had been founded on multi-racial principles, its own advocacy of 'black/white polarization',[66] and its clear abandonment of the strategy of multiracialism, that solidified this trend. After the dissolution of UCM, SASO's links to multi-racial groups were effectively severed, and it moved into an ideology that bore more simi-larity to the Africanism of the Pan Africanist Congress (PAC) than to any other liberation movement in South Africa.

SASO and Black Consciousness modified the Africanism of the PAC in important ways, however: it shared some influences from African nationalists and philosophers like Frantz Fanon, but it also drew on ide-ologies expressed by black Americans like Stokely Carmichael and James Cone, as discussed above. In addition, it broadened its target audience, addressing a more encompassing group of 'blacks' rather than Africans, or Bantus as apartheid had categorized them. While the PAC conceived of Africans only as black Africans, and particularly those within South Africa's ethnic groups, Black Consciousness defined black as something much broader: it included Indians, coloureds, and all those who were oppressed by the apartheid state. It largely excluded whites, however. Though SASO had white sympathizers – many of the activists who had been involved in the UCM, for instance – they were explicitly excluded from membership because they did not experience the oppression that the state meted out based on race.

[64] Ibid.
[65] Ibid.
[66] Ibid.

Black Consciousness itself was an ideology rather than an organization; it had no card-carrying members, but it targeted everyone who had
been psychologically subjected to the doctrines of racial superiority and
inferiority on which apartheid was built. Still, even in its broader conception of who 'counted' as black, the Black Consciousness Movement
with its emphasis on self-reliance and psychological liberation adopted
and advanced some key tenets of Africanism as it had been identified in
earlier decades. Anton Lembede, the father of South African Africanism
and former member of the ANC Youth League, wrote in 1946, of the
'symptoms of a pathological state of mind' that affected black Africans
in South Africa: 'loss of self confidence, inferiority complex, a feeling
of frustration, the worship and idolization of white men, foreign leaders and ideologies', and called for people to free themselves from this
pathology.[67] Twenty-six years later, Lembede's inheritors had managed
not only to rally an important segment of the black population around
this idea of psychological liberation, but, as demonstrated by the UCM
leadership, they had persuaded a segment of the white population (albeit
a very small one) for that need as well.

After the UCM dissolved, Black Theology became a primary project
of SASO, and the UCM donated office furniture and supplies, as well as
its remaining funds, to its fellow student organization.[68] Until the end,
these two groups were closely linked ideologically, with many points of
intersection in shared projects and members, but UCM's ecumenism,
multiracialism, and more limited mobilization strategy resulted in its
own dissolution, while SASO went on to become the most significant
mobilizing force in student politics at Turfloop of the 1970s.

The South African Students' Organization

The South African Students' Organization (or SASO) was founded in
December of 1968 at the University of Natal – Black Section.[69] Its birth
was the result of dissatisfaction among some black students about the
ability of the existing national student organization, the National Union
of South African Students (NUSAS), to represent the interests of a black
constituency. Harry Nengwekhulu, a Turfloop student and founding
member of SASO, describes discontent among black students in NUSAS

---

[67] A. Lembede, 'Policy of the Congress Youth League', *Inkundla ya Bantu*, May
1946, in Gerhart, *Black Power in South Africa*, p. 58.
[68] Letter to Barney Pityana from Chris Mokoditoa. 6 November 1972 [HPRA
AD1126/J].
[69] S. Biko, *I Write What I Like* (Oxford, 1988), p. 2.

over issues like language and flags of delegates, but points to a particular tipping point at a 1968 NUSAS Conference:

> [T]he idea came initially from the conference of NUSAS at Rhodes University. Big problem again with that – normally at those conferences NUSAS would say 'We must fight apartheid; we must sleep in the white areas.' We [black delegates] were doing that at very great risk of being arrested. When we went to Rhodes we said, 'No, this time we're all going to sleep at the [African] location.' [...] And it became a major issue, because why should we have [the] risk of being arrested by going to sleep in a white area, and you [white delegates] are not willing to? If you are fighting the system, you must come and sleep with us.[70]

Contention over this and similar issues that persistently divided black NUSAS members from white led finally to the 1968 formation of SASO. Writings of its founders and early leaders detail the key aims of the organization, which focus on the needs, aspirations, identity, and morale of black students on South Africa's campuses.[71]

Clive Nettleton, a former NUSAS vice-president, acknowledged the disaffection of black NUSAS members at the time SASO was founded, admitting 'that NUSAS was founded on White initiative, is financed by White money, and reflects the opinions of the majority of its members who are White'.[72] Few of NUSAS' members approached the founding of a 'rival' student organization with Nettleton's equanimity, however. There was much internal debate and contention over the fact that SASO, an organization founded specifically for the needs of 'non-white' students, flouted the non-racial policies that NUSAS itself supported. However, Nettleton's analysis is apt; in spite of its non-racial ideology, NUSAS was predominantly an organ of liberal white activism. In an effort to distance themselves from white liberals and, more importantly, to build a forum through which black students could politically engage, SASO set itself up as 'the custodian of non-white interests'.[73] They did so unapologetically, leading a crusade for psychological liberation among South African blacks that eventually developed into the Black Consciousness Movement.

At Turfloop, SASO had a somewhat variable beginning. Its inaugural national conference was held there in July 1969, and it was then

---

[70] Author's interview with Harry Nengwekhulu (a).

[71] Biko, *I Write What I Like*, p. 4.

[72] C. Nettleton, Racial Cleavage on the Student Left' in H.W. Van der Merwe and D. Welsh (eds.), *Student Perspectives on South Africa* (Cape Town, 1972), p. 134.

[73] Biko, *I Write What I Like*, p. 6.

and there that Steve Biko was elected the organization's first president. Under the leadership of Harry Nengwekhulu and Petrus Machaka, the Turfloop SRC elected to use its own funds to support the conference, which brought them into conflict with the university registrar who was concerned about SASO's ability to repay the money.[74] But the SRC was entitled to spend its student dues as it saw fit, in support of various student organizations. From the outset, it made a commitment to support SASO not just politically, but financially as well. But no sooner had SASO rooted itself at the University of the North than it began to encounter resistance from the university administration, similar to that faced at that time by the UCM.

Students at Turfloop had been disallowed from affiliating with NUSAS in 1968 after a protracted battle between university officials and the SRC. In fact, two former rectors at the time were 'encouraging students to "shake off the yoke of NUSAS" and to establish their own … organization.'[75] According to Nengwekhulu, Professor Engelbrecht, who was a professor of philosophy and the acting rector in early 1969, cautioned his students, 'Don't allow yourself to be used by NUSAS; you are not instruments.'[76] Gessler Muxe Nkondo, a young lecturer on campus at the time, also recalled the administration's initial support for SASO's apparent racial separatism.[77] SASO's on-campus leaders used this to their advantage. They garnered the tacit permission of Engelbrecht and the university administration to operate on campus by arguing that by forming their own organization they would not be 'used' by NUSAS. The administration was especially sympathetic to SASO's antipathy to white liberal NUSAS, because there was deep-seated mistrust between white liberals and the nationalist government.[78]

The formation of SASO, then, presented a conflict for the university administration: on the one hand, the formation of an all-black student organization, to supplant the older non-racial national union, aligned neatly with the ideals of separate development, which underlay the founding of the university itself. It also marked a point of intersection – surprisingly, perhaps – between the politics of SASO and the vast majority of white university staff in its anti-white liberal (and by extension, anti-NUSAS) stance. Until this point the administration of the University of the North had taken a cautiously permissive approach

[74] Author's interview with Harry Nengwekhulu (a).
[75] Wolfson, *Turmoil at Turfloop*, p. 12.
[76] Author's interview with Harry Nengwekhulu (a).
[77] Interview with Muxe Nkondo by Tshepo Moloi, 10 June 2017, Pretoria.
[78] Author's interview with Harry Nengwekhulu (a).

to student political activism: When students were dissatisfied with the prefect system of representation the administration permitted the establishment of an SRC. The UCM was allowed to operate on campus for nearly a year after officials expressed overt suspicion towards it, and in fact, Turfloop was the last of the black universities to ban the UCM on its campus.[79] Though university authorities would clamp down on politics when deemed necessary (as eventually happened to UCM), in early 1969 they had demonstrated a 'wait and see' philosophy to student groups on campus.

During this period of relative laxity on the part of the university administration, SASO built a strong presence on campus at Turfloop and at other black campuses throughout South Africa. They did so by a process of holding frequent and regular branch meetings, local formation schools, executive meetings, and annual General Students Councils (GSCs).[80] Branch meetings, on the smallest and most local scale, built up SASO's organizational capacity on individual campuses. Though, in its own words, SASO's reception after its launch in 1969 was 'mixed' nationally, Turfloop was one of its most prominent vocal and financial bases of support.[81]

Turfloop, then, was an early bastion of SASO support both politically and monetarily. Affiliation was arranged *en masse* through the SRC rather than on an individual membership basis (an important change from the mobilizing mechanisms of earlier groups like the UCM), and as the above quote indicates, the Turfloop student body overwhelmingly supported it. As has been mentioned, Turfloop was the site of SASO's inaugural congress, and many 'formation schools' went on to be held in surrounding locations (like the Kratzenstein Lutheran Mission Station, north-east of Turfloop), attracting Turfloop students and others from local and regional areas. These were essentially workshops geared at deepening political education for existing SASO members, and extending it to new ones. Such formation schools formed the next tier of SASO's organization: they allowed prominent local student activists to liaise with one another on a scale above the very local (that of the campus or the township) and acted as an important mechanism for publicizing SASO to new groups and members. These were run by local activists and frequently attended by national leaders to ensure that SASO

---

[79] Letter from Colin Collins to Rev. R. Selby-Taylor, 23 April 1969 [HPRA AD1126/G2].

[80] SASO meeting minutes, c. 1969–1976 [HPRA AD1126/J, A2176/4].

[81] Minutes of the SASO Executive Meeting, 3–5 December 1969, University of Natal, pp. 1–2 [HPRA AD1126/J].

ideology was taught as widely and cohesively as possible. In order to increase its reach and impact, SASO also began to publish and disseminate a monthly newsletter in 1970. In this, organizational leaders wrote campus news reports and topical articles about current projects (reports on Black Theology featured prominently in early editions[82]).

Campus and national leaders corresponded regularly by letter and telegraph, as well as travelling and convening at the local and regional formation schools. This frequent correspondence and a few highly mobile individuals (including a role of travelling general secretary) allowed SASO to be quickly responsive on a national scale to issues that arose on local campuses. The leadership also convened several times a year for National Executive Council meetings, and annually for a General Students Council (GSC) meeting. The GSC included delegates from all active SASO chapters. In order to create even broader solidarity among members, SASO also held annual Intervarsity days during the winter holidays. These brought together SASO members from around the country to participate in sports and games. This ensured that students from disparate and distant campuses – like Turfloop and the University of Zululand, for instance – could forge acquaintances, friendships, and political solidarity. SASO leaders would also use these occasions to address the assembled students about their programmes, and contemporary political events.[83]

In its early years, then, SASO effectively established networks of student activists throughout South Africa, and it built an especially strong branch at Turfloop. It was able to do so in part thanks to the university administration's initially ambivalent response to its founding: SASO's ostensible adherence to many of the University's own founding principles of separation earned it some room to operate at Turfloop in the very early 1970s. However, as it became evident that SASO's politics were as radical as the UCM's had ever been, and as its leaders began to articulate an ideology of Black Consciousness that drew heavily on the writings of men like Stokely Carmichael and the American Black Power movement, rather than on the separatism of apartheid, the new organization increasingly gave the administration cause for concern. The first manifestation of this concern came in early 1972, when in February the rector took steps to censor an SRC publication that contained SASO material in it. Rector Boshoff prevented the distribution of this 'Student

---

[82] SASO Newsletters 1(3) (August 1971) and 1(4) (September 1971) [HPRA AD1126/J].

[83] Author's interview with Pandelani Nefolovhodwe, Germiston, 27 September 2011.

Diary' until two articles, the SASO Policy Manifesto and a Declaration of Student Rights, had been removed. This caused the student body to call for his resignation, and to defend their right to print and distribute the materials. An SRC resolution declared 'that since the university administration recognizes their affiliation to SASO, their distribution of the SASO policy manifesto and other literature cannot be restricted'.[84] In an open letter to all students and staff, Boshoff expressed his feeling that 'the two articles are of a controversial nature, and a diary is no place for controversial articles'.[85] He did not, however, consider the SRC's failure to request his permission before printing the diary 'in a very serious light', and decided that the university would bear the cost of reprinting. This incident marked the Turfloop administration's first overt step against SASO on campus, but it did not hold the student body or even the SRC responsible for SASO's message. Very shortly this would no longer be the case.

As the example of the inclusion of SASO documents in a general student diary indicates, by 1972 SASO was deeply enmeshed in the fabric of student politics at Turfloop. It had built upon the work of the campus branch of the UCM and made effective use of affiliating with the entire student body through the SRC, rather than recruiting individuals. Their tiered levels of meetings – structured from the local to the national – encouraged cohesion within and between local branches.

Perhaps most importantly, the Turfloop SRC itself was a bastion of SASO politics. In 1970–1 it was led by Onkgopotse Ramothibi Abraham Tiro, a SASO activist and later a member of the SASO national executive. Under Tiro's administration the SRC led the Turfloop student body in protest over the university's proposed academic autonomy from the University of South Africa (UNISA), which had been responsible for setting the curriculum and granting degrees at Turfloop since its founding in 1959. In January 1970, that link was severed as Turfloop ceased to be the University College of the North and became the University of the North.

This change of name and ostensible autonomy changed relatively little in the governing structure of Turfloop; though UNISA no longer conferred the degrees of its graduates, the new university was autonomous in name only. The University of the North Act No. 47 of 1969

---

[84] 'Rector must resign – students', *Rand Daily Mail*, 4 March 1972 [HPRA AD1912/239].

[85] Memo from J.L. Boshoff to All Members of Staff and All Students of the University of the North, 'The Student Diary: Deletion of Articles' [National Archives of South Africa, hereafter NASA, BAO X109/6/4(42)].

(section 14) reaffirmed the control of the Minister of Bantu Education over appointments to and decisions made by the University Senate and Council, its two governing bodies. In addition, the university required approval from the minister for any donations or bequests it received.[86] The veneer of independence was thin at best; though the university was not beholden to UNISA's standards any longer, it was still clearly under the jurisdiction of the Department of Bantu Education and subject to the apartheid-style ethnic segregation of its founding.

In September 1970, when invited to take part in celebrations for this independence and the investiture of the university's first chancellor,[87] students boycotted the celebrations in protest. The alleged autonomy, they contended, was a farce: 'another calculated move by the Government to drive the Non-white students into a life of isolation, despair and perpetual frustration'.[88] Independence from UNISA was considered 'premature', and designed not to liberate the university but to further isolate it from its peers in South Africa. To this end, the SRC resolved

> That if independence has to be true to its meaning, such independence should also relate not only to academic independence of this College [but also to independence] from Government control [...].[89]

As a result of these resolutions, the entire student body boycotted the celebrations. Though the boycotts were resolved without expulsions or similar punishments, they indicate the increasing activism that was brewing on campus as the ties between the SRC and SASO grew. In 1972 the SRC presidency was taken over by Tiro's deputy, Aubrey Mokoena, and his SRC continued the criticism of university governance his predecessor had begun. Their outspoken politics were to bring the tensions that had been brewing between SASO, the SRC, and the administration to a head in autumn 1972.

---

[86] Quoted in White *From Despair to Hope*, p. 122.
[87] The first Chancellor of the University of the North was Dr W.W.M. Eiselen, who was Commissioner-General of the Northern Sotho before the creation of Lebowa as a self-governing Bantustan in 1972.
[88] Telegraph to the President of the UCM from A.R. Tiro, President of the SRC of the University of the North, 30 September 1970, Sovenga [HPRA AD1126/F].
[89] Ibid.

The Tiro incident[90]

On 29 April 1972, the University of the North graduated its third class as a fully autonomous university, and Onkgopotse Abraham Tiro, the former Student Representative Council president who had led the campaign against autonomy from UNISA, spoke as the elected speaker for the graduating class. Tiro had been a prominent student leader on campus since his arrival in the late 1960s, and was a member of the SRC and of the South African Students' Organisation. At the time of his selection as speaker he had completed his bachelors degree in education, and was working towards a postgraduate diploma in education.[91] By this time Tiro was already very politically engaged. His activism had early roots: he had been exposed to political protest at the age of 12 when, in 1957, his local primary school in the village of Dinokana, near the Botswana border, was closed as thousands of local women protested the introduction of pass laws.[92] This led to a frequently interrupted education in a series of schools in the Western Transvaal and Soweto. By the time he completed matric at Barolong High School in Mafikeng, he was already a student leader, and was elected to speak at the leavers' party. 'According to [Barolong] Principal Lekalake, 'Tiro's speech about the conditions the pupils were subjected to was so influential that dramatic changes were made immediately in the make-up of the school's administration.'[93] This gift for transformative oratory was to become his hallmark at Turfloop and beyond.

Tiro's invitation to speak at the 1972 graduation was issued at the behest of the sitting Student Representative Council, then under the leadership of Aubrey Mokoena (who had been Tiro's Vice-President the previous year). The role of such speakers was traditionally to support the university and its policies. According to one student who was present, 'Speakers at graduation were always custodians of the ideology of the time.'[94] Bearing witness to this, Mokgama Matlala, the chief minister of the Lebowa Bantustan who also spoke that day, gave a speech

---

[90] Some of this material has been explored in my article, A. Heffernan, 'Black Consciousness' lost leader: Abraham Tiro, the University of the North and the seeds of South Africa's student movement in the 1970s', *Journal of Southern African Studies*, 41(1) (2015), 173–86.

[91] Author's interview with Pandelani Nefolovhodwe.

[92] A. Lissoni, 'Student organizations in Lehurutshe and the impact of Onkgopotse Abram Tiros', in *Students Must Rise: Youth struggle in South Africa before and beyond Soweto '76*, ed. A. Heffernan and N. Nieftagodien (Johannesburg, 2016), pp. 34–44.

[93] Heffernan, 'Black Consciousness' lost leader', p. 176.

[94] Reuel Khoza, quoted in A. Butler, *Cyril Ramaphosa* (Oxford, 2008), p. 48.

advocating the policies of Bantu Education.[95] Tiro, however, did not conform to this tradition. His speech was a damning critique of Bantu Education and the broader discriminatory policies of apartheid, particularly its manifestations at Turfloop.

Tiro's speech married the structural injustices of Bantu Education, and indeed apartheid itself, with the local realities faced by students at Turfloop, and it was laced with the hypocrisy he saw there. He criticized apartheid on its own terms, beginning with a quote from South African Prime Minister John Vorster: 'Addressing an ASB congress in June last year Mr Vorster said: "No black man has landed in trouble for fighting for what is legally his." Although I don't know how far true this is, I make this statement my launch pad.' Tiro went on to critique the failures of apartheid in its manifestation at Turfloop: the fact that an ostensibly black university was run by white administrators and staffed predominantly by white faculty; that, absurdly, its bookshop was only open to whites; that it awarded university contracts for food supply to a white administrator rather than a local black supplier; and that vacation jobs on campus were allocated to white students 'when there are [Turfloop] students who could not get their results due to outstanding fees'.[96] He decried the indignities that parents of the graduates were forced to undergo, being kept outside the hall while white dignitaries sat in the front rows; he called for a black university to have black leadership, and to allocate jobs and contracts for its functioning within the black community. 'The system is failing,' Tiro declared. 'It is failing because even those who recommended it strongly, as the only solution to racial problems in South Africa, fail to adhere to the letter and spirit of the policy.'[97] Though his critique was deeply political, and enmeshed in local grievances, it was also framed by Christian values: he opened the speech quoting an American lay preacher on the centrality and importance of the truth, and he closed it on a ringing note of warning to university and apartheid authorities, with evangelical echoes of Martin Luther King Jr., saying, 'In conclusion Mr Chancellor I say: Let the Lord be praised, for the day shall come, when all men shall be free to breathe the air of freedom and when that day shall come, no man, no matter how many tanks he has, will reverse the course of events. God bless you all!'[98]

---

[95] Ibid., p. 48.
[96] G.M. Nkondo, *Turfloop Testimony: The dilemma of a Black University in South Africa* (Johannesburg, 1976), p. 91.
[97] Ibid., p. 92.
[98] Ibid., p. 93.

The aftermath of this speech was in some ways predictable, and in others extraordinary. Appalled at what they perceived as the abuse of the platform he had been given, the Rector and Advisory Council of the university expelled Tiro. The University Senate, all members of which were white, concurred. In response, following a mixed meeting of both black and white staff, the black academic staff of the university walked out in protest, students at Turfloop boycotted lectures, and the national committee of the South African Students' Organisation (SASO) began to mobilize. Tiro's expulsion set off protests of solidarity, not only at Turfloop, but also elsewhere around South Africa at other black universities and colleges. Though the University of the North insisted that Tiro was the only culprit to be blamed, this was a clear miscalculation. They failed to realize that his words had had an electrifying and galvanizing effect. Percy Mokwele, a young black lecturer in Education who was present, recalled, 'When Tiro addressed the graduation ceremony we were there in the hall. And during his talk students cheered, cheered and accepted what he was saying. And some black members of staff – especially the younger ones – also cheered.'[99]

Indeed, the expulsion of Tiro marked a turning point, not just for the students of Turfloop, but for the staff as well. Until 1972 academic staff at the university had co-existed in a joint Staff Association, the *Dosentvereniging* or Lecturers' Union, which was responsible for academic management and making recommendations to the Rector and University Senate. Though social activities and living quarters remained firmly separated by race under the ethos of apartheid, academic and administrative matters were undertaken and debated by this joint body.[100] In an emergency meeting after the 1972 graduation ceremony (mentioned above), this union faced the question of whether to support or condemn the university administration's decision to expel Tiro. As remembered by Percy Mokwele, it was a fraught discussion:

> During the discussions of what Tiro said, there was great tension in the meeting place [...]. The chairman was, of course, white and he wanted the staff association to condemn what Tiro said. But the black members of staff said nothing to him – they wouldn't agree. They didn't support that motion of condemning what he [Tiro] said and that the university [was] doing well by expelling him. It was great tension. And eventually when,

[99] Author's interview with Percy Mokwele, Turfloop, 20 September 2011.
[100] Author's interview with Percy Mokwele; 'Turfloop: Growing University of the North', *The Star*, 16 May 1968 [HPRA AD1912/258.16].

because white members were in the majority,[101] when they voted they won that motion of condemning Tiro and supporting the administration for expelling him, the black members of staff marched out, led by the most senior black member of staff: Professor Kgware, who was the most senior.[102]

This walkout was the fissure that led to a fundamental and lasting division between black and white staff at Turfloop for many years. It precipitated the formation of the Black Academic Staff Association (BASA), and by default a white academic staff association of the old *Dosentvereniging*. In the mid-1970s BASA became a vehicle for black staff to express their political support and solidarity with student causes. As tensions heightened at Turfloop the polarization between the white administration and staff, and the black staff and students became entrenched.

Before the formation of BASA, racial politics were already a facet of life at Turfloop, as has been discussed with regard to the UCM and SASO earlier in this chapter. By the time Tiro stood at the graduation podium in April 1972, the university authorities were highly suspicious of SASO. This was evidenced by Rector J.L. Boshoff's censoring the two SASO documents for distribution on campus in March 1972. That incident indicates the disintegration of the tacit consent with which the university administration had previously treated SASO's emergence in student politics, but as I have argued above it was a moderated response and no disciplinary action was taken against students. In a dramatic turn to more aggressive punitive measures, the administration banned SASO from campus in the aftermath of the 'Tiro incident'.

Aggressive action marked the general approach of the University of the North administration to Tiro's speech, and it was to become a hallmark of the relationship between the university and its students throughout the 1970s and 1980s. In reaction to Tiro's expulsion, students organized a boycott of lectures in protest 'until such time that Mr. Tiro be readmitted or tried before a tribunal'.[103] In response to this, the university administration summarily expelled *all* students from Turfloop and required each to apply for readmission. This heavy-handed tactic allowed administrators to pick and choose whom to readmit, with some knowledge of which student leaders played especially influential and

---

[101] In 1972 white academic staff outnumbered black at Turfloop by approximately three to one.
[102] Author's interview with Percy Mokwele.
[103] SASO memo from Rubin Phillip, 24 May 1972 [HPRA A2176/3].

political roles. In the end, the entire SRC and other influential students were denied readmission for a period of at least two years.[104]

Banning SASO on campus proved as ineffective as banning the UCM before it. These two organizations and their political platforms had already made an impact on the Turfloop student body. After the expulsion of Tiro and so many other student leaders in 1972, other students proved willing and able to step into their shoes. Whereas once anti-apartheid politics had been the province of a radical minority, now, according to student leaders from disparate groups, the majority of the student body supported them.[105] Thanks to SASO's bulk-affiliation method through the SRC, and to its frequent and widespread meetings and formation schools, most were conscientized[106] to the political situation. But another significant factor in the mobilization of students lay at the feet of the university administration itself: their strict punishment of Tiro, and the extreme reaction of expelling all students, served to galvanize not just the students and staff of Turfloop, but also their fellows at black universities across the country. The formation of the Black Academic Staff Association has already been mentioned. For the students' part, boycotts and protests on campus became frequent, almost routine. In the winter of 1972 students at Turfloop were out of lectures almost as much as they were in. Following a declared 1 June return-to-classes, protests resumed within days.

It is worth noting that the depth of conscientization varied; not all students became core SASO activists, and many (though by no means all) left their activism behind after university and went into administrative jobs sometimes in the very structures against which they had protested. But in the context of the very local and specific concerns of life at Turfloop – the overreach of the university authorities, and the effective mobilization by groups on campus like SASO and the SRC – students protested in huge numbers with stay-aways, boycotts, and walkouts.

---

[104] Author's interview with Pandelani Nefolovhodwe.
[105] Author's interview with Pandelani Nefolovhodwe; author's interview with Sydney Seolanyanne, Parktown, Johannesburg, 24 November 2011.
[106] Conscientization refers to a process of political awakening and education within a particular ideology or worldview. It was used widely by groups like SASO and the UCM in the 1960s and 1970s, similar to the way the term 'woke' is used today.

The Alice Declaration and student solidarity

The impact of these protests was felt well beyond Turfloop's walls. On 13 May 1972, in the weeks following the mass expulsion at the University of the North, delegates at a SASO Formation School being held at the Federal Theological Seminary (FedSem) in Alice in the Eastern Cape adopted what became known as 'The Alice Declaration'. Forty SASO delegates from black institutions and universities attended the Formation School, with the majority likely coming from FedSem itself and the nearby University of Fort Hare. The Alice Declaration, referring to incidents of unrest throughout the country, took particular notice of the recent expulsion of the entire Turfloop student body, and called for students at other black universities to shut down their own institutions in solidarity, by boycotting classes.[107]

The Alice Declaration was taken up by students at the Universities of Fort Hare, the Western Cape, Zululand, and Durban-Westville, and students on these campuses engaged in solidarity boycotts. Daniel Massey, in his institutional history of Fort Hare, has detailed how events at Turfloop dovetailed with Fort Hare students' frustration with their own rector, who they perceived as exacerbating tensions in the student body and 'as a mouthpiece of Pretoria'.[108] 'Angry at [Rector] De Wet's failure to address them and eager to display sympathy with the students of Turfloop, the Fort Hare students began a sit-in strike on 22 May with approximately 800 of the 900 students boycotting lectures.'[109] Turfloop's reach had extended far beyond the small farm in the Northern Transvaal, thanks in large part to the organizational capacity of SASO.

Quick responsiveness and the ability to mobilize their highly politicized base were two of SASO's great organizational advantages, both of which were displayed in its response to the expulsion of Tiro and the Turfloop student body following the 1972 graduation controversy. However, sometimes these mechanisms enabled such quick responses that the SASO executive was unable to control them. The Alice Declaration was one such instance. As it was initiated at a formation school by ordinary delegates with no electoral mandate, and not by the SASO executive, or indeed by representatives of the relevant SRCs, it caused some controversy. At a special meeting in June 1972 of SRC presidents, the SASO Executive Committee, and campus representatives of SASO,

---

[107] SASO, 'A Fact Paper: The Student Crisis', 1972, p. 1 (emphasis original) [HPRA A2176/6.20],
[108] Massey, *Under Protest*, p. 214.
[109] Ibid., p. 214.

the adoption and publication of the Alice Declaration the previous month 'came under serious discussion'. Concern was raised because 'this decision was published in the Sunday press even before the SRCs were consulted'. Some SRC leaders argued that this had allowed university officials to 'pre-arm' themselves, and perhaps had intimidated students before 'the students [had] planned themselves',[110] but the Alice Declaration also usurped some of their power to dictate the course of student protests. Though these and other significant concerns were raised over the timing and manner of the Alice Declaration, the leadership also recognized 'that students actually responded to the Alice call when they protested in June and fully aligned themselves with student resentment of authoritarian universities throughout the country'.[111] The SASO mechanisms for mobilization, then, were highly effective, although difficult to harness.

The university administration was not without leverage in the face of such student protests, however. In order to be readmitted, it required students to sign statements agreeing that '(1) Mr. A. R. Tiro will not be readmitted, (2) The Students Representative Council has been suspended, and (3) The Constitution of the SRC has been suspended including the committees and also the Local Committee of SASO'.[112] Over the course of the winter holidays most students eventually signed these declarations in order to return to the university, which caused contention in activist circles. At the 1972 SASO General Students Council meeting some of these students who were in attendance were accused of 'tactily [sic] accept[ing] that SASO be suspended on campus'. Turfloop's expelled SRC president Aubrey Mokoena brought a motion demanding that these students be requested to leave the conference.[113] Though the motion was withdrawn before a vote was held, it is indicative of the division that university authorities were able to foster by qualifying the readmittance of each individual student. In spite of this disagreement and the fact that most students at Turfloop did eventually return to lectures with their demands unmet, the mass-action in response to Tiro's expulsion marked a turning point in protest and politics at the University of the North, and was to shape the face of protest at the university for the

---

[110] Minutes from the Meeting of SRC Presidents (constituted in Johannesburg on 31 May 1972), SASO Executive Committee, and representatives of SASO on campuses, 17 June 1972, p. 1 [HPRA A2176/4.2].

[111] Ibid., p. 1.

[112] SASO, 'A Fact Paper: The Student Crisis', 1972, p. 3 [HPRA A2176/6.20].

[113] Minutes of the Proceedings of the 3rd General Students Council of the South African Students' Organisation, St Peter's Seminary, Hammanskraal, 2–9 July 1972 [HPRA A2176/5.2].

next two decades. The 1972 General Students Council meeting, at which Aubrey Mokoena lobbied for the expulsion of some Turfloop students, also marked a fraught moment in SASO's own politics. In addition to Mokoena and other SASO stalwarts decrying the collaboration of students who had returned to classes at the University of the North, a bigger scandal was brewing in the SASO executive itself between those favouring boycotts and isolation and those who were more willing to work within the framework demanded by the University authorities: Themba Sono had been elected as the third SASO president the preceding year. A former Turfloop student, Sono came from outside the original core of SASO leadership. Harry Nengwekhulu and Barney Pityana, then SASO's national organizers, had brought him to the attention of the executive as a presidential possibility. Even though Sono was selected as candidate by the SASO executive he turned out to be an unpredictable leader. Looking back, Nengwekhulu suggests that he was an unknown quantity, even though he had been proposed by members of the leadership:

> [I]n SASO we never really had democratic elections. We had democratic elections but they didn't exist, because we [the members of the executive] vetted – and we made sure that we know [who the candidate(s) would be]. [...] So Sono was a surprise candidate, something that had never happened.[114]

A surprise candidate was, it transpired, not something SASO knew how to handle. Soon suspicions of Sono had been raised: he was nowhere to be found when the other members of the SASO executive wanted him to represent the organization at the funeral of a colleague from the South African Institute of Race Relations, and the SASO secretary reported that he would not let her transcribe his speech notes in the lead-up to the General Students Council.[115] Rumours had begun to germinate that he might be informing to the police. But the real surprise that Sono presented was when he gave the presidential address at the 1972 General Students Council: rather than conforming to the standard SASO position on non-cooperation with 'The System' as the apparatuses of the apartheid state were called, he called for SASO to work through organizations within the Bantustans to further their programme of Black Consciousness and the elevation of black South Africans. It was a highly controversial speech that resulted in immediate calls for Sono's removal from the presidency and expulsion from SASO itself. Steve Biko, watching from the audience, drafted a motion that Sono's speech be struck

---

[114] Author's interview with Harry Nengwekhulu (a).
[115] Ibid.

from the record, to prevent it being reported in the press and associating SASO with any form of collaboration.[116] Following the speech, Biko's motion to suppress its contents, and a further motion calling for Sono's expulsion, were passed. Shortly thereafter Sono left South Africa to pursue further education in the United States. The allegations of collaboration increased as his former SASO colleagues speculated about the speed and apparent ease with which he received a passport to make the trip.[117]

Speaking obliquely about the incident a year later with an interviewer in New York, Sono argued again for the revolutionary potential inherent in the Bantustan system, noting the *de jure* and *de facto* power that Bantustan leaders had over eight million rural Africans. He argued that these figures could lead a real struggle for land and independence against Pretoria.[118] Sono, then, contends that he advocated cooperation with the Bantustans specifically to thwart the apartheid state, while those in the audience at the 1972 GSC heard only a protagonist of collaboration. This might have been an unfair critique of Sono, and indeed of Bantustans; at the time that Sono held the SASO presidency Bantustan leaders like Mangosuthu Buthelezi in KwaZulu and Cedric Phatudi in Lebowa were engaging to some degree with broader anti-apartheid forces. Beinart has argued they could be highly critical of the South African government, and even investigated the idea of forming a unified black South African state at a 1973 meeting.[119] That same year Hudson Ntsan'wisi, chief minister of the new Gazankulu Bantustan in the Northeastern Transvaal, gave a speech at Turfloop itself criticizing the very premise of a segregated university.[120]

But SASO had drawn a clear line on Bantustans and their leaders, even as some of those leaders began to articulate increasingly anti-apartheid politics. Even this was perceived as a boon to the South African state. Of the new rhetoric being used by Buthelezi and others, Biko wrote, 'Bantustan leaders are subconsciously siding and abetting in the total subjugation of the black people of this country. By making the kind of militant noise they are now making they have managed to confuse the

---

[116] Author's interview with Harry Nengwekhulu (a).

[117] Ibid.

[118] Sono, *Origins of Black Consciousness*, p. 126.

[119] W. Beinart, 'Beyond "Homelands": Some ideas about the history of African rural areas in South Africa', *South African Historical Journal*, 64(1) (2012), 5–21 (11).

[120] H. Ntsan'wisi, 'Opening address to the University of the North, Academic Year 1973', in *Deeds Speak* (Nelspruit, 1987), p. 38.

blacks sufficiently to believe that something great is about to happen.'[121] He further blamed the white press for publicizing the statements of Bantustan leaders, which, he argued, gave the misleading impression that South Africa protected free speech and that Bantustans offered a political challenge to the apartheid state, which the state was not actively repressing.[122] Biko argued that, in this way, reporting the limited criticism from Bantustan leaders actually propped up the legitimacy of the apartheid state to outside observers.

From the SASO perspective, cooperation in any form was interpreted as collaboration; no scope for changing apartheid from within its own structures – like Bantustans – existed. In the same General Students Council where Sono had given his controversial speech, a motion was brought that described Bantustans as 'nothing else but toy-telephones presumably meant to cheat black people into believing that they had communication-links with Pretoria', and resolved 'to call upon the leaders of Bantustans to forthwith withdraw from this system effort to preserve their own dignity and to demonstrate with the struggle of the black people'.[123] The motion was carried unanimously, 'with acclaim'.

The incident surrounding Sono's speech, and the starkly different perspectives on each side even decades later, indicates the highly charged atmosphere in SASO during the early 1970s, and the seriousness with which any threat of collaboration was dealt. Sono, the first presidential candidate who had not been tightly vetted by the founders of SASO, had used language that sent up alarms within the organization that he might be a collaborator with the apartheid state and the core of the SASO executive moved swiftly to protect the organization from this perceived taint. Ideological purity about the doctrine of non-cooperation was paramount for SASO, and this exacting measure sometimes took its toll: on those students who accepted university restrictions and returned to classes after the Tiro protests, and even at the very highest reaches of the organization.

The Students' Christian Movement

Christianity played a critical role in student politics at Turfloop as they were mobilized by both the UCM and SASO. The Black Theology of

---

[121] Biko, *I Write What I Like*, p. 85.

[122] Ibid., p. 85.

[123] Minutes of the Proceedings of the 3rd General Students Council of the South African Students' Organisation, St Peter's Seminary, Hammanskraal, 2–9 July 1972 [HPRA A2176/5.2].

James Cone that many students had embraced demanded political activism from its adherents, and Onkgopotse Tiro's pivotal speech had been peppered with evangelical, as well as political, language. The convergence of these two important strands in the student body gradually crystallized in another on-campus Christian group, the Students' Christian Movement (SCM). The SCM had been founded as an offshoot of the South African Students' Christian Association (SCA). The SCA was an all-white apolitical, evangelical body. After a national tour around late 1964, its founder Graham Mackintosh decided that black, Indian, and Coloured universities and high schools also had need of such an ecumenical Christian organization, and he set up branches of the SCA for each of South Africa's four racial groups.[124] These became independent, autonomous movements in January 1965, and in 1966 the Bantu Section of the SCA adopted the new name of the Students' Christian Movement of South Africa.[125]

In contrast to the UCM, the SCA and the SCM were always racially segregated, and their theology emphasized evangelical Christian ecumenism rather than Black Theology. The SCA drew its membership from a cross-section of Christian groups with strong roots in the 'mainstream' Protestant Churches (particularly Methodists, Lutherans, and Anglicans). The SCM also incorporated members from Pentecostal churches, like the Apostolic Faith Mission (AFM), and from some African Initiated Churches, like the populous Zion Christian Church (ZCC), with its headquarters very near Turfloop.[126] In its ecumenism, it was similar to its successful predecessor at Turfloop, the UCM, but arguably wider in its reach as UCM membership had always been heavily concentrated among the five mainstream churches that offered it support.[127] However, during the period of their co-existence, the theology of the Turfloop branch of SCM was much more conservative than that of UCM and its members were less politically active. Initially this was by the design of the top levels of the organization: in the words of founder Graham Mackintosh in a 1968 letter to former SCA travelling secretary Ruth Schoch, 'SCM is quite rightly not prepared to touch UCM with a barge pole and we are the only people who can give them [the SCM] the help

---

[124] Butler, *Cyril Ramaphosa*, p. 51.
[125] Correspondence between J.J. Viljoen and Rev. B.H.M. Brown announcing the formation of the SCM, 18 August 1966 [HPRA AC623/3.6].
[126] Author's interview with Sydney Seolonyanne.
[127] These were the Methodist Church, the Anglican Church, the Presbyterian Church, the Catholic Church, and the United Congregational Church.

they need to establish a Biblical witness on the campusses [sic] and to counter the UCM's excessively political slant.'[128]

In addition to its apolitical bent, and in another contrast to the UCM (which was the product of university students, chaplains, and staff), the SCM was most deeply rooted in secondary schools throughout South Africa. Though Mackintosh had established branches both on university campuses and at schools, it was in the latter environment that SCM particularly thrived. In Soweto it was one of many important Christian student groupings that linked students from key secondary schools like Sekano Ntoane, Morris Isaacson, and Naledi.[129] Elsewhere, as with Mphaphuli High School in Sibasa, Venda, it was the largest student organization at the school, and attendance at its meetings was compulsory in the late 1960s.[130] Branches at schools engaged in prayer meetings and bible study, but also in film and games meetings, and evangelical outreach to nearby communities. Initially these activities were explicitly Christian in focus: films were ordered from SCM-approved Christian providers, quiz nights consisted of opposing teams answering timed questions on biblical passages in front of an audience, and members were encouraged to bring in records and share music, but 'Preferably Christian choral or vocal works should be presented'.[131]

In this assortment of events, bible study was given pride of place: 'Without hesitation it may be stated that Bible Study is and should be the most important aspect of the practical work of every branch.' A guide outlined important passages and things to emphasize in this work; in contrast to the UCM's exegetical development of passages like Luke 4: 18, which focuses on Christ's coming to grant freedom to prisoners and the oppressed, the SCM took a much more literal approach to their interrogation of the text. The SCM generally dealt with the bible in much greater specifics than the UCM, and the two frequently focused on different passages, but where common themes can be identified, the two groups diverged in their interpretations: where the UCM advocated a Christian struggle against the evil of apartheid and racial segregation with overt political action, when SCM addressed the issue of battle, in regard to a passage in Judges 7: 1–25 in which Israelites fought the Midianites, the lesson to be taken away was that the contemporary battles of

---

[128] Letter from Graham Mackintosh to Ruth Schoch, 26 December 1968 [HPRA AC623/3.6].

[129] Glaser, *Bo-Tsotsi*, p. 162.

[130] Butler, *Cyril Ramaphosa*, p. 29.

[131] Handbook for the Students' Christian Movement of South Africa, May 1970 [HPRA AC623/3.6].

SCM members were 'too great for us. Unless we realise our helplessness in the face of the powers of Satan, we will never win the battle against him.'[132] The weapons to be used in such battles were always identified as spiritual weapons, never political ones. In another passage from the guide, SCM members are advised to 'Be angry and sin not. Anger is required, we must be angry about sin and injustice. But we must not be angry just to satisfy our own needs.'[133] The overall tone of SCM's theology emphasized the doctrine of individual salvation and responsibility, rather than the collective interventionist Christianity of the UCM. In its early days, SCM clearly identified the primary struggles its members faced as against sin and Satan, not the injustices of the South African state.

This barrier to political engagement began to slowly dissolve as SCM existed in schools and on campuses that were becoming increasingly politically aware, and as its members were exposed to the Black Theology being propagated by the UCM and SASO. In Soweto schools in the early 1970s some members began to jettison their apolitical stance and to engage with SASO and its affiliates.[134] Its growth at the university level owed a great deal to those roots; at Turfloop, many students who had been members while at school continued to be actively engaged in the organization.

These adherents were not initially enough to give the group credibility at Turfloop as the campus became increasingly politicized and tensions heightened. Though as an established group the SCM predated the UCM, by the late 1960s the increasing politicization on campus had made the conservative SCM something of a pariah among the bulk of Turfloop students. It was increasingly ostracized on campus by students for its apolitical 'emphasis on the gospel of individual salvation'.[135] In 1970 and 1971 those students who were SCM members were forced to meet secretly in lecture halls, or in the fields outside campus.[136] The organization was widely considered a 'sell-out' by politicized students in the very early 1970s, and was contrasted to the politically active and radical UCM, much as it had been contrasted by Mackintosh, although from a different perspective.

---

[132] 'Outlines for Group Bible Study', Students' Christian Movement of South Africa, undated c. early 1970s, p. 2 [HPRA AC623/3.6].
[133] Ibid., p. 2.
[134] Glaser, *Bo-Tsotsi*, p. 162.
[135] Butler, *Cyril Ramaphosa*, p. 50.
[136] Ibid., p. 51.

The tide began to turn for the SCM with the arrival of a new class of students in 1972. Like those before them, many among this class had been actively involved in the SCM at the school level; among these were the devoutly religious Frank Chikane and Cyril Ramaphosa. Ramaphosa particularly was well known for his evangelical work during secondary school in Sibasa, Venda, as well as for his personal charisma and leadership capabilities. Chikane had played an important role as mediator in conflicts – sometimes violent ones – between Christian and other, increasingly political, students at his high school in Orlando, Soweto.[137] By the time they both arrived at Turfloop in 1972, the situation for politically active Christians on campus was in flux; the UCM had been banned on campus and was also in the process of dissolving itself, as SASO assumed responsibility for programmes like Black Theology. Confronted with a radical and disintegrating UCM and a broadly reviled SCM, Ramaphosa rejected the politically pure position of joining UCM, and instead worked to reform the SCM's Turfloop branch.[138] Given that Ramaphosa's arrival on campus coincided with the last few months of the UCM's existence before dissolution, this proved to be a prescient choice. But beyond pragmatism, Ramaphosa's loyalty to the SCM, and that of many of his peers in their first year at Turfloop, including Chikane, Ishmael Mkhabela, and Lybon Mabasa, was rooted deeply. All had been involved in the organization's branches at their secondary schools in Soweto, and, in Ramaphosa's case, Sibasa. Their approach to the SCM was markedly different from the organization's profile on campus and incorporated a new focus on evangelical activism in local communities.

Men like Ramaphosa and Chikane brought this activism with them from their school days and were instrumental in spreading it to other Turfloop SCM members: this cohort arrived at Turfloop in early 1972, just months before Onkgopotse Tiro's pivotal speech, and at a moment when a space was opening in the political arena on campus. In the aftermath of Tiro's rousing (and explicitly Christian) speech and the mass expulsions, and with the UCM and SASO both now banned on campus, some SCM members also began to move away from a singular emphasis on salvation and the organization began to attract more politically active members.

But this shift within the group was gradual and, in some senses, incomplete. As contemporary SCM member and leader Sydney Seolonyanne

[137] F. Chikane, *No Life of My Own: An autobiography* (Johannesburg, 1988), p. 48.
[138] Butler, *Cyril Ramaphosa*, p. 51.

put it, the SCM on campus encompassed students of radically different political views: conservatives, fundamentalists, and those who took a pragmatically political stance, arguing, 'You know the life we live here in South Africa, [...] if you're black it affects you, regardless if you're a black fundamentalist or an ordinary Christian believer.'[139]

The early 1970s saw a shift in power between these factions – from the more fundamentalist, conservative base to a more politically active engagement pioneered by SCM's new leaders at Turfloop. SCM's theology began to incorporate contemporary issues and to address injustices faced daily by blacks in South Africa. According to Ishmael Mkhabela, his generation of SCM, 'were not just people who believed in fellowship and reflection. [...] We also consciously confronted the situation that we need to make our people, the students, raise their [political] awareness.'[140]

Ramaphosa particularly worked to restructure the SCM at Turfloop, and in so doing, he gave it a new political ethos. 'He produced a new constitution, and his fellow members were obliged to debate its contents endlessly. In this constitution, [Ramaphosa] inserted a "doctrinal basis" section that explicitly repudiated racism and the unjust system of apartheid.'[141] The structure of this new constitution and the process of forming it brought the SCM and its members at Turfloop more firmly into the arena of political action, while their intense programme of social activism involved close contact with the needs and problems of local communities. Sydney Seolonyanne articulates the shift this way:

> [W]hen I arrived [in 1970, the campus profile of SCM] was not as influential on student life as two years later, when these other youngsters: Ishmael, Lybon, Cyril, came. [...] it became very strong and influential; let's say from '72 onwards.[142]

This political awakening of the SCM was fortuitous in its timing for anti-apartheid activists at Turfloop. By 1972 both the UCM and SASO were banned on campus, and the UCM was only months away from its own dissolution. While SASO remained a powerful force off-campus, by 1974 the SCM had become the most significant group that was still unbanned and politically active within the campus walls. Though less

---

[139] Author's interview with Sydney Seolonyanne.
[140] Author's interview with Ishmael Mkhabela, Killarney, Johannesburg, 21 October 2011.
[141] Butler, *Cyril Ramaphosa*, p. 51.
[142] Author's interview with Sydney Seolonyanne.

closely associated with SASO than the UCM had been, the SCM and
SASO also had a working relationship and overlapping membership –
in 1974 Ramaphosa became the chairman of the off-campus branch of
SASO in addition to his leadership of SCM.

By the time of the publication of the Snyman Commission Report
into campus unrest in 1975,[143] the SCM, though still more conservative than the UCM had been, was increasingly recognized as a radical
student organization, having absorbed some of the UCM's members on
campus and adopted a modified version of its Black Theology. According to the report:

> During May 1973 the first signs of the political orientation of [the Stu-
> dents' Christian Movement] began to manifest themselves when an SCM
> poster appeared on the students' notice board on the campus. On the
> poster Christ was referred to as the 'Popular leader of a liberation move-
> ment'. This poster was prepared by the Chairman of the local SASO
> branch [Cyril Ramaphosa] and the witness Frank Chikane [the campus
> chairman of the SCM] referred to above. This was followed by symposia
> with topics such as Christianity and the Political, Cultural, and Social
> Problems of our Time, Religion in a Black Society and Black Theology.[144]

The SCM's increased political profile did not end at Turfloop's gates,
either. By the mid- 1970s, the Students' Christian Movement's increased
politicization had filtered out of universities, and back into schools
where it had already been a substantial organizing presence for Christian students. But while in the late 1960s, when Chikane, Mkhabela,
Mabasa, and Ramaphosa were schoolboys and adherents of SCM, the
organization was still primarily and almost singularly focused on religious salvation, by the early 1970s Ramaphosa's 'reforms' to the Turfloop branch of SCM had permeated well beyond the university itself.
It had become widely politically active, cooperating with SASO activists
in schools, and in many cases embracing Black Theology. Important
student leaders of the Soweto 1976 student uprising, including Tsietsi
Mashinini, were members of SCM.

There are direct links between this rising politicization of SCM in
schools and the Turfloop Christian student activists. As Magaziner has
noted, 'At SCM meetings [in secondary schools], members listened to
veterans of the turmoil at the University of the North and talked about

---

[143] The Snyman Commission and Report are discussed more fully in Chapter 3
(pp. 112–17).

[144] J.H. Snyman, *Report of the Commission of Inquiry into Certain Matters Relating to the University of the North* (Pretoria, 1975), p. 75.

Black Theology and the martyrdom of Christ.'[145] Clive Glaser points to the influx of 'politically conscious Turfloop students (many of them expelled before finishing their studies) who took up jobs as teachers in Soweto's high schools' as an important influence on growing political movements in Soweto schools in 1974 and 1975. (These people and their roles inside and out of Turfloop will be examined further in Chapter 2.)

At Turfloop, student politics across groups as disparate as SASO and the SCM relied on articulations of Christianity to muster support for their platforms; by the same token, previously apolitical Christian groups like SCM had to write politics into their agendas in order to gain and maintain support in the student body. Christianity and politics at Turfloop, then, were mutually reliant on one another to mobilize student support.

Conclusion

In the decade and a half since its inception in 1959, Turfloop had gone from its planners' ideal of a cradle of Bantustan 'civilization' to, in reality, a hothouse for anti-apartheid and anti-Bantustan activists. This transformation was neither linear nor inevitable, though. The constraints of geography and tight control through the department of Bantu Education did exert significant pressure on those in and around Turfloop to conform to these founding ideals: in a 1973 speech at the Turfloop graduation ball, Collins Ramusi, a Johannesburg lawyer and Lebowa politician, made an appeal for graduates to 'involve themselves in the development of their respective homelands':

> I'm appealing to you to be prepared to serve the people not theoretically, but practically because the people are suffering. They need doctors, clothes and food. There's hardly water for them. [...] You can shun the people if you want to, but you have no right to refuse to assist us, although this business of homelands is embarrassing in so much that the educated people find it difficult to move freely and with dignity. But what can we do?[146]

Ramusi's appeal encapsulated the intractable situation created by apartheid's homelands: though he decried the policy as 'embarrassing', he appealed for university recruits with a sense of desperation, positing the 'practical' needs of suffering people against the 'theoretical' contribution

---

[145] Ibid., p. 158.

[146] M. Nonyane, 'Give help in homelands, students told', *Rand Daily Mail*, 5 July 1973 [HPRA AD1912/258.16].

of the political movements that advocated disengagement. But by the time of his speech, Ramusi was far to the right of the political trend at Turfloop. He was decried and dismissed as a collaborator, much as Themba Sono had been the previous year.

Turfloop student activists in SASO and SCM (after it was radicalized) pressed forward in their campaigns of political conscientization through Black Consciousness and Black Theology (in SASO), and in social outreach and activism to citizens in surrounding communities (in both). In this work, their twinning of politics and Christianity was an important mechanism in successful outreach to fellow students and to local communities, and it followed closely on the earlier example set by the UCM. A 1974 commission of inquiry report had a purely political reading of the University Christian Movement: 'UCM's secret objective was to train the Black people of South Africa for an armed revolution against the Whites.'[147] However, given that the UCM never made any moves towards armed struggle, this reading of the situation misses the point. The UCM was a radical organization that politicized and arguably secularized religion for its aims, but its currency among activists, and particularly students at the University of the North, was due to its combination of politics with religion – not simply the use of religion in service of politics. This pattern was replicated in different ways in organizations like SASO and the SCM. As Anthony Butler has noted, perhaps in rebuttal to the fairly secularized literature on student politics in South Africa, 'It was an inescapable fact forgotten by radicals that almost all of the students on a campus like Turfloop were or had been active members of Christian organizations.'[148]

SASO itself followed this example; activist Nkwenkwe Nkomo frequently described SASO and other Black Consciousness activists as 'prophets..., bishops..., ministers [and] evangelists'.[149] Magaziner has called this 'the interpenetration of politics and religion', and suggests that in Black Consciousness and SASO it was rooted in the fact that the overwhelming majority of leaders were, like Nkomo, Christian.[150] This interplay was clearly at work at the University of the North in the early 1970s. Not only was Christianity central to Black Consciousness and SASO because it was a constitutive element of those organizations' leadership, but Christianity extended the political influence of those groups on campuses like Turfloop, because it spoke to a fundamental

---

[147] Wolfson, *Turmoil at Turfloop*, p. 12.
[148] Butler, *Cyril Ramaphosa*, p. 52.
[149] Magaziner, *The Law and the Prophets*, p. 55.
[150] Ibid., p. 56.

characteristic of the students they sought to mobilize. Religion played a key role in political recruitment as well as personal conscientization. Christianity and politics were necessary bedfellows for activists of the time.

The University of the North at Turfloop, in spite of its small size, and relative geographic isolation, was a crucible for student protests in 1970s South Africa, years before the iconic Soweto uprisings of 1976. It became a site for integrating many levels of protest: through the closely intertwined roles of Black Consciousness, politics, Black Theology, and Christianity in student organizations like the University Christian Movement, the Students' Christian Movement, and especially the South African Students' Organization. It was the cumulative effect of all these that gave activists at Turfloop currency, and the scope to mobilize protests. Neither Christianity nor Black Consciousness alone would have provided as powerful an ideological motivator to the bulk of Turfloop's students, and SASO was ideally placed to channel that motivation into mobilization that had ripples of influence beyond Turfloop's campus and throughout South Africa.

2

Centre of the Storm

By the early 1970s the University of the North at Turfloop was growing increasingly prominent as a centre of student resistance against the
apartheid state, or 'the system' as student activists called it. This was due
in large part to a number of high-profile student activists who had cut
their political teeth with campus groups like the South African Students'
Organization, the Students' Christian Movement, and the earlier University Christian Movement, as discussed in the previous chapter. For
these individuals, and for the majority of the student body of Turfloop,
Christianity and political resistance to the system went hand in hand.
These activists also served an important role in representing Turfloop,
and the radical politics that had developed on campus, to the rest of
South Africa and to other student and political activists in the anti-
apartheid cause.

These developments occurred against a backdrop of changes in the
way that protest politics were being enacted throughout South Africa.
In his recent book *The Road to Soweto*, Julian Brown explores these
changes and argues that the decade preceding the 1976 Soweto Uprising
was marked by increasingly confrontational forms of politics. He contends that the shift towards confrontational protest originated on white
university campuses in 1966 and 1968; he points to the aftermath of
Tiro's expulsion in 1972 as the first move towards such confrontation on
black campuses, and the Viva-FRELIMO rallies of 1974, one of which
was held at Turfloop, as the culmination of this trend at black universities.[1] Building on Brown, who is primarily concerned with the form of
these protests and linking them to national trends, this chapter situates
them in the context of life and campus politics at Turfloop. It seeks to
understand the ways in which student protests on campus came to incorporate broader political concerns around national liberation, and argues

[1] J. Brown, *The Road to Soweto: Resistance and the Uprising of 16 June 1976*
(Oxford, 2016); see particularly Chapter 1, 'White Student Activism in the
1960s', Chapter 3, 'Confrontation, Resistance and Reaction', and Chapter 6,
'The Pro-Frelimo rallies of 1974'.

for their impact on developing ideas of nationalism and African solidarity that influenced political developments far beyond Turfloop itself.

This chapter considers Turfloop's increasingly prominent place as a centre of student activism, SASO's growing organizational capacity and public profile, and how these two phenomena interacted with one another. It centres on the stories of prominent activists, the roles they played both at and outside of Turfloop, and their importance in South African student politics in the middle of the 1970s – perhaps the most important period of student activism in the country's history. It also considers the impact of two major and related events – the 1974 Viva-FRELIMO rallies, and the resulting arrest and trial of the SASO 9 – on the trajectory of SASO's organizational history.

Turfloop's student-teacher activists

In 1972 Turfloop's most high-profile student activist was Onkgopotse Tiro, author of that year's controversial graduation speech in April. Tiro's stand against the inequality he encountered at the university, at the graduation itself, and throughout South Africa resulted in his expulsion, the temporary closure of the university, and solidarity protests at Turfloop and on campuses throughout the country. The speech and its immediate aftermath at Turfloop and beyond have been discussed in Chapter 1; now we pick up Tiro's continuing role as an activist after he left university. The dramatic closure of the university and summary expulsion of all Turfloop students resulted in a carefully orchestrated readmission process that allowed the university authorities to exclude Tiro, the entire SRC, and other politically prominent students. After his expulsion, Tiro left campus and moved to Soweto where he stayed with his mother, who was living there at the time.

Tiro continued his activism in student politics immediately, unhampered by his expulsion from Turfloop. He became a key organizer for SASO at the executive level, and was paired with Permanent Organizer (and fellow ex-Turfloop student) Harry Nengwekhulu as part of SASO's tiered approach to leadership. These tiers were designed to create stables of leadership within the organization that permeated beyond the most visible leaders like Steve Biko and Barney Pityana. From its inception, the founders of SASO understood their tenuous position as an above-ground activist organization. They were aware of the banning of other political groups, including the African National Congress and the Pan Africanist Congress, less than a decade earlier, and realized the risks of directly challenging the state. One way they successfully sought to delay this clash was to target a mutual enemy: white liberals. As I argued in

Chapter 1, at Turfloop this allowed the fledgling SASO room to develop without immediate interference from university authorities. But targeting white liberals first was at best a delaying tactic – conflict with the state would come, SASO activists knew; it was only a matter of when. Harry Nengwekhulu described early debate among SASO founders over whether their new organization should operate above ground or underground. The founders worried that an above-ground SASO would be banned in a matter of weeks, but they knew that starting underground would significantly hamper their ability to organize students. Nengwekhulu recalls that a decision was taken to try to 'mobilize almost everybody' in SASO's first few years, so that if they had to go underground, their base would already be formed.[2]

> In order to maximize their influence and mobilization in those first years SASO devised strategies to prolong their existence and influence. One of these strategies was the layering of leadership, pairing each member of the executive with one or more deputies who could step into the key role quickly in the event that a prominent leader was banned. At its height, Nengwekhulu says, 'We were six layers! So even if they burned the first layer, the second layer – the third layer could take over immediately.'[3]

Abraham Tiro was part of this backbench of leaders, prepared to step seamlessly to the fore if Nengwekhulu was banned or otherwise incapacitated. He travelled within and even outside South Africa in the course of this work, bringing SASO's message with him. In a 1973 speech in Lesotho he reiterated SASO's position against white liberalism: 'We have no use for liberals. We reject their help. They have no part to play in the struggle for liberation. Their policy of multi-racialism is useless.'[4]

Mzamane, Maaba, and Biko have argued that effective leadership training was a key SASO strength, and that formation schools in particular facilitated the growth of a cohort of leaders who were able to expand Black Consciousness ideas beyond SASO itself.[5] But I would contend that the greatest strength of its leadership training was contained within SASO itself, in the depth of leadership it included at a given time and its approach to apprenticeship. Gerhart argues that ideological cohesion was a key product of the layered-leadership approach, which resulted

---

[2] Author's interview with Harry Nengwekhulu (a).

[3] Ibid.

[4] 'Tiro's goal was black liberation', *The Star*, 4 February 1974 [HPRA AD1912/239].

[5] M.V. Mzamane, B. Maaba, and N. Biko. 'The Black Consciousness Movement' in *SADET, The Road to Democracy in South Africa, Volume 2, 1970–1980* (Pretoria, 2006), p. 138.

in 'a level of political education and ideological diffusion never before achieved by any black political organization'.[6] SASO's strategy to prevent banning of its leadership and to prolong the organization's existence, then, also served to promote more thorough and deep-reaching indoctrination in its ranks. Students were a natural audience for the intellectual message of Black Consciousness, which emphasized psychological liberation before physical revolution. With education at its core, targeting this demographic enabled SASO to achieve the deep diffusion of political ideas across campuses and even schools that Gerhart indicates. Other liberation organizations (including the ANC) working across more disparate class, race, generation, and geographic groups could not achieve the same levels of ideological cohesion, even as they exceeded SASO's organizational capacity in other areas.

Indeed, SASO itself was unable to maintain high levels of ideological cohesion and organizational effectiveness once it moved beyond the bounds of educational institutions, though its activists were also engaged in reaching outside SASO's ranks to spread the message of Black Consciousness. As Harry Nengwekhulu said, 'within five years we should have been able to mobilize almost everybody'.[7]

An important, albeit much later implemented, part of SASO's goal to mobilize 'almost everybody' came about with the development of its sister organization, the Black People's Convention (BPC).

The BPC was conceived as a political party to carry SASO's message of Black Consciousness and Africanization (the move to replace white with black leadership in core African institutions, like Turfloop) to a more diffuse group than the existing system of working through students allowed. It was meant to be a platform for organizing those who were outside SASO's remit – namely adults who were outside the educational system.[8] The organization was planned by the student leaders of SASO, and fleshed out by their executive,[9] but it was to stand apart as its own independent organization. In order for this new party to embody its different demographic from SASO, it made its first new head Winifred Motlalepula Kgware, wife of Turfloop professor William Kgware and mother of activists Ben, Manana, and Pinky.[10]

---

[6] Gerhart, *Black Power in South Africa*, p. 270.

[7] Author's interview with Harry Nengwekhulu (a).

[8] Black People's Convention, First National Congress, 16–17 December 1972 [HPRA A2177].

[9] Author's interview with Harry Nengwekhulu (a).

[10] The Kgware family's role in politics and activism at Turfloop is more thoroughly discussed in Chapters 1 and 3.

Winifred Kgware had been deeply involved in the Turfloop branch of the University Christian Movement during the late 1960s, but had been more removed from direct political action since the UCM's dissolution. She had no personal involvement with SASO, though her daughter Manana had been part of the early executive in 1969. Kgware's transition from wife and mother to activist and figurehead of a party is instructive in several ways: her Christian beliefs were the impetus that prompted her own politicization through the University Christian Movement. She agitated for more press coverage of student protests at Turfloop, and of what she perceived as the persecution of the UCM by the then Rector, whom she described as unscrupulous and unfair.[11] In the face of that persecution, though, she helped students smuggle information inside programmes for events, and through letters to other UCM colleagues out to the press, in spite of her fear that she might face retribution 'from all sides, including my employers, the Bantu Ed. Dept.'[12] In addition to her political activism, Mrs Kgware was a teacher at Mankweng's Hwiti High School, just outside the Turfloop gates. Here she helped expose her students to some of the political movements that were blossoming on the nearby campus. As a mother, wife, and teacher she was an ideal figure to lead the BPC because she encapsulated an age group and demographic as a middle-aged woman that the more radically active students in SASO hoped to reach: Winifred Kgware was very much part of the profile of Harry Nengwekhulu's 'almost everybody'.

In spite of such concerted efforts, however, BPC never achieved the organizational success of its sister body SASO; it remained one of the many groups under the Black Consciousness Movement remit, but it failed to mobilize the non-student population the way SASO had done with students. In part this must be attributed to the unique character of students themselves. Particularly at an institution like Turfloop, where, as Tiro's stinging critique had clearly indicated, the rhetoric of self-rule and institutions for Africans met the harsh reality of apartheid oppression and inequality, students formed a ready cohort for politicization. The intellectual curiosity and sharing of ideas that characterize university life for students around the world were also present for those at Turfloop and its fellow 'bush' colleges in the early 1970s. The development of an ideology like Black Consciousness, which presented exciting intellectual engagement and addressed students' personal circumstances,

---

[11] Letter from Winifred Kgware to Colin Collins, 23 September 1968 [HPRA AD1126/F].

[12] Ibid.; letter from Manana Kgware to James Moulder, 15 August 1968 [HPRA AD1126/F].

proved very popular and expanded beyond universities to schools. But its outreach to other groups – through the BPC and other organizations – never achieved the same success. Theories of psychological liberation were harder to market to non-students outside the black intelligentsia; Magaziner has described the 'vague' political platform of the BPC:

> [t]he BPC was SASO's philosophical approach in another form. Its program to 'oppose vigorously' and 'negate' racism resonated with SASO's existentialism-infused calls to negate nonwhiteness and assume an oppositional stance.[13]

The very vagueness that enabled SASO's message to intellectually excite students also hampered its ability to politically mobilize their parents and older generations.

As Winifred Kgware was becoming more politically active in the BPC, her husband William Kgware was distancing himself from the activism that most of his family had embraced. A motivating factor in this move may have been the death of their son Bob, in 1968. According to UCM leader Reverend Basil Moore, Bob, an active student leader in the University Christian Movement, was murdered 'by unknown assailants (but presumably the security police)' shortly after their return from a UCM conference in the United States.[14] That same year, William Kgware withdrew his membership from the UCM, which at the time was becoming increasingly politically outspoken. This move also marked a shift to focus on his career as an academic; by 1969 he had risen to become head of the Department of Didactics, and younger staff respected him as the most senior black academic on campus.[15] He still endeavoured to straddle the disparate worlds of black political emancipation and the constrained Bantustan system of which he found himself part, and which, though it was tightly controlled, offered the possibility of social and career advancement.[16] It was Professor Kgware who led the black academic staff of Turfloop in their walkout from the May 1972 meeting in which Tiro's expulsion was debated. Percy Mokwele, a young lecturer in education at the time, remembers following Kgware out of the meet-

---

[13] Magaziner, *The Law and the Prophets*, p. 143.

[14] B. Moore, 'Learning from Black Theology', speech given at Rhodes University Graduation, 8 April 2011. [http://www.ru.ac.za/media/rhodesuniversity/content/ruhome/documents/Basil%20Moore%20Speech%20%20-%20Black%20Theology.pdf] (parentheses original) Accessed 15 August 2012.

[15] Author's interview with Percy Mokwele.

[16] For instance, Kgware's contemporary on the staff at Turfloop, Professor Hudson Ntsan'wisi, left the university in 1969 to contribute to the founding of the Gazankulu Bantustan, of which he later became Chief Minister.

ing: 'I was new of course at that time, and my attitude was that if he goes out, I go out with him.'[17]

But in spite of such moments of political protest, Kgware more commonly preached caution and discretion as students agitated against the oppression and segregation imposed by apartheid. In an article published in October 1974, entitled 'Education of the Africans in South Africa', Kgware discussed the roots of Bantu Education policy, the boom in primary education that had occurred since its implementation, the 'disturbingly high drop-out rate' among black pupils, and the inadequacy of government funding for black schools.[18] He did so without challenging the premise of racially segregated education, never linking the specific inadequacies to the injustice of the system as a whole, something his Turfloop students had long been doing. Indeed, he described the development of eight Bantustans as a 'welcome and inevitable' development, indicating that South Africa's own African independence was on its way to completion; all that remained to be achieved was a 'commensurate development of human and natural resources'.[19]

Though he advocated African independence, increased development, and, most vociferously, improved educational opportunities for black students, Kgware advocated pursuit of these agendas through the Bantustan system and not through conflict with the South African state. His family, in contrast, became increasingly politically radical: his daughters Manana and Pinky were both active in SASO on campus at Turfloop; Manana was part of the first SASO executive under Steve Biko, and continued her activism as a teacher when she graduated from Turfloop and moved to Thaba 'Nchu in the Orange Free State. Winifred had remained an active member of the University Christian Movement until its dissolution in 1972; in December of that year she became the first president of the BPC, and later tried (but failed) to set up a BPC branch at Turfloop.[20]

In addition to its work through BPC to conscientize adults, SASO sought to reach out to younger students who had not yet arrived at university. This effort became a main priority in 1972, and after his expulsion Onkgopotse Tiro was deeply involved in this approach. In addition to his continued activism with SASO, he got a job as a teacher in Soweto's Morris Isaacson High School. In spite of his expulsion from

---

[17] Author's interview with Percy Mokwele.
[18] William Kgware, 'Education of the Africans in South Africa', *South Africa International*, October 1974 [HPRA A2675/III/943].
[19] Ibid.
[20] SASO 9 Trial Transcripts, p. 5296 (Lekota) [HPRA AD2012/14.1].

Turfloop, Tiro had a bachelor's degree and had partially completed his university diploma in education. In the context Kgware had described – of the booming numbers of school children and inadequate resources and staff to teach them – Tiro's political past did not preclude his employment. The principal at Morris Isaacson, Lekgau Mathabathe, hired Tiro to teach English and History.

Once they were involved in school structures, Tiro and other SASO activists found that a framework for political organization was already established within some schools. The African Students Movement (ASM) had emerged in the late 1960s[21] at Diepkloof High School in Soweto. It spread to a limited number of neighbouring schools and drew together students primarily from Christian youth groups like Y-Teens, Leseding, and Youth Alive.[22] Furthering this Christian identity, the ASM in its early days had links to the University Christian Movement. UCM members like Tom Manthata, then a teacher at Sekano Ntoane High School in Soweto, encouraged the fledgling group and provided them 'access to literature on developments in Africa'.[23] As with the University Christian Movement, ASM's Christian associations did not preclude its political development, and redressing the perceived apolitical nature of youth organizations (including those that had fed into ASM) in Soweto became one of its goals. Its political development focused on Africanism in its early years (thanks in part to literature from people like Manthata). The first Organising Secretary of SASM described that ideological formation: 'We were grappling and experimenting with Africanism and did this on our own, without reference to the PAC [Pan Africanist Congress]. [...] We were just trying for ourselves to work out what it means to be African.'[24]

Africanism, the philosophy developed by Anton Lembede for the early ANC Youth League, was what Gerhart has called 'a first attempt to formulate a creed of orthodox nationalism for black South Africa', and as this implies, Lembede's vision informed a number of subsequent nationalist movements. The Pan Africanist Congress (PAC) was its most overt inheritor, founded by Lembede's Youth League colleagues, A.P. Mda and Robert Sobukwe. That organization emphasized the racial singularity that Lembede had borrowed from Marcus Garvey, but also advocated Pan-African unity over ethnic differences. As the quote above

---

[21] Nozipho Diseko ('Origins and Development of SASM') and Clive Glaser (*Bo-Tsotsi*) date this as 1968.

[22] Diseko, 'Origins and Development of SASM', p. 43.

[23] Ibid., p. 43.

[24] P. Lenkwe, quoted in Diseko, 'Origins and Development of SASM', p. 43.

from Lenkwe, the Organising Secretary of SASM indicates, however, Africanism was a wider philosophy than the PAC captured, and by the early 1970s a generation of students were grappling with what it might offer them. In this their primary influence was Black Consciousness. The Black Consciousness Movement and SASO had adopted tenets of Africanism, particularly, as discussed in Chapter 1, Lembede's focus on psychological liberation as a precursor to political autonomy. It was these ideas of what it meant to be an African that galvanized many of the students in SASM. According to Anthony W. Marx, this was an aspect of Lembede's ideology that the PAC did not share: 'Indeed, BC's focus on reshaping ideas was criticized by the PAC's founder, Robert Sobukwe, as an elitist concern.'[25] For school students, though, as for students at Turfloop, a focus on the politics of ideas was a natural extension of their education and it led them to consider large questions like what it meant to be African.

They also grappled with national identity: by the early 1970s, the ASM was focusing more concretely on the situation inside South Africa. This was reflected in its 1972 change of name to the South African Students' Movement (SASM), which coincided with the efforts of SASO to conscientize school students. Tebello Motapanyane, one of the key leaders of the June 1976 uprising, described how the name change reflected the organization's growth out of Soweto and into schools around the country: 'By 1972 it was decided that since the movement was now national, it should be known as the South African Students Movement, that is SASM.'[26]

Clive Glaser has argued that the name change also represents a growing identification with SASO, and its 'more inclusive interpretation of black identity'.[27] The decision to adopt the new name, with its links to SASO and its nationalist undertones, marked an increasingly political focus within SASM. Of students' political awareness at this point, Motapanyane said:

> We were, of course, very alive to the fact that we as Black people were being oppressed. The students especially were quite sensitive to this and we were all the time trying to find a way to do something about it. It was

---

[25] A. Marx, *Lessons of Struggle: South African internal opposition, 1960–1990* (Oxford, 1992), p. 50.
[26] Tebello Motapanyane, 'How June 16 demo was planned', *Sechaba*, 11(2), 1977 [HPRA A2953].
[27] Glaser, *Bo-Tsotsi*, p. 162.

just unfortunate that we were not so clear about how to show our anger and resentment in a clear political way.[28]

The ASM became SASM, providing an outlet for political expression in high schools, just as political protest was beginning to heat up on black university campuses. Tiro's expulsion and the subsequent protests at Turfloop, Ngoye, Fort Hare, and others, were the first public signs of major dissatisfaction at the 'bush' colleges. These developments had important implications for the growing politicization among school students, even beyond symbolic resonance.

As I have noted, just months after his expulsion Tiro moved to Soweto where he secured a job teaching history at Morris Isaacson High School; teaching became an outlet for many politically active university students who were expelled in waves of protest at places like Turfloop between 1972 and 1974. In his testimony after the Soweto Uprising, Aubrey Mokoena, former Turfloop student and president of the SRC, noted that 'BPC and SASO had some of its members teaching in schools. [...] It was the duty of these people to conscientize students with regard to the struggle for liberation.'[29] Among these teachers, Mokoena noted Tiro at Morris Isaacson, himself at Orlando North Secondary, Tom Manthata at Sekano Ntoane High School, and Cyril Ramaphosa and Lybon Mabasa at Meadowlands High School. In addition, Frank Chikane worked informally as a maths tutor with learners at Naledi High School.[30] All of these except Manthata had been students at Turfloop and were expelled for their political activities.

Their work was effective, because by 1973 SASM had established a cooperative relationship with SASO and its brand of politics, and was using the language of Black Consciousness. Nozipho Diseko has argued persuasively that SASM did not develop as a school wing of SASO, and that it in fact predated the development of Black Consciousness as an ideology, to counter the way that much of the literature has conflated these two movements.[31] Though SASM did not develop as a subset of SASO and did have its own autonomous identity, I would contend that development within the two organizations was closely related and eventually converged in the early 1970s. The style of Africanism espoused by

---

[28] Motapanyane, 'How June 16 demo was planned', *Sechaba*, 11(2), 1977, p. 2 [HPRA A2953].

[29] Deposition of Aubrey Mokoena taken by Justice of the Peace D.L. Aspelling in Johannesburg. Undated (c. early 1977) [HPRA A2953].

[30] S. Mkhabela, *Open Earth & Black Roses: Remembering 16 June 1976* (Johannesburg, 2001), pp. 30–1.

[31] Diseko, 'Origins and Development of SASM'.

SASM and by SASO developed in tandem, and with related influences – the University Christian Movement being a significant early one – so that by 1973 they were well positioned to work together. Teachers from the Black Consciousness Movement who were teaching in schools with SASM branches fostered this ideological symmetry. Most prominently, Tiro, in his role at Morris Isaacson, was perhaps the closest SASO member to the workings of SASM. Tiro acted as liaison between the organizations, and under his watch an official wing of SASM was created for SASO and older members; from the SASO perspective there was SASM (Junior), which was the original South African Students' Movement, based in schools, and SASM (Senior), which consisted of the affiliated older membership of groups like SASO that supported SASM's efforts to conscientize and organize school students. Tiro became the first president of SASM (Senior),[32] a semi-formalized position that was designed to facilitate cooperation between SASM and other organizations in the Black Consciousness Movement like SASO and the BPC.

As a teacher and in his capacity as SASM liaison, Tiro worked to seek out politically curious and motivated students, and strove to conscientize them in the SASO mould. The students who passed through Tiro's classes, and under his wing, were to become some of the most prominent figures in the next generation of student political actors. One, Tsietsi Mashinini, later became the chair of the influential Soweto Students' Representative Council (SSRC), which played a critical organizational role in the June 1976 Soweto uprising and its aftermath. Another of Tiro's students was Esau Tshehlo Mokhethi: older than Mashinini, he had already moved from Morris Isaacson to Turfloop by 1976, where he was involved in the reorganization of the SRC at the university, and later became an activist and exile for the Azanian People's Organisation (AZAPO).[33] Such direct links to students like Mashinini and Mokhethi are evidence of how, in a short time, Tiro's influence had been expanded by his work at Morris Isaacson.

Other students expelled in the aftermath of the Alice Declaration stay-aways found themselves in similar situations. In an interview with Clive Glaser, Jake Msimanga, a student at Soweto's Sekano Ntoane High

---

[32] Composite Executive Report to the 6th GSC, 7 July 1974, p. 2 [HPRA A2176]; deposition of Aubrey Mokoena taken by Justice of the Peace D.L. Aspelling in Johannesburg. Undated (c. early 1977), p. 20 [HPRA A2953]; T. Mashinini, 'Behind the Growing Upsurge in South Africa', *Intercontinental Press*, 15 November 1976 [not paginated] [HPRA A2953].

[33] K. Dikobo, 'Esau Mokhethi Reburial Speech'. [http://azapo.org.za/esau-mokhethi-reburial-speech/] Accessed 27 March 2012.

School in 1972, 'recalls that ex-Turfloop students played a key role in the "conscientisation process". "There were about four or five young teachers from Turfloop; some had been expelled and some had graduated".'[34] Though Soweto was a hotspot for such activism – the urban areas of the Rand attracted a large number of expelled Turfloop students – it existed elsewhere as well. Pandelani Nefolovhodwe, a member of the SRC committee that had invited Tiro to speak, also found employment as a teacher, in Sibasa, Venda in 1973.[35] Even though he was teaching maths and science, Nefolovhodwe strove to conscientize his students politically by encouraging them to read daily newspapers, and instituting weekly discussions of current events. He especially aimed to conscientize those who would go on to join SASO at the university level:

> I would add my own political activism.[...] [I focused on] these ones who may finish schools and go to universities, so I was trying to link them with the activities already at a higher level. So that is what I used to do, and it went very, very well. There are a lot of others [among my former students] who went on to go to university and became very good activists [...].[36]

Scholars including Nozipho Diseko and Clive Glaser have highlighted the role that these teachers played in transmitting Black Consciousness philosophy into township schools.[37]

Morris Isaacson, in particular, was a major and early centre for student politicization in Soweto. The ASM had been active in the school since the late 1960s, as had the Students' Christian Movement. By the time that ASM was changing to SASM, and incorporating itself more fully into the Black Consciousness Movement, the SCM was shifting firmly into the political arena – at Turfloop (as discussed in Chapter 1) but also in schools like Morris Isaacson and some of its Soweto fellows. 'The concerns of the SCM [in schools] were primarily Christian but it was increasingly exposed to, and intertwined with, Black Theology, the Christian arm of the emerging Black Consciousness movement. [...] Christianity gave cover to mounting political awareness and debate.'[38] It was into this already increasingly political environment that Tiro

---

[34] Clive Glaser, '"We must infiltrate the tsotsis": School politics and youth gangs in Soweto, 1968–1976', *Journal of Southern African Studies*, 24(2) (June 1998), 301–23 (305).

[35] Author's interview with Pandelani Nefolovhodwe; SASO 9 Trial Transcript, p. 5561 (Nefolovhodwe) [HPRA AD2021/14.1].

[36] Author's interview with Pandelani Nefolovhodwe.

[37] Diseko, 'Origins and Development of SASM', p. 57; Glaser, *Bo-Tsotsi*, p. 162.

[38] Glaser, 'We must infiltrate the tsotsis', p. 303.

and others arrived, following the expulsions and unrest of May 1972. The environment was ripe for such politically active teachers: 'Mary Mxadana, who studied and taught at [Morris Isaacson], recalls that students talked enthusiastically about Tiro's teaching. He asserted the need to move away from rigid syllabi, "to challenge the poison of Bantu Education".'[39] He also became a sought-after advisor and speaker for student groups like SASM.

As significant as this influence was, it was short-lived in terms of direct student–teacher contact. The Department of Bantu Education exerted pressure on schools to fire trouble-making teachers, though Glaser has noted that 'they were often able to make a major impact even in the few weeks or months of their stay'.[40] Tiro was dismissed from Morris Isaacson less than a full year after he had started. In her testimony to the Truth and Reconciliation Commission, his mother said of his dismissal from the teaching job:

> The school [Morris Isaacson] closed and they reopened and I saw [Ongkopotse] coming home. [...] he said to me Mamma they expelled me again from school. And I asked him again why have you been expelled? No they just said I should get out of the school, I will teach my fellow schoolmates wrong information.[41]

Tiro's 'wrong information' was the SASO and Black Consciousness ideology that he had been imparting to his students, which had drawn the attention of government officials beyond the school itself. According to a *Rand Daily Mail* article, 'In February [1973], after months of confrontation between the local school committee and officials of the Bantu Education Department, Mr. Tiro was sacked from his teaching position at Morris Isaacson High School in Soweto.'[42] The timing of his dismissal coincided with a nationwide crackdown on SASO and Black People's Convention activists: in early March 1973 banning orders were issued against the most prominent leaders in both groups including, among SASO's top tier of leadership, Biko, Pityana, and Nengwekhulu. After their banning Nengwekhulu was restricted to Venda, in the far north of the Northern Transvaal, and tried to organize covertly for SASO while there. Given the restrictive terms of his banning, though, he made little headway. After months in isolation at a house near Tshilindzini in Venda,

[39] Ibid., p. 305.
[40] Glaser, *Bo-Tsotsi*, p. 162.
[41] TRC Testimony of Moleseng Anna Tiro, 29 April 1996. [http://www.justice.gov.za/trc/hrvtrans%5Cmethodis/tiro.htm] Accessed 12 May 2011.
[42] 'Bomb kills ex-Saso leader', *Rand Daily Mail*, 4 February 1974 [HPRA AD1912/239].

Nengwekhulu fled in the middle of one September 1973 night, making for the Botswana border. He met Tiro, along with Bokwe Mafuna and some other SASO activists in Zeerust, very near the border and where Tiro had grown up. Together they went into exile in Botswana.[43]

Tiro and Nengwekhulu remained active in their efforts to bolster student resistance within South Africa, and to raise support for their cause within Botswana. Tiro had not been banned and had papers allowing him to move legally between South Africa and Botswana, so he assumed Nengwekhulu's role of Permanent Organizer, when exile prevented the other man from fulfilling the role. SASO's tiered leadership allowed for minimal disruption to their work even as banning and exile sidelined major leaders. Tiro had little time to pursue this work, however. He was killed in Botswana by a parcel bomb on 1 February 1974, under suspicious circumstances, only five months after fleeing South Africa. The parcel bomb that killed him allegedly had markings from the International University Exchange Fund (IUEF) in Geneva, but among friends of Tiro and officials in Botswana alike it was widely believed to have been sent by agents of the South African government.[44] The package was addressed in longhand, and hand-delivered by a priest with whom Tiro was living, just south of Gaborone.[45] For its part, IUEF denied that the package had originated with them, saying, 'the fund's correspondence to Southern Africa never carries any indication of its origin'.[46]

The public reaction following Tiro's death speaks to the impact of his activism both in South Africa, and in Botswana, for the short time he was there. In a memorial to him at their General Students Council that year, SASO said, 'Circumstances surrounding Tiro's death have [not] been made absolutely clear, but one thing [is] certain, he died at the violent hands of agents of imperialism.'[47] The Transvaal regional secretary for SASO noted, 'It is a real tragedy to have one of the most able and dedicated leaders brutally and ruthlessly murdered,' going on to describe the culprit as 'the enemy'.[48] In a statement, the Office of the President of Botswana said:

---

[43] Interview with Harry Nengwekhulu (a); 'Top SASO men flee the country', *The Star*, 6 October 1973 [HPRA AD1912/239].

[44] 'Tiro bomb "a real killer"', *The Star*, 4 February 1974 [HPRA AD1912/239].

[45] 'Bomb kills ex-Saso leader', *Rand Daily Mail*, 4 February 1974 [HPRA AD1912/239].

[46] 'The Tiro mystery', *Sunday Times*, undated, c. 10 February 1974 [HPRA AD1912/239].

[47] Composite Executive Report to the 6th GSC, 7 July 1974, p. 2 [SASO A2176].

[48] Transvaal Region Report to the 6th GSC, p. 1 [SASO A2176/5.5].

Mr Tiro had, during the last few years of his life been an outspoken critic of a so-called South African way of life under which Black South Africans are subjected to racial discrimination and many other indignities. And in speaking out against the denial to Black South Africans of their human rights, Mr Tiro had incurred the deep displeasure of certain powerful circles in South Africa. Mr Tiro's sudden and cruel death will in no way depart from the validity of his criticism of the politicians in South Africa. Nor will it intimidate others from speaking out in that country. For its part, the Botswana Government strongly condemns the inhuman and dastardly manner in which Mr Tiro's life was taken. The Botswana Government wishes to state unequivocally that this kind of terrorism will not make it change its attitude towards those who seek refuge in Botswana from oppression in their own country.[49]

This statement itself ignited controversy, as South African newspapers took up the gauntlet that had been thrown down by the government of Botswana. An editorial in the *Sunday Times* called it 'a slur on South Africa which the Government should not allow to hang in the air unanswered. If our police are, as they should be, making every possible effort to establish the truth, then the Prime Minister should say so.'[50] In fact, the South African government did allow the statement from their northern neighbour to 'hang in the air unanswered'. South African police were not involved in the investigation into Tiro's killing, which was handled by the police in Botswana. No one was ever charged with the crime.

Activists inside South Africa did not let the event pass unmarked, however. When the news reached SASO's branches in the Transvaal, 'Members from alll [sic] over the region started flooding into the office and became involved in several undertakings that were geared at the burial of our brother. Fundraising lists were prepared and widely distributed around the regions.'[51] Memorials for Tiro were held at Regina Mundi Catholic Church in Soweto, one of the country's largest churches, as well as in Kimberley and at Turfloop itself. Students from SASO 'and other black organizations' raised more than R2000 in support of a memorial held in Tiro's home village of Dinokana, and many, including those in the acting executive, travelled to this remote area of the north-western Transvaal to attend.[52] Meanwhile, more than 1200 people attended a

---

[49] 'Botswana hits at Tiro killing', *Rand Daily Mail*, 6 February 1974 [HPRA AD1912/239].

[50] 'The Tiro mystery', *Sunday Times*, undated, c. 10 February 1974 [HPRA AD1912/239].

[51] Transvaal Region Report to the 6th GSC, pp. 1–2 [HPRA A2176/5.5].

[52] Ibid., p. 2.

special ceremony in Tiro's memory at the Roman Catholic cathedral in Gaborone, Botswana.[53]

The loss of Tiro was a blow to SASO, as well as to Turfloop and school students for whom he had been a formative figure in their political education; but rather than dampening student activism for his cause, his death furthered the resolve of the organizations with which he had worked. As the SASO Transvaal regional secretary at the time noted, 'The enemy must have really joyfully felicitated for the brutal and cold-blooded murder, though at least realising that on that very point in time a hundred Tiros emerged and decided to join hands with those who are involved in the fighting against oppression.'[54]

Turfloop, 1972–1974: disquiet between the storms

Though Tiro and other expelled students had left Turfloop, the campus remained a restive place after most students returned to campus in June 1972. They met with greater suspicion and harsher control exerted by the university authorities. As mentioned in the previous chapter, all read-mitted students (and their parents) were required to sign a pledge that they would not participate in any demonstrations or political activities, and acknowledge that particular students (including Tiro and the SRC) would not be readmitted. Refusing to sign was grounds for their application to be rejected. Additionally, the university authorities banned SASO from campus in the aftermath of the Tiro controversy, and they refused to reconstitute an SRC on campus following the expulsion of all sitting members of the previous SRC under Aubrey Mokoena. In lieu of an SRC the Rector, Professor J.L. Boshoff, 'appointed a committee to represent student interests but they [the student body] rejected the nominees, electing their own men'.[55] This was likely done by mass meeting, which was the vehicle for much student political action at Turfloop at the time. The elected representatives were not given official standing as an SRC, however, and were therefore limited in their power to negotiate on behalf of students with university administrators and authorities.

Discontent with this usurping of student representation was one of the main factors influencing a stay-away from the 1973 diploma ceremony. In April of that year, 82 of 97 students scheduled to receive their diplomas from the faculties of nursing, commerce, and education

[53] '1200 Mourn Tiro', *The Star*'s Africa News Service, 9 February 1974 [HPRA AD1912/239].
[54] Transvaal Region Report to the 6th GSC, p. 1 [HPRA A2176/5.5].
[55] '82 Students boycott at Turfloop', *The Star*, 2 April 1973 [HPRA AD1912/258.16].

boycotted the ceremony and persuaded their parents to do the same. Only fifteen graduates crossed the stage in a ceremony palpably at odds with the packed auditorium that Tiro had addressed the previous year; its very emptiness spoke volumes of the same discontent among students that his speech had highlighted.

In addition to enforcing stricter rules about student politics and activism on campus, the University of the North administration undertook an investigation into the 1972 protests. The Wright Commission it established completed its report in March 1973, and though the university refused to publish or release its findings, some details were leaked to the press. The commission determined that lack of communication was 'the main cause of the trouble' after Tiro's speech in May 1972. It also pointed to student impatience with the slow pace of Africanization at the university following its ostensible autonomy, and particularly to the election of W.W.M. Eiselen, a controversial white member of staff with close ties to the government and the National Party, as the new Chancellor.[56]

Following the Wright Commission's conclusions, and the boycotts of the 1973 diploma ceremony, the university reconstituted the Students' Representative Council and allowed students to elect their own officers. Isaac Nkwe became president of this new SRC in the winter of 1973, but his position was to be short-lived.[57] By autumn 1974, students had become disillusioned with Nkwe's leadership. They complained that the SRC had failed to execute its mandate in a variety of areas. Of particular note were complaints about failing to advocate for student accommodation, about inadequate dialogue between the SRC and students, and the SRC and the Rector, and about abuses of power by installing SRC members as primarii, in prefect-style leadership roles.[58] This was controversial because the role of primarius provided remuneration, so the installation of SRC members in the positions, apparently at their own instigation, had a whiff of nepotism to it. But it was also problematic because historically the SRC had been created explicitly to bring democratic representation into a closed power system between the university administration and its handpicked prefects. The reconflation of these roles caused an outcry among the student body.

[56] 'Turfloop unrest probed', *Rand Daily Mail*, 14 March 1973 [HPRA AD1912/258.16].

[57] SASO 9 Trial Transcripts, p. 5567 (Nefolovhodwe) [HPRA AD2021/14.1].

[58] SASO 9 Trial Transcripts, p. 5574 (Nefolovhodwe), and p. 5858 (Sedibe) [HPRA AD2021/14.1].

Another grievance was the way in which the SRC had dealt with the popular issue of Africanization at the university. In late March 1974 students petitioned the SRC for an emergency meeting on its conduct; the petition noted, among other complaints, that the SRC had been 'tactless' in its approach to the Rector to advocate for Africanization of university staff. 'This may result in the deterioration of the student/White lecturers relationship in general, and the consequence that can crop up on the part of the student body.'[59] This note in the petition is revelatory of the tension students experienced, pushing the university for change but cognizant of doing so in a way that would not incite backlash, if possible. The petition was initially brought by a single student, Peter Gaele, but at the meeting called by the SRC it was clear that Gaele was supported more broadly in his concerns. At the mass meeting the students in attendance made a no-confidence vote, and ousted the sitting SRC under Nkwe in what Mosiuoa Lekota later described as a 'coup'.[60] In its place, the students present appointed a three-person electoral committee to temporarily 'occupy the SRC offices for the purpose of running new elections of the SRC'.[61] Law students Cyril Ramaphosa and John Nkadimeng were two of the electoral officers chosen.[62]

In the weeks preceding the ousting of the SRC, political activism was once again fomenting at Turfloop, but for the first time it was primarily taking place off campus: in the middle of March 1974 Lekota, a former Turfloop student who had recently been elected SASO's permanent organizer,[63] arrived in Mankweng to set up an off-campus branch of SASO. This was designed to circumnavigate the university's still-standing ban against SASO on campus.[64] A meeting was held in the local Roman Catholic church, and was advertised widely to students through the SRC. An estimated 300–400 students came to the meeting, and there they elected Pandelani Nefolovhodwe as chairman of their new local

[59] SASO 9 Trial Transcripts, p. 5575 (Nefolovhodwe) [HPRA AD2021/14.1].
[60] SASO 9 Trial Transcripts, p. 5567 (Nefolovhodwe), and p. 5261 (Lekota) [HPRA AD2021/14.1].
[61] SASO 9 Trial Transcripts, p. 5575 (Nefolovhodwe) [HPRA AD2021/14.1].
[62] SASO 9 Trial Transcripts, p. 5576 (Nefolovhodwe) [HPRA AD2021/14.1]; author's interview with Pandelani Nefolovhodwe.
[63] Lekota stepped in to fill the post, which Tiro had occupied before his death in February 1972 (SASO 6th GSC minutes, p. 4 [HPRA A2176/5.5]).
[64] SASO 9 Trial Transcripts, p. 5259 (Lekota), and p. 5570 (Nefolovhodwe) [HPRA AD2021/14.1].

SASO branch.[65] A week later he was also elected president of the new SRC, following the vote of no-confidence in Nkwe.

The timing of these two meetings is significant: the new Mankweng SASO branch was formed in the middle of March, and less than a week later student discontent on campus resulted in the ousting of the SRC.[66] The key SASO members involved in constituting the local branch – Terror Lekota and Pandelani Nefolovhodwe – both maintained (at their later trial for trying to overthrow the state) that SASO itself had not instigated the coup. [67] In his testimony, however, Lekota admitted, 'Of course, I also tried to make some propaganda here for our organization here by suggesting that because the student body had subsequently elected Accused No. 6 [Nefolovhodwe] as president of the SRC that this was in a way a declaration of confidence by the student body in the organization SASO itself.'[68] Beyond 'making propaganda', Lekota was drawing an important point. Though SASO had not been directly involved in the ousting of the SRC, its imprint could be found on the whole episode: students moved to replace their SRC almost as soon as a viable alternative was available. SASO was a popular organization at Turfloop (attested by the level of attendance at the off-campus meeting, which attracted between a quarter and a third of the student body), and arguably the most popular.[69] Well-known SASO supporter Cyril Ramaphosa was selected as one of three electoral officers who were charged with running the elections of the new SRC.[70] Nefolovhodwe's selection as chairman of the local SASO branch and then shortly after as president of the new SRC also emphasizes the critical role that SASO was playing in student politics at Turfloop.

> [I]n that meeting I was elected SRC president. So in that sense I was no longer worried about having to run the affairs of SASO outside campus. I had then a legitimate position of SRC President, to propagate whatever I wanted to propagate within the student body. So together with the new

[65] SASO 9 Trial Transcripts, p. 5262 [HPRA AD2021/14.1]; also SASO 6th GSC minutes Res. 11/74, p. 25 [HPRA A2176/5.5].

[66] SASO 6th GSC minutes, Report of the Permanent Organizer, p. 2 [HPRA A2176/5.5].

[67] SASO 9 Trial Transcripts, p. 5571 (Nefolovhodwe), and p. 5261 (Lekota) [HPRA AD2021/14.1].

[68] SASO 9 Trial Transcripts, p. 5261 (Lekota) [HPRA AD2021/14.1].

[69] As Pandelani Nefolovhodwe described its importance, 'There was no other student organization of black people. It was the central organization throughout' [author's interview with Pandelani Nefolovhodwe].

[70] SASO 9 Trial Transcripts, p. 5576 (Nefolovhodwe) [HPRA AD2021/14.1].

SRC we then went on activities that were consistent with [SASO] – against apartheid.[71]

This cooperation was to become even more critical later in 1974, as, amid heightening tensions, the links between SASO and the Turfloop SRC became more closely intertwined.

Under Nefolovhodwe the new SRC embarked on a distinctly SASO-driven platform. One of its earliest priorities was to negotiate the return of SASO as an organization allowed on campus. Nefolovhodwe described it thus, 'Well, once I was SRC president, in a subsequent meeting of the SRC, the students urged that we should step into the steps that had already been taken by the previous SRC in negotiating with the Rector for the bringing back of SASO on campus.'[72] The Black Academic Staff Association also supported this move.[73] After conferrals with the university council, members of whom were as far afield as Pretoria, the Rector approved Nefolovhodwe's request, and SASO was once again permitted to operate on campus in June 1974. There is no record of why this decision was taken, but it may have been an attempt to appease students and preempt further protests.

By this stage Nefolovhodwe was straddling dual roles as president of the SRC and chairman of the local branch of SASO. Widespread support of SASO among the Turfloop student body seems to have prevented this from posing a perceived conflict of interest among students; in fact three of the members of the local SASO committee were elected to the new SRC.[74] On his visit to Turfloop in April/May of 1974, SASO's national president Muntu Myeza noted, 'The SRC and the newly constituted [SASO] Local Committee Executive [...] enjoy the following and support of the student body.'[75]

From 30 June to 6 July 1974 SASO held its annual General Students Council in Roodepoort, on the West Rand. Here the Turfloop situation was hailed as a success, having thrown off 'more than eighteen months of inactivity' following the unrest and upheaval of mid-1972.[76] Terror Lekota described the constitution of the new SASO branch as

---

[71] Author's interview with Pandelani Nefolovhodwe.

[72] SASO 9 Trial Transcripts, p. 5578 (Nefolovhodwe) [HPRA AD2021/14.1].

[73] SASO 6th GSC minutes, Report of the Permanent Organizer, p. 3 [HPRA A2176/5.5].

[74] SASO 9 Trial Transcripts, p. 5696 (Nefolovhodwe) [HPRA AD2021/14.1].

[75] 'Report of the President Presented at the 6th GSC', SASO 6th GSC minutes, pp. 207–8 [HPRA A2176/5.5].

[76] SASO 6th GSC minutes, Report of the Permanent Organizer, p. 2 [HPRA A2176/5.5].

'a breath-taking event', and Nefolovhodwe in particular was roundly applauded for his efforts in revitalizing SASO at one of its core campuses.[77] Following the carefully orchestrated way in which SASO elections were handled, as discussed in the previous chapter, it is perhaps unsurprising that Pandelani Nefolovhodwe was elected the new national president of SASO at the end of the 6th GSC in July 1974. For a short time, Nef, as he was known, also retained his position as president of the Turfloop SRC, and as chairman of the local SASO branch. In August this conglomeration of positions was diffused: Cyril Ramaphosa was elected to lead the Turfloop branch of SASO, which was once again allowed to operate on campus, and Gilbert 'Kaunda' Sedibe was elected as president of a new SRC, which was inaugurated on 13 September.[78] In spite of devolving these three positions from one person (Nefolovhodwe) to three (Nefolovhodwe, Ramaphosa, and Sedibe), the links between SASO and the Turfloop SRC were still extremely close. Ramaphosa, the new campus leader of SASO, had acted in the role of electoral officer during the SRC's emergency elections in March of 1974 – the same elections that had resulted in Nefolovhodwe's rise to the position of SRC president (while he already chaired the off-campus branch of SASO). Sedibe, an active member of SASO, had been present at Nefolovhodwe's election to both offices and he worked closely with his predecessor after taking over the SRC presidency. These relationships allowed the two organizations to coordinate their efforts in promoting anti-apartheid politics to an unprecedented degree on campus. The intricate ties between the Turfloop SRC and SASO on a local and national scale were to become of paramount importance in the months to come.

The Viva-FRELIMO rallies

FRELIMO, the Front for Liberation of Mozambique, took power in that country on 25 September 1974. This event reverberated beyond Mozambique itself, and was seized on by activists across the border in South Africa as an opportunity to celebrate and herald the turn to majority rule in the region.

By late 1974, SASO had increased the scope of its activism to regional and local chapters not necessarily affiliated directly with universities, had begun outreach in schools, and had made serious efforts to extend its reach beyond the student population with the development of the BPC. These two groups coordinated a series of rallies around the country

---

[77] Ibid., p. 2.
[78] SASO 9 Trial Transcripts, p. 5861 (Sedibe) [HPRA AD2021/14.1].

to celebrate FRELIMO's victory. These 'Viva-FRELIMO' rallies were planned for major cities – Durban, Cape Town, and Johannesburg, as well as for the black university campuses of Fort Hare, the University of Zululand, the University of the Western Cape, and the University of the North at Turfloop. Though accounts differ, as many as seven rallies were planned to occur across South Africa and in some of its Bantustans.[79] To publicize the events, SASO announced that several FRELIMO leaders would be crossing the border to address South African crowds at the rallies. They also posted placards with pro-FRELIMO and anti-Apartheid slogans. One of these placards 'so incensed' Cornelius Koekemoer, a Durban resident, that when he saw it two days before the scheduled rally he tore it down and sent a telegram to Prime Minister Vorster asking for government intervention to prohibit the planned demonstration. Koekemoer counselled against 'supporting terrorists whilst citizens of all races are sacrificing lives on [the] country's border', and claimed 'Thousands of Whites ready to take necessary steps to prevent demonstration,' in a letter that was picked up by the local press.[80]

Koekemoer's telegram made it to the office of Minister of Justice Jimmy Kruger, where on 24 September – one day before the scheduled rallies – the minister issued a comprehensive ban on the rallies, under the Riotous Assemblies Act. It prohibited any public gatherings 'encouraged or promoted by or on behalf of' SASO and the BPC, effective immediately, and until late October.[81]

It is hard to be certain of the causation behind the banning order; it is likely that police were already monitoring the preparations for the rallies – particularly the highly publicized Durban one – but Koekemoer's telegram, and perhaps more importantly the publicity it gained in the press, seems to have influenced Kruger's decision to proceed with the ban (as much was indicated by the judge during the trial of the SASO 9 after the rallies).[82] The order amounted to an effective ban on all SASO and BPC meetings, movements, and events for nearly a month – though both SASO and the BPC were still legal organizations at the time. In scope it reached well beyond the Viva-FRELIMO rallies themselves, but

---

[79] 'Kruger to stop mass Saso rally', *Rand Daily Mail*, 24 September 1974 [HPRA AD1912/239].

[80] 'Whites urged to stay away', *City Late*, 24 September 1974 [NASA MJU 727 MP17/2/3].

[81] *Republic of South Africa Government Gazette*, Vol. III, No. 4415. Cape Town, 25 September 1974 [NASA MJU 727 MP17/2/3].

[82] SASO 9 Trial Transcripts, p. 5635 (Nefolovhodwe) [HPRA AD2021/14.1].

there was no suggestion that its purpose was anything other than to ban public displays of support for the FRELIMO victory.

As word began to circulate about the ban, SASO hit back swiftly, releasing a joint statement with the BPC, saying that press reports had aggravated the situation and distorted the planned rallies by saying that the FRELIMO leaders would be 'smuggled or sneaked into the country'; SASO maintained that the guest speakers 'were going to come through normal channels'.[83] On the morning of 25 September, Muntu Myeza, SASO and BPC's joint publicity officer based in Durban, announced to reporters that, in spite of Kruger's ban, 'This afternoon's rally will go ahead as planned and the Frelimo leaders will be there.'[84]

The escalating tension was played out in local and national newspapers. A Durban *Daily News* editorial referred obliquely to Koekemoer, stating that, 'one White citizen telegraphed an objection to [Minister Kruger], who forthwith manufactured instant alarm'.[85] When asked if his decision had been influenced by the telegram, Kruger acknowledged that it had been a factor, though he contended, 'It was not the only consideration. I have taken all sorts of things into consideration.'[86] He said the rallies had 'evoked a strong emotional reaction among certain sections of the public.'[87] The *Daily News* editorial countered that the rally had actually evoked 'a strong emotional overreaction on the part of the Minister. What he has achieved now is to focus national, perhaps international, attention on what could well have been a damp squib of a meeting.'[88]

Whatever the Viva-FRELIMO rallies might have been – in the absence of Cornelius Koekemoer, the heated press coverage, and the banning order – what they actually were was fundamentally shaped by these factors. Of the many rallies planned to take place across the country, on the afternoon of 25 September only two of the rallies went ahead: the first was held at Curries Fountain Stadium in Durban, and was the one that Mr Koekemoer had threatened to disrupt with 'thousands of

[83] 'Kruger to stop mass Saso rally', *Rand Daily Mail*, 24 September 1974 [HPRA AD1912/239].

[84] '"Frelimo" Secrecy', *Durban Daily News*, 25 September 1974 [NASA MJU 727 MP17/2/3].

[85] 'Cheers and boos', *The Daily News*, 24 September 1974 [NASA MJU 727 MP17/2/3].

[86] 'Kruger to stop mass Saso rally', *Rand Daily Mail*, 24 September 1974 [HPRA AD1912/239].

[87] 'Cheers and boos', *The Daily News*, 24 September 1974 [NASA MJU 727 MP17/2/3].

[88] Ibid.

whites'. It was at the epicentre of the controversy, as SASO and the BPC both had their national headquarters in Durban, and many of their most prominent activists were based there. It was the Durban *Daily News* that was primarily responsible for the press coverage before the rallies took place, and Durban's proximity to Lourenço Marques, the capital of Mozambique, also helped to focus attention there given the anticipated arrival of FRELIMO leaders.

The second Viva-FRELIMO rally that proceeded in spite of the ban was nearly a thousand kilometres away, at the altogether less likely rural campus of the University of the North. In contrast to events in Durban, Turfloop was almost entirely ignored in the pre-rally controversy. The announcement of Minister Kruger's ban did not reach the area until the evening of 24 September; it initially arrived by radio broadcast from the nearest town of Pietersburg, 30 kilometres away, and took some time to filter through to key people on campus.[89] According to Pandelani Nefolovhodwe, the Turfloop student who was also the national president of SASO, news of the broadcast did not reach him until midday on the 25th, and then it was by word of mouth from an SRC member.[90]

In fact, under cross-examination during his treason trial in 1975, it became clear that Nefolovhodwe and other key SASO activists had, in fact, heard about the possibility of the ban the previous evening (24 September). Communication across its leadership was an important facet of SASO's organizational capacity. Though access to phones and other office equipment was scarce outside SASO headquarters in Durban, local leaders were able to use resources at their various institutions to stay in touch with one another. At Turfloop, this was one benefit of the close relationship of SASO to the SRC, who provided access to important facilities like their telephone and photostat machines.

It was via the SRC phone, on the evening of 24 September, that Nefolovhodwe was first alerted to the possibility that the Viva-FRE-LIMO rallies might be banned. Muntu Myeza, SASO's general secretary who was based in Durban at the time, informed Nefolovhodwe of the press coverage surrounding the rally there and Minister Kruger's response – that 'the necessary steps will be taken' – which both men considered ambiguous enough to provide a loophole for the rallies.[91] (This conversation had been bugged and recorded by security police,

[89] SASO 9 Trial Transcripts, p. 5633 (Nefolovhodwe) [HPRA AD2021/14.1].
[90] SASO 9 Trial Transcripts, p. 5608 (Nefolovhodwe) [HPRA AD2021/14.1].
[91] The conversation was bugged and recorded by the security police, and a transcript of it later introduced at the trial of the SASO 9, in which both Nefolovhodwe and

and was later admitted as evidence in Myeza and Nefolovhodwe's trial for treason.) In addition, at Turfloop they had the extra cover of being a step removed from the organization of the rally, which was explicitly under the coordination of the SRC, while the ban had only specifically named SASO and BPC. The students decided to proceed with their plans; Nefolovhodwe explained this decision to the judge in their trial: 'until such time the Minister bans the rally categorically in the Government Gazette you continue as though nothing has happened.'[92] Continue they did, even when the printed ban reproduced in the *Rand Daily Mail* reached campus on the morning of the 25th.[93]

So while Durban was braced for a conflict, Turfloop remained relatively quiet. But by late 1974 protests and class boycotts had become commonplace at Turfloop, and the campus was ripe for political confrontation led by their increasingly coordinated SRC and campus branch of SASO.[94] As well as having produced high-profile activists like Tiro, Nengwekhulu, and Nefolovhodwe, Turfloop was home to a burgeoning group of new activists, including the SRC president Gilbert Sedibe, local SASO chapter chairman Cyril Ramaphosa, and Students' Christian Movement leaders Frank Chikane, Lybon Mabasa, and Ishmael Mkhabela. As I have argued, by September 1974 the links between SASO and the Turfloop student leadership were unprecedentedly close. It was a highly politicized student body, peppered with prominent activists, that made the decision to hold the Viva-FRELIMO rally in spite of Kruger's banning order. They were the only group to do so besides Durban – where tensions had been brought to boiling by external factors before the rally.

If the tension at Turfloop was less than in Durban leading up to the rally, that was certainly not the case on the day itself. On the morning of 25 September students and staff at the University of the North awoke to find their campus plastered in political slogans and placards. Posters were everywhere, and slogans had been painted directly onto buildings. 'Those entering the campus from outside were greeted with the slogan "Voetsek [piss off] Vorster and his pigs".'[95] In an interview

---

Myeza were defendants [SASO 9 Trial Transcripts, pp. 5634–40 (Nefolovhodwe) [HPRA AD2021/14.1]].

[92] SASO 9 Trial Transcripts, p. 5636 (Nefolovhodwe) [HPRA AD2021/14.1].

[93] Republic of South Africa, *Government Gazette*, Vol. 111, No. 4415 [NASA, MJU 727 MP17/2/3].

[94] The Snyman Commission chronicles at least 13 incidents of student protest and activism in the two years between Tiro's expulsion and the Viva-FRELIMO rally at Turfloop.

[95] Snyman Commission Report, p. 106 (6.3.1).

nearly forty years later, Pandelani Nefolovhodwe declared that students had independently undertaken a placard-making campaign during the night of 24 September. 'When we woke up in the morning, we were all eyes on [...] these things.'[96] Some of the slogans were inflammatory, like the poster that read 'Frelimo killed. South African blacks?', prompting the idea that SASO should embark on an armed or violent struggle.

At 9am Lieutenant Viljoen of the Security Police arrived at the Rector's office and told him that 'they had information that SASO had arranged a pro-Frelimo rally in contravention of the Minister's prohibition for 2 o'clock that afternoon in the students' hall'.[97] This appears to have been the first the Rector learned of the possibility of a rally on his campus that would contravene Kruger's ban.

The details here are still a matter of contention: the students involved in coordinating the Turfloop rally said they did so with the blessing of the University Rector. But in the aftermath of the rally Rector Boshoff 'denied it, and said he had warned the students against holding a meeting', because he was concerned it would bring them into conflict with the state.[98] In fact, this warning was not issued until 12:30pm on the day of the rally itself, at which point the students decided to proceed with their plans. They defended their case by arguing that Kruger's ban did not apply to the Turfloop rally, which, they contended, had been organized under the auspices of the Student Representative Council and was not a SASO or BPC event. After the SRC had received word of the ban on the morning of the 25th, the president Gilbert Sedibe consulted several senior law students to determine the legality of proceeding. 'They also assured me that the banning of the SASO and BPC rallies would not affect our SRC rally.'[99] The Black Academic Staff Association (BASA) further defended the students after the rally took place. In a memo from its chairman BASA argued that 'such [police] intervention would have been called for were the celebration organized by the South African Students' Organization; as it is, there is no evidence that this was not a purely SRC affair'.[100]

[96] Author's interview with Pandelani Nefolovhodwe.

[97] Snyman Commission Report, p. 108 (6.3.4).

[98] 'Rector "warned students"', *Rand Daily Mail*, 26 September 1974 [HPRA AD1912/258.16].

[99] SASO 9 Trial Transcripts, p. 5884 (Sedibe) [HPRA AD2021/14.1].

[100] 'Whites must share blame, says rector', *Rand Daily Mail*, 30 September 1974 [HPRA AD1912/258.16]. Boshoff's contention to the press was that 'in contact situations the blame never lies on one side only. [...] There are too many Whites who reject apartheid and the Blacks in their relationships.' The article further

In fact, there was rather a lot of evidence that it was not purely an SRC affair. The rally had been coordinated by the SRC, but, as I have argued above, in September 1974 the Turfloop SRC was wholly affiliated to SASO. The recent transfer of SRC office to SASO member Gilbert Sedibe from SASO's national president Pandelani Nefolovhodwe did not represent an ideological shift away from SASO politics in the SRC. Nefolovhodwe was still a student at Turfloop, and closely involved in student politics. He also addressed the rally on the afternoon of 25 September, and he was joined in speaking by Sedibe and a female student, N.C. Tshoni, who was a member of both SASO and the SRC.[101]

It is interesting that the organizers of the Turfloop rally took such a different approach to the outright defiance displayed in Durban, where the Curries Fountain rally was never billed as anything other than a SASO/BPC event. Though there were many similarities between the rallies – motivation and organizational tactics, and police response – a primary difference is that Turfloop was a university campus. Until this point it had enjoyed a measure of shelter from the direct intervention of the state into student affairs. Though students had a history of conflict with the university administration, their protests and actions had thus far been a step removed from state penalty or retribution. Even Onkgopotse Tiro's high-profile expulsion had not prevented him from getting a job as a teacher under the Department of Bantu Education (short-lived though it was). Perhaps by claiming that the SRC had organized the rally the students sought to maintain that distance, whereas in Durban there was no distance to maintain; perhaps the Rector's belated warning not to go ahead with the rally was the first sign that such protection – if it can be called that – would no longer be possible.

Shortly after Nefolovhodwe was told about the ban by an SRC member, in the hour leading up to the 2pm start of the rally, 82 policemen - from both the South African and Lebowan police forces, as well as men from the Bureau of State Security (BOSS) - assembled at the Mankweng police station, which sits just outside the western campus gates of Turfloop.[102] All of them were armed with rubber batons, and each of the white officers was also armed with a service revolver. Some of the police had dogs, 'which were controlled with long leashes'. The

---

explains that 'by apartheid he understood the pragmatic adjustment to a contact situation'.

[101] SASO 9 Trial Transcripts, p. 5863 (Sedibe) [HPRA AD2021/14.1].

[102] These numbers and times are taken from police reports submitted into evidence to the Snyman Commission of Inquiry, which was held to uncover the causes of unrest at Turfloop.

acting District Commandant of the South African Police, Major Erasmus, was commanding them. At 1:45pm, Major Strydom of the Security Police 'moved to the campus [...] and saw that the students intended to go ahead with the rally. He reported immediately to Major Erasmus.'[103]

At 2pm, as students were gathering in the hall for the beginning of the rally, the Rector left the main campus to play golf with the Registrar. In his absence no member of the university staff or administration was designated to liaise with the police who were amassed outside campus. Meanwhile students had gathered in the hall, and the turnout was so large that many had to amass outside the building itself and listen to the proceedings from there.[104] Gilbert Sedibe, president of the SRC, was the first to take the floor, and he reflected on the importance of the FRELIMO victory in Mozambique for South Africans, and particularly for South African students. He emphasized that the assassinated president of FRELIMO, Eduardo Mondlane, had been a student himself in the Northern Transvaal before going to the University of the Witwatersrand and subsequently being expelled from South Africa.[105] (Mondlane attended the Douglas Lain Smit Secondary School – a Swiss Missionary school south-east of Louis Trichardt – in Lemana from 1944 to 1948, before moving to the Jan H. Hofmeyr School of Social Work in Johannesburg and, finally, to the University of the Witwatersrand. He left in 1950 without completing his degree, expelled by the new Nationalist government of South Africa.[106]) Sedibe's remarks were followed by a brief address from Pandelani Nefolovhodwe, who endeavoured to make clear that he spoke only in his capacity 'as an individual member of the student community' and not as the national president of SASO.[107] His efforts were undermined, however, by the fact that programmes for the rally – printed before Kruger's ban – listed him as representing SASO at the meeting.[108] The final speaker, N.C. Tshoni, a member of both SASO and the SRC, took the stage, and like Sedibe, she drew important links between South African student activists and FRELIMO, as well as other pan-African examples. Her fellow SRC member, Jonas Ledwaba, recalled her appealing to the legacies of Kenneth Kaunda, Julius Nyerere, and Mobutu Sesi Seko – saying South African students were

[103] Snyman Commission, p. 110 (6.3.12).
[104] SASO 9 Trial Transcripts, p. 205 (Ledwaba) [HPRA AD2021/14.1].
[105] SASO 9 Trial Transcripts, p. 5613 (Nefolovhodwe) [HPRA AD2021/14.1].
[106] Biography of Eduardo Chivambo Mondlane. [http://www.oberlin.edu/archive/holdings/finding/RG30/SG307/biography2.html] Accessed 24 June 2012.
[107] SASO 9 Trial Transcripts, pp. 5614–15 (Nefolovhodwe) [HPRA AD2021/14.1].
[108] SASO 9 Trial Transcripts, p. 5613 (Nefolovhodwe) [HPRA AD2021/14.1].

disappointing these African leaders by not fighting for their freedom. 'Then she further said that don't students demanding [sic] something similar[ly] dramatic as the South African Mau Mau.'[109]

Tshoni's speech was the most radical of the three, as she drew direct parallels between student activism in South Africa and violent guerilla liberation movements elsewhere on the continent, but all three speakers made an effort to explicitly link the work of student activists in South Africa to the liberation movement in Mozambique (and in Tshoni's speech, beyond). As demonstrated by the placards around campus that called for immediate – and often physical – action, the rhetoric of the Viva-FRELIMO rally was more militant and less psychological than SASO events that preceded it; it had also lost the explicit Christian over-tones of Onkgopotse Tiro's graduation speech two years earlier. This marked a shift in mobilizing factors SASO was employing, if not an outright one in ideology.

At approximately 2:20pm the police unit entered campus and moved to the hall in a convoy of police cars. When they reached the hall they found the rally was already in progress, and Tshoni's speech was in full flow. Major Erasmus entered the hall, addressed the assembled students through a megaphone, and ordered everyone to disperse within 15 min-utes. An estimated 1200 students were gathered, and according to evi-dence submitted to the Snyman Commission, 'absolute pandemonium broke out, during which the SASO salute (a clenched fist) was given by many students and slogans such as "Viva-FRELIMO" and "Free-dom" were shouted'.[110] The students did leave the hall, but many of them (approximately 700) reconvened on the sports grounds. Here the details of the archival record and personal recollections get fuzzier.[111] Students claim that they congregated on the sports ground to conclude the rally with the singing of the African anthem, *Nkosi Sikelel' iAfrika*. The police reports say the students 'gave the SASO (or Black Power) salute and marched up and down', refusing to disperse.[112] The police allege that at this point a group of male students began to throw stones and bottles at them. 'Major Erasmus then gave an order for the students to be dispersed. A baton charge followed and the students ran away but soon afterwards they again formed a unit.' Students countered this nar-rative, saying that bottles and stones were only thrown after the police

---

[109] SASO 9 Trial Transcripts, p. 207 (Ledwaba) [HPRA AD2021/14.1].

[110] Snyman Commission, p. 111 (6.3.15).

[111] The previous information is generally confirmed both by evidence given to the Snyman Commission, by press reports and in interviews.

[112] Snyman Commission, p. 112 (6.3.17).

baton charge, in retaliation. Clashes between students armed with bottles and stones, and police armed with batons and dogs, continued for several minutes; in the chaos one student was attacked and wounded by a police dog. The students were finally dispersed when the police fired teargas at them; they left the sports ground and retreated to their residences, but many returned. In the conflict three students – including the one attacked by the dog – had been arrested. The SRC leaders returned to the sports ground and demanded the release of the arrested students, and at this stage the Rector arrived on the scene. He had been called back to address the situation, and he successfully negotiated the release of the arrested students, the withdrawal of the police, and the dispersal of the students.

The détente was premature, however; some groups of students moved to other sections of campus, and began to try to barricade areas. Two white staff members and two white tradesmen, travelling in three different cars, were attacked and stoned by students. Two of the men sustained injuries, and one was 'permanently disfigured' when a stone thrown through the broken window of his car struck his face. The police were once again called to campus, but 'when the students saw them they dispersed and disappeared into residences'.[113]

The Viva-FRELIMO rally represents a turning point in protest at Turfloop: it is the first use of state force against the students on campus as well as the first incident of student violence against the university staff. In this it was part of a larger trend towards confrontational politics across South Africa, which Julian Brown has explored. Brown suggests that the violence employed on both sides during the Turfloop rally 'short-lived and ineffectual as it may have been – represented a new form of confrontation'.[114] For students, consequences of the rally also marked a major departure from previous campus conflicts. On the one hand, with the intervention of the Rector in negotiating the dispersal of both students and police from the sports ground, the university administration had reinserted itself in the narrowing space between students and state. But this was fleeting – only a few hours after the Rector's efforts, campus again devolved into clashes directly between students and the police.

The university authorities found themselves similarly impotent in the aftermath of the rally. Two meetings of the university disciplinary committee failed to pass a resolution disciplining the SRC, as the members of the Black Academic Staff Association insisted (in a majority vote) 'that the SRC could not be held responsible in any way for any of the

---

[113] Snyman Commission, p. 115 (6.3.26).
[114] Brown, 'Public Protest and Violence', p. 286.

incidents on 25 September 1974'.[115] The Rector and white staff largely disagreed, and the University Council made the decision to shut the university for two weeks in October to consider how best to address the situation.[116] In the end they turned to the state. After meeting in Pretoria on 8 October the Council 'decided to request the Minister to appoint a judicial commission of inquiry'.[117] From this request the Snyman Commission was appointed. As noted earlier, following the student unrest after the Tiro incident in 1972, the University had appointed its own commission of inquiry, resulting in the secret Wright Report. The failure of the university to be similarly proactive in the aftermath of the Viva-FRELIMO rally suggests that the university authorities no longer had confidence in their own ability to maintain order on campus.

The state had no such qualms: in the weeks following the rallies, police conducted sweeping arrests of SASO and BPC activists involved in the Turfloop and Durban rallies. Gilbert Sedibe was arrested and held in the Mankweng police station, while Pandelani Nefolovhodwe was arrested at the SASO headquarters in Durban, where he had travelled to help arrange bail for Muntu Myeza, Terror Lekota, and others.[118] In a protest march from Turfloop campus to the Mankweng police to demand the release of Sedibe, Cyril Ramaphosa was also arrested. Of the activists gathered in this roundup, nine – including Nefolovhodwe and Sedibe – were eventually tried for terrorist activities in the SASO/BPC trial.

On 17 October the SRC resolved to hold a sit-in until Sedibe, Nefolovhodwe, and Ramaphosa were released from police custody. They blamed the Rector for 'selling our rightful leaders to the system'.[119] The resolution was undertaken at a mass meeting and enjoyed the support

---

[115] Snyman Commission, p. 118 (6.4.7).

[116] The University Council was the body charged with governing the university, and was composed of senior administrators on campus as well as educators and bureaucrats outside the structure of the university itself; at its inception in 1960, it was an all-white, all-male group. It was 'assisted' by an Advisory Council of no fewer than eight non-white members, who were appointed by the Governor General of the Council. Both bodies' decisions were subject to approval and veto by the Minister of Bantu Education. It was not until 1975, with the publication of the Jackson Report, which advocated Africanization of Turfloop's leadership, that these demographics began to shift and Africans were included in the highest reaches of the university's administration. [White, *From Despair to Hope*, pp. 85–9, 116–20.]

[117] Snyman Commission, p. 119 (6.4.9).

[118] Author's interview with Pandelani Nefolovhodwe; SASO 9 Trial Transcripts, p. 34 (Nefolovhodwe) [HPRA AD2021/14.1].

[119] Wolfson, *Turmoil at Turfloop*, Annexure O, p. 68.

of the majority of the student body, but there was also some dissent, demonstrating the increasingly polarized nature of politics at Turfloop. Only approximately fifty students on a campus of more than 1200 actively contravened the SRC sit-in, while a large majority participated. Small groups of students in pharmacy and nursing passed resolutions dissenting from the SRC's decision to hold the sit-in. In the case of the pharmacy students, they even explicitly supported the student body in its aim of Africanization, but objected to the approach:

> The procedural machinery has failed to allow us to bring forth our views in a mass meeting. We feel it is our right to differ. We feel that we should dissociate ourselves from the popular stand of holding a sit-in because we consider it to be a cause of self-destruction and facilitates the aims and objects of the very system [of apartheid]. [...] We all cherish the idea of the system of Africanisation of this University, but a sit-in will destroy the very means of achieving this ideal.[120]

The nursing students, in contrast, dissociated themselves from the aims and movements of the student body completely: they requested to write their examinations, declaring,

> We are professional people, civil servants, sent by our employing authorities and sponsored by the South African Nursing Association. We are answerable for our behaviour to the South African Nursing Council. As such we are not party to what is taking place concerning the Student body.[121]

The SRC responded to each of these minority resolutions; to the pharmacy students it was conciliatory, conceding 'that, rather than calling the dissenters to appear before the SRC Disciplinary Committee, they should be called to give their views to the house and to assure them of the fullest protection they will enjoy as the house is eager to have them in the deliberations.'[122] But to the more confrontational stand taken by the nurses it responded angrily, decrying 'the self-evident reactionary collaboration between the SA Nursing Council and our Administration'; the nurses themselves were understood to be caught in an impossible position, between their employer, the South African Nursing Council, and the student body of which they were part. To settle the conflict, the SRC resolved 'to recognise that nurses are not part of this Student Body, since an employee is subject to instructions from the employer'.[123] As

---

[120] Ibid., Annexure P, p. 69.
[121] Ibid., Annexure Q, p. 70.
[122] Ibid., Annexure R, p. 71.
[123] Ibid., Annexure S, p. 72.

the nurses were no longer considered part of the student body, they were also not bound to abide by SRC resolutions. But this demonstrates the drastic steps that could be taken to ensure near-universal support – the SRC went as far as redefining who constituted a student in order to maintain this. Turfloop's growing history of large student protests and class boycotts, beginning with the protests over university autonomy in 1970 and epitomized by the protests over the expulsion of Onkgopotse Tiro in 1972, exerted significant pressure for students to participate in these highly politicized events. There were sometimes allegations of coercion surrounding such protests.

The Trial of the SASO 9

The Trial of the SASO 9, or the Black Consciousness Trial, as it came to be called, began in July 1975, nearly nine months after the October 1974 detentions of a wide scope of political activists associated with SASO, BPC, and the Student Representative Council of the University of the North. As remembered by defendant Pandelani Nefolovhodwe:

> [A]ll of us were taken to the Pretoria Central Prison, where Steve Biko finally died. We were locked up there as a large group, and they went on to interrogate us, put us in solitary confinement [...] and finally they selected a few of us to become the accused on a terrorism charge. We were then charged under the Terrorism Act, we were fomenting hostility against white people, emulating FRELIMO... We were thirteen in number when we were charged, and finally the charges for four others don't stick, so we ended up with nine.[124]

Those nine defendants came to play a pivotal role in the broader public conception of SASO as an organization, and in a growing political conscientization among certain sections of the population. In his historical analysis of this trial, Michael Lobban has argued that it offers particular insights into how the South African state sought to 'use a political trial to control its opponents'.[125] In this section, I shall argue that the trial also demonstrates the way that young activists used the court system and attendant press coverage (especially important for those from Turfloop who were under a gag-order on campus, and for those who were banned from publishing or public speech) to propagate their own political agenda. Similarly to Tiro before them, these defendants came to be

---

[124] Author's interview with Pandelani Nefolovhodwe.
[125] M. Lobban, *White Man's Justice: South African political trials in the Black Consciousness era* (Oxford, 1996), p. 77.

the public face of student resistance to 'the system' at the outset of their trial in 1975.

The government's crackdown on the defiance displayed at Turfloop and Durban during the pro-FRELIMO rallies – evidenced by the first use of force by police on the university campus and in the sweeping detentions and arrests that followed – was designed to clamp down on SASO's mobilization and activism. Instead the trial provided a platform to highlight their cause. South Africa's longest terrorism trial played out over the course of seventeen months and garnered substantial press coverage. Magaziner has said that 'the trial was more farce than tragedy, and reasoning that some sort of conviction was inevitable, the defendants treated it like theater'.[126] While theatricality did play a role in how the defendants presented themselves on the stand, there were serious motives behind this performance. More than a stage, the defendants used the stand as a microphone, and indeed a pulpit from which to propagate their message.

Famously, Steve Biko, SASO's founder and figurehead, took his opportunity on the stand as a witness for the defense to expound on the birth of SASO and the philosophy of Black Consciousness as the guiding principle for SASO and the BPC. In his explanation to presiding Judge Boshoff, he states:

> [B]asically Black Consciousness refers itself to the Black man and to his situation, and I think the Black man is subjected to two forces in this country. He is first of all oppressed by an external world through institutionalised machinery: through laws that restrict him from doing certain things, through heavy work conditions, through poor education, these are all external to him, and secondly, and this we regard as the most important, the Black man in himself has developed a certain state of alienation, he rejects himself, precisely because he attaches the meaning White to all that is good, in other words he associates good and he equates good with White. This arises out of his living and it arises out of his development from childhood [...]. This is carried through to adulthood when the Black man has got to live and work.[127]

Redressing this psychological conditioning formed the core thrust of the Black Consciousness Movement. Over the course of five days of testimony in May 1976 Biko articulated the process of forming SASO as an organization and the challenges that had been faced by black student activists in the 1960s; he ranged from discussing the psychological grounding of the SASO slogan 'Black is beautiful' to the importance of

---

[126] Magaziner, *The Law and the Prophets*, p. 153.
[127] SASO 9 Trial Transcripts, pp. 4362–3 (Biko) [HPRA AD2021/14.1].

disinvestment in South Africa by foreign firms. Over those days, Biko articulated his position not just to the lawyers, judge, and accused in the courtroom, but to a much broader audience through the platform provided by the press. Banned to a location outside King Williams Town in the rural Eastern Cape since 1973, and further restricted from public engagement and publishing in 1975, Biko seized the opportunity to use the witness box at the trial as a pulpit for the movement. He was not the only one to do so – many of the defendants followed this lead.

In debunking the state's case that the Viva-FRELIMO rallies had revolutionary capacity, Lobban has argued that at the outset of the trials, SASO and BPC did not have 'coherent confrontational strategies or ideologies';[128] but the psychological, and indeed, theological aspects of Black Consciousness were coherent among students on campuses like Turfloop, as I have argued in this and the previous chapter. Lobban is correct that prior to the Viva-FRELIMO rally SASO did not have a coherent revolutionary strategy. I would argue that such a strategy was just beginning to be articulated at the rally itself – in the speeches of SRC members like N.C. Tshoni. But a revolutionary ideology of overturning white rule was deeply entrenched and widely held in the organization by late 1974. It had been realized in the philosophy of Black Consciousness and the theology of Black Theology. When they came to the stand, the SASO 9 defendants were able to articulate aspects of these platforms. In his testimony, defendant Mosiuoa Lekota gave a detailed explanation of Black Theology, as SASO preached it:

> I think, M'Lord, the importance of Black Theology is one because of the prime interest of Black people in spiritual health. Perhaps one can just generalize and say so, what Black Theology in fact attempts in my view to do is to suggest to Black people that the fact that for instance they are in the ghettoes, that they live in those conditions and so on, is not a God-created kind of situation. What in fact Black Theology seeks to say there is that God is not approving of the oppression of Black people or their desolate situation. It seeks to draw from the Bible the liberatory message that is in there, and putting into context Black people in relation to God. If I may just be literal, what they would really seek to say would be that God is involved with the Black people, he is involved with the Black experience, and that therefore Black people must see themselves as an extension if I may so say of God – I mean an embodiment of God.[129]

Theologically this bears comparison to other religions that preached of a people 'chosen' by God. Though often associated with Judaism, this

---

[128] Lobban, *White Man's Justice*, p. 77.
[129] SASO 9 Trial Transcripts, p. 5265 (Lekota) [HPRA AD2021/14.1].

was also a key tenet of Afrikaner Christianity in the Dutch Reformed Church (NGK). But in contrast to the theology of the NGK, Black Theology was corrective rather than exclusive; it did not say that blacks were chosen by God to the exclusion of other peoples; rather it sought to redress their own exclusion from the way that Christianity had historically been practised in South Africa.

Lekota's testimony recalls the significance of Christianity to SASO as a whole, and also specifically at Turfloop. When forced to operate outside campus in setting up a new branch of SASO, Lekota himself, who was an alumnus, had arranged the meeting at the local Catholic church in Mankweng. Biko also described the spirituality that was exhibited at SASO gatherings, in his testimony about SASO memorials on Heroes Day and the Day of Compassion, using explicitly Christian imagery:

> Certainly the way SASO conducted the various services in our campus it was mainly a sermon, and we called various distinguished ministers to conduct a service, and I have no doubt that the majority of people there were moved by the way the whole thing was handled. In a way they tended to relate it to a biblical sacrifice, you know, to say that these people died for us.[130]

Those commemorated on Heroes Day included the victims of the Sharpeville Massacre in 1960, Ahmed Timol and those who had died in detention, Onkgopotse Tiro, and others; with its religious overtones of sacrifice and selflessness, this day essentially enshrined a set of martyrs to the struggle against apartheid.[131] The Day of Compassion sought to highlight suffering in communities that were victims of natural disasters (like flooding) and the disastrous circumstances of poverty in which some South Africans found themselves. As Biko explained it, 'In a sense, the main theme in Compassion Day was to get students to develop a social conscience, to see themselves as part of the community, and to direct their energies at solving problems of the nature we were thinking about on Compassion Day.'[132]

SASO leaders worked to draw direct links between Christian theology and liberation. This linkage between student politics and Christianity was not restricted to the early days of the movement, when it was most closely associated with overtly Christian groups like the University Christian Movement. On the Day of Compassion (17 August) in 1974, Lekota travelled to Turfloop to address the crowd on Black Theology.

---

[130] SASO 9 Trial Transcripts, p. 4359 (Biko) [HPRA AD2021/14.1].
[131] Ibid.
[132] SASO 9 Trial Transcripts, pp. 4360–1 (Biko) [HPRA AD2021/14.1].

As Jonas Ledwaba, a member of the Turfloop SRC who was in the audience that day recalled, '[Lekota] said […] as we go to the Holy Bible we find that the true God is a God of justice who took care of the children of Israel when they were under Egyptian oppression, and so if these churches can get the right God, then that God will take care of people under oppression'.[133]

Events at Turfloop, ranging from the Day of Compassion up to and including the rally, comprised an important focus of the trial, and once again drew national attention to the rural campus of the University of the North. Two of the defendants in the SASO trial were accused for their roles in the Viva-FRELIMO rally at Turfloop – Gilbert Sedibe and Pandelani Nefolovhodwe – and a third, Mosiuoa Lekota, was a Turfloop alumnus who helped organize the Durban rally and had been active as a SASO organizer on campus earlier in 1974.

Of simultaneous public interest was the Snyman Commission of Inquiry, which had been appointed to investigate the causes of unrest at the university. Its hearings were also well publicized, and thanks to reports of the trial and the commission in 1975 Turfloop found itself featuring as the pinnacle of student unrest in newspapers throughout the country. Rector Boshoff publicly called the situation 'extremely serious' in an interview with *The Star*, where he described escalating racial tension on campus: 'We are doing all we can to sort things out here by consultation with the people concerned. But many of the students come here with anti-White ideas and these are encouraged by some members of the Black academic staff.'[134] Such perceptions were reinforced by articles like an editorial in *The Star* by Jean Le May, 'Turfloop has been a trouble spot for years', which reiterated the campus's history of unrest during the Tiro episode, and earlier student protests surrounding its split from UNISA to become an 'independent' university in 1970.[135] In the wake of the rally increased tensions on campus were rarely out of the headlines: 'Turfloop Students Boycott Classes', 'White "home guard" on patrol in Turfloop', 'Police keep watch as Turfloop sit-in goes on'.[136]

---

[133] SASO 9 Trial Transcripts, p. 216 (Ledwaba) [HPRA AD2021/14.1].

[134] 'Turfloop situation is now "serious"', *The Star*, 30 September 1974 [HPRA AD1912/239].

[135] 'Turfloop has been a trouble spot for years', *The Star*, 8 October 1974 [HPRA AD1912/239].

[136] 'Turfloop Students Boycott Classes', *The Star*, 17 October 1974 [HPRA AD1912/258.16]; 'White "home guard" on patrol in Turfloop', *Sunday Times*, 20 October 1974 [HPRA AD1912/258.16]; 'Police keep watch as Turfloop sit-in goes on', *Rand Daily Mail*, 21 October 1974 [HPRA AD1912/258.16].

But while such press coverage may have inspired fear and worry in some South Africans, for others the increased coverage of Turfloop as a centre for resistance, and of the defiant defendants in the SASO 9 Trial, was inspiring. The trial positioned youth as a model for courageous resistance.[137] The courtroom was routinely full of onlookers in the gallery, a mix of supporters and the curious. The prosecutor, Mr Rees, noted the composition of spectators in the court in his cross-examination of Pandelani Nefolovhodwe: 'You have your Turfloop friends here, you have had Ramaphosa comes [sic] and visit you regularly [...].'[138] This support extended beyond personal friends and fellow SASO activists, as well. Following the convictions of all nine defendants in December 1976, with sentences ranging from five to six years' imprisonment, 'Shouts of Amandla by the nine convicted men were met with a chorus of Awethu from a packed gallery of about 200 people after sentence was passed in the Saso terror trial [...].'[139] Two white students from the University of Cape Town were detained by security police for handing out pamphlets to spectators outside the Pretoria courthouse on the day of the verdicts, and police with dogs entered the Palace of Justice itself when 'a crowd of spectator [sic] had an altercation with police guarding the courtroom door'.[140]

During the course of the trial the Soweto student uprising began in June 1976, marking a critical turning point in South Africa's history when school children took to the streets in mass protest against the Bantu Education policy of teaching in Afrikaans. Among them were those who had been taught by Tiro and many other expelled Turfloop students. With the uprisings in Soweto all student protest was cast into sharper relief throughout the country, and heightened public interest in the SASO 9 Trial reflects this. Though all of the nine were convicted and given sentences of between five and six years on Robben Island, their trial had provided such an important platform for proliferating SASO's message that the imprisonment of the bulk of its leadership was a steep but worthwhile cost. When the trial ended, student protest and conscientization in the Black Consciousness mould had never been stronger.

---

[137] Gerhart, *Black Power in South Africa*, pp. 298–9.
[138] SASO 9 Trial Transcripts, p. 5705 (Nefolovhodwe) [HPRA AD2021/14.1].
[139] 'Nine get 51 years' jail over rally plot', *The Daily News*, 22 December 1976 [HPRA AD1912/239].
[140] Ibid.

The Snyman Commission of Inquiry

The middle of the 1970s was a time of unparalleled prominence for the South African Students' Organization and other Black Consciousness organizations. As argued above, the trial of the SASO 9, taking place over seventeen months from July 1975 to December 1976, provided an exceptional platform for the SASO leadership to broadcast their messages of equality, self-sufficiency, and African nationalism. Just preceding the trial, another event had also put SASO in headlines regularly, particularly with regard to its role at the University of the North. The Commission of Inquiry into Certain Matters Relating to the University of the North (or the Snyman Commission, as it has been called for its head Justice J.H. Snyman), held hearings from November 1974 to June 1975 in order to determine the root causes of unrest at the university. The constitution of this committee, as has been mentioned, was requested by the university council after the Viva-FRELIMO rally on 25 September 1974. Between the rally itself, the hearings held by the commission, and the trial of the SASO 9, SASO and Turfloop were rarely out of the national press between late 1974 and the end of 1976. In concert with the Soweto uprisings of June 1976 that spread across the country and carried the ideology of Black Consciousness with them, this served to make 1976–7 a pinnacle moment for Black Consciousness and Africanist politics in South Africa.

This period of prominence wrought tangible changes in life at Turfloop: in the aftermath of the Viva-FRELIMO rally of September 1974, some of the most noticeable changes were influenced by the hearings of the Snyman Commission. The hearings were initially held publicly near campus, and later moved to Pretoria in January 1976. Students and staff were regularly in attendance at these hearings between November and December 1975, while they were held in Lebowa government administrative offices in Mankweng. The press described the crowded events: 'the 200 seat auditorium was crammed to capacity'[141] and 'students and staff turned out in force at the inquiry'.[142]

Initially, though, there was some debate on campus about whether students would participate in the commission at all: Justice Snyman came to campus in late November to address a mass meeting of students about the importance of hearing all sides of the circumstances

---

[141] 'Turfloop Inquiry hears of slogans', *Pretoria News*, 19 November 1974 [HPRA AD1912/258.16].
[142] 'Turfloop students to give evidence', *Rand Daily Mail*, 20 November 1974 [HPRA AD1912/258.16].

surrounding the Viva-FRELIMO rally. He came at the invitation of the SRC. 'I asked the students to back their SRC [in testifying], because I did not want one-sided views or a one-sided report,' Snyman said to a reporter.[143] Eventually the students voted to allow student testimonies: two days into hearings 'an SRC spokesman said they had now been given a mandate by the 1000-strong student body to appear before Mr Justice J. H. Snyman'.[144] The Black Academic Staff Association (BASA) also agreed to give evidence; both BASA and the SRC were led in their submissions by legal counsel.[145]

In spite of the students' mandate to testify, student participation in the commission was minimal. Evidence came primarily from staff and from the submission of documentary evidence and affidavits; only one student, Frank Chikane, actually took the stand before the commission. In part this lack of representation can be attributed to the quick back-lash that had already hamstrung the student and SASO leadership at Turfloop following the rally. In the weeks following the Viva-FRELIMO rally the presidents of the SRC, and of SASO both locally and nation-ally (all of whom were Turfloop students) were detained. Pandelani Nefolovhodwe, the national president of SASO and former Turfloop SRC president, recalled the frustration of not being able to participate in the commission of inquiry during his detention and trial as one of the 'SASO 9':

> But in the meantime, while we were in here [in Pretoria] standing trial, Turfloop established a commission of inquiry on the activities that took place during our time before we were arrested. We kept on asking that we should be allowed to give evidence to that commission of inquiry, but the apartheid government refused. So we who were leaders of the students were never given a chance to state our case, we were not given a chance to state our case at our own trial.[146]

But it is also clear that the student body was concerned with presenting a cohesive story, and a united front to the commission. The SRC leader-ship refused to testify until mandated to do so by a majority vote at their mass meeting; even once the mandate had been secured, they decided to

---

[143] 'Judge appeals to students at Turfloop', *Rand Daily Mail*, 19 November 1974 [HPRA AD1912/258.16].

[144] 'Turfloop students to give evidence', *Rand Daily Mail*, 20 November 1974 [HPRA AD1912/258.16].

[145] S. Duval, 'Who's who at the Turfloop inquiry', *Rand Daily Mail*, 30 November 1974 [HPRA AD 1912/258.16].

[146] Author's interview with Pandelani Nefolovhodwe.

have only one student represent their case in verbal testimony, rather than to open the opportunity to testify to all students.

It fell to Chikane then, not one of the rally's organizers, but a student of some prominence on campus, a member of SASO and of the executive of the Student's Christian Movement, to speak for the student body. He confined his testimony to the events on the day of the rally, speaking concretely about the order of events and the chaos that erupted on the sports fields in confrontation with the police.[147] He explained – in justifying the decision to hold the rally – that the students were confident the ban from Minister Kruger on SASO gatherings did not apply to their SRC-organized event. And he described police perpetrating violence in the confusion after the event: 'As I was running [from the police] I noticed one of the students I had been walking with earlier being knocked to the ground by the police. I realised he would need help. It took all my courage to go back and help him.'[148]

Aside from Chikane's testimony, other student evidence was amassed by letters and motions by the SRC that were submitted to the commission, and these too stuck very closely to the subject of what happened as the rally was broken up by the police. Rector Boshoff read one such letter aloud at the hearing in his own testimony. In it, the SRC defended their right to hold the rally and declared that 'the police who came and interrupted the rally had no cause to believe that law and order would be disturbed, and the police disturbed the peace of the campus by the use of dogs, batons, and teargas'.[149]

Student submissions to the commission focused on creating a narrow and consistent narrative of a peaceful rally that turned to violence when police used force to disperse it. In contrast to this, some staff recognized the opportunity that the Snyman Commission afforded to express their views about Turfloop publicly, beyond its specific remit of the events surrounding the Viva-FRELIMO rally. Arguably the single most significant piece of evidence submitted to the Commission was the compiled survey of the Black Academic Staff Association (BASA), who elected to respond to Snyman's written survey of university staff *en masse*, rather than individually. The fifty-two members of BASA signed this collective memorandum, raising issues from pay parity and promotion scales between black and white staff to the lack of white staff involvement

---

[147] 'Student tells of unrest at Turfloop rally', *Rand Daily Mail*, 27 November 1975 [GPP].

[148] Ibid.

[149] Quoted in 'Police accused of disturbing peace', *Natal Witness*, 20 November 1975 [HPRA AD1912/258.16].

in students' extracurricular clubs.[150] From BASA the Snyman Commission heard evidence on university life broadly defined, considering the breadth of student societies and activities from SASO to religious groups, the Students' Choral Society, and African Arts Week.[151]

Conclusion

The mid-1970s became the hallmark period of student protest in South Africa's history. Though the pivotal Soweto uprising has come to epitomize this era, the concerted work of the South African Students' Organization that predated the uprisings of students in the townships played an important role in laying the foundations for June 1976. The University of the North at Turfloop also occupied a critical place in the national landscape of student protest, and particularly in the rise of Black Consciousness throughout the country. Brown has demonstrated how the use of confrontational protest in the Viva-FRELIMO rallies ushered in a new era in the form of South African protest politics. In this chapter I have extended that case and argued for the role of Turfloop specifically in propagating both new form and content of protest on a national scale. Highly publicized events like the student protests after Tiro's expulsion and the Viva-FRELIMO rally demonstrated Turfloop's politics – which combined an important mix of local grievances with broader anti-apartheid rhetoric – to a national audience, while student activists strove to bring the message of Black Consciousness to local communities throughout South Africa.

High-profile figures like Onkgopotse Tiro and the SASO 9 were able to leverage their positions as student activists and amplify the SASO message of Black Consciousness to a broad audience. From Tiro's work as a teacher in Soweto, to travelling around South Africa and to frontline neighbours like Botswana and Lesotho, his enduring impact belies the relatively short time he occupied the activists' stage. His role as mentor to some of the students who led the 1976 protests is testament to his achievement in mobilizing and conscientizing his students. The SASO 9 were many of Tiro's contemporaries, and had almost all been longtime activists by the time of their arrests after his death. But it was their prolonged trial that provided them an unparalleled platform from which to speak. Aware that it might be their last opportunity to do so, many of the defendants used the witness stand to articulate principles of Black Consciousness and Black Theology.

[150] Nkondo, *Turfloop Testimony*, pp. 25, 27.
[151] Snyman Commission, pp. 45, 75–6.

Of equal importance to the high-profile figures that were the public face of Turfloop, of SASO, and of student resistance to the state, organizational mechanisms played a critical role in facilitating this work. SASO's tiered approach to leadership enabled the organization to react quickly and efficiently to the sidelining and loss of its leaders. The role of permanent organizer in the early-mid 1970s is an example of this: Harry Nengwekhulu occupied it until his exile in September 1973, when Onkgopotse Tiro stepped into the breach until he was killed in February 1974. Mosiuoa Lekota assumed the role immediately following the death of Tiro. Throughout the period and under each man, the role of permanent organizer continued to be a major force for SASO's organizing capacity, benefiting, especially in the case of Nengwekhulu and Tiro, from the layered leadership model that had paired the two men as work partners long before Nengwekhulu's banning. All travelled widely as long as they could do so, and worked to bring the message of Black Consciousness to new communities in South Africa, as well as to maintain its presence in strongholds like Turfloop. An important by-product of the tiered leadership was the ability of SASO to deeply diffuse ideology throughout its ranks, ensuring that the movement was ideologically cohesive.

Ideological cohesion actually reached beyond SASO itself at the University of the North in 1974: the close ties between SASO at a local and national level and the Students Representative Council resulted in what amounted to a cooperative effort between the organizations in mounting the Viva-FRELIMO rally on campus. This was the biggest planned protest event to take place at Turfloop since the university's founding, and it marked the first clash of students directly with agents of the state – in this case the police. Far from being an isolated incident, police and state intervention in everyday life at Turfloop went on to become a common occurrence over the next twenty years. In the 1980s Turfloop became the first university in South Africa to have military troops garrisoned on its campus. The Viva-FRELIMO rally was the first moment in the university's development that made that eventuality possible.

3

Africanization: The New Face of Turfloop

The violent confrontations between students and police during the Viva-Frelimo rally attracted national attention to Turfloop in the middle of the 1970s. They also caused a great deal of concern within the government about the future of Bantustan universities. Increasingly even the Department of Bantu Education was confronted with the fact that Turfloop was far from the paragon of Bantustan civilization it had been founded to become. In response to student unrest, the government commissioned two inquiries – one, the Jackson Commission, was commissioned in the wake of Tiro's speech and the subsequent protests, but its report was initially withheld and eventually tabled in parliament at the same time as the second, more substantial, Snyman Commission report. Justice Snyman was tasked with reporting on the factors at Turfloop that had led to the political showdown with police in September 1974. The reports of both the Snyman and Jackson Commissions, and the collective submission to the Snyman Commission by Turfloop's Black Academic Staff Association (BASA), act as both source and subject for this chapter. The reports and their reception, both at Turfloop and more broadly, and the later controversy over the publication and distribution of BASA's submission, illuminate the disagreements about running the university that arose between the university administration, the staff, the students, and the government. Previous scholarship on black student activism has suggested that Turfloop's significance waned after the Viva-Frelimo rally of 1974.[1] But I argue that contestation at the university contained the seeds of changes that were significant both on campus and more widely during and beyond the mid-1970s.

It was certainly at the forefront of Africanization – the move to put Africans in positions of authority, in this case, at universities. As a result of pressure from both the Jackson and Snyman Commission Reports, Africanization at its highest level was achieved at Turfloop in 1977, when Professor William Kgware was installed as the first black rector

---

[1] Magaziner, *The Law and the Prophets*, pp. 152–4; Gerhart, *Black Power in South Africa*, pp. 298–9.

of any university in South Africa. However, the appointment of Kgware did not result in the political shifts that some students and activists had envisioned. These unmet expectations, and the frequent conflicts with both students and staff that dogged Kgware's administration, are a primary focus of this chapter.

The Snyman and Jackson Reports and the push for Africanization at Turfloop

The report of the Snyman Commission, released in February 1976, called for important changes at Turfloop. Though it broadly affirmed the principles of separate development and segregated education, and said that 'the development of the University of the North as a university has been sound since its inception and its establishment has been justified',[2] it also called for major changes in the structure of the university itself, to address the discontent among students and black staff.

Many of these seem to have been drawn from BASA's recommendations to the commission in its submission. The changes suggested included parity of pay between black and white staff, greater financial autonomy for the university (like that enjoyed by its white counterparts), and a reorganization of the (white) council that ran the university:

> The commission visualises a university controlled by a council consisting of a majority of Blacks designated by the homeland governments concerned, while the teaching and administrative functions will be the joint responsibility of Whites and Blacks. The Blacks would thus have the predominant say in the control of the university established for them.[3]

These proposed changes were supported, in part, by testimony from the student and staff bodies; both vocally supported the process of 'Africanization' at the top levels of the university. In its submission to the Snyman Commission, the Black Academic Staff Association criticized the inequitable practices of employment and promotion for black and white staff at Turfloop,[4] and the system of advancement governed primarily by racial, rather than academic, qualifications. They criticized this as the incursion of white South African apartheid policy on an ostensibly black, Bantustan university:

[2] Untitled, *Rand Daily Mail*, 10 February 1976 [HPRA AD1912/258.16].
[3] 'Equal pay with help to ease tension', *Rand Daily Mail*, 10 February 1976 [HPRA AD1912/258.16].
[4] Nkondo, *Turfloop Testimony*, pp. 28–31.

[T]he University of the North continues to express and extend views of white supremacy often to be found outside the homelands. [...] Fundamental in this regard is also the Black man's desire that the University must be controlled and administered by Black men of ability. The choice of White personnel in positions of authority will then be made by them in exercise of their own sovereignty and free will, not imposed from without.[5]

In broad agreement with BASA, the SRC issued a statement on 16 October 1974 declaring 'the need for a black rector for the University of the North could not be overemphasised'.[6] However, for students race was not to be the only salient factor in the appointment of a new rector. 'The rector of the university should not be a member of any political body *that was not representative of the Black people*,' read the SRC's statement.[7] Race alone could not displace political ideology as a qualifying factor. This insistence is a reminder of Turfloop's place as a catchment of students from four separate homelands, and the fact that it was purpose-built to educate the future elite of these areas. While BASA had indicated that homelands represented an arena that was protected from attitudes of white supremacy, the SRC remained suspicious of them, and this reflected the position of many students and student organizations. SASO, in particular, distrusted members of the black elite who participated in the Bantustan system (as demonstrated by the backlash against Themba Sono when he proposed cooperating with the Bantustan authorities). Its dominance on campus likely played a role in the SRC's insistence that any black rector have what they considered an appropriate political background. For his part, Justice Snyman had little sympathy for SASO's influence on campus, saying that it could not be described as a true students' organization, but was closer to a political party. The bitterness expressed in its politics, he judged, 'can only bedevil relations, especially between students on the one side and the White staff on the other'.[8]

Gessler Muxe Nkondo, head of BASA, also called for blacks to take 'complete control of the university', rather than just nominal or symbolic posts. Nkondo was a member of a politically active family from the Northern Transvaal by way of Soweto; one of four sons, his brothers entered various forms of political life. Zinjiva had been a student

---

[5] Ibid., pp. 39–40.
[6] 'Students call for Black rector', *Natal Mercury*, 22 November 1974 [HPRA AD1912/258.16].
[7] Ibid. (emphasis mine).
[8] Snyman Commission Report, pp. 54–6.

at Turfloop and an organizer for the Black Consciousness group Black
Community Programmes (BCP) before going into exile in 1977; he was
later arrested and detained by security police when he returned to South
Africa in 1979.[9] Brother Ephraim joined *Umkhonto we Sizwe* (MK) but
allegedly criticized some leaders (Joe Modise and Mzwai Piliso were
named in a later exposé article) and was later tortured and presumed to
have been killed in 1984 at MK's notorious camp in Angola, Quatro.[10]
Curtis, the most politically prominent of the brothers, also entered education as a profession, and as a teacher in Soweto he was supportive of
the students' 1976 uprising. He went on to become the first president
of AZAPO, and his role in that organization is discussed further in the
next chapter. Of the Nkondo brothers, Gessler Muxe was the most aca-
demically successful, and he melded this success with political activism
similarly to his brother Curtis. He was one of the University College of
the North's earliest cohort, and became the president of its first SRC
in 1961. He was later appointed to a junior lectureship at Turfloop in
1966, after the completion of his honours degree.[11] After earning masters degrees at UNISA (1968) and then at Leeds University in the UK
(around 1972), Nkondo returned to Turfloop as a senior lecturer and
quickly became a leading member of the black faculty. He became the
chairman of BASA, and gained prominence beyond the campus as the
spokesman for black staff in the aftermath of the 1974 Viva-FRELIMO
rallies. He was the editor of BASA's joint submission to the Snyman
Commission.

In spite of many points of commonality, Nkondo and other staff did
not always completely align with the concerns of the SRC in their testimony. Rather than adhering to SASO's ideological denigration of the
homeland system, Nkondo was willing to use it as a justification for the
goal of complete Africanization, saying, 'This [complete black control
at Turfloop] should not be regarded as an unreasonable request since
it is in line with Government policy for the homelands.'[12] Even many
of Turfloop's white staff supported the move to Africanization (though
perhaps a version less 'complete' than that advocated by Nkondo and
BASA), hoping that it would ameliorate the 'bad relations' between

---

[9] 'Where is Zinjiva, asks brother', *Argus*, 19 December 1979 [GPP].
[10] 'The execution of a camp commander', *Mail and Guardian*, 30 October 1998
[GPP].
[11] Tshepo Moloi's interview with Muxe Nkondo, 10 June 2017, Pretoria.
[12] Quoted in 'White Staff quitting Turfloop over disturbances', *The Star*, 11 October 1974 [HPRA AD1912/239].

blacks and whites on campus.[13] This view was supported by BASA's joint submission to the commission, which argued that '[...] the abolition of discrimination between Black and White at the University and the power to administer and control the University by Blacks, are considered to be the basic foundations on which improved co-operation can be built'.[14]

Snyman's findings reflected this nearly universal support within the university community for the process of Africanization. His report called for substantive changes in the way Turfloop was structured and run, thus validating many of its students' complaints. Despite being tame by SASO's standards, the Snyman report was praised for its calls for change by the liberal press; a *Rand Daily Mail* editorial declared that '[Snyman] has provided not only the incentive but also the opportunity to introduce change without fanning political tempers'.[15] The editors of the *Rand Daily Mail* were particularly pleased by the muted response from the government to the commission's report, noting that Minister of Bantu Education M.C. Botha 'implicitly accept[ed] some guilt for the situation by promising to do "everything possible and within the powers of existing legislation" to improve things [at Turfloop]'.[16]

This cautious acceptance of the report was echoed by the University Council, which endorsed its recommendations for Africanization and autonomy. According to Turfloop's public relations director Casper Squier, speaking two months after the report's release, implementation of the recommendations 'was now obviously out of the university's field of competence. It is over to the government department concerned [Bantu Education] and we all hope that the Minister will speedily decide to implement the recommendations.'[17] But this was not to be the case; though Minister Botha paid lip service to the recommendations, no timeline was adopted for implementation and, in spite of support from quarters as diverse as the *Rand Daily Mail* editors and the University Council itself, many of the recommendations were never implemented after the report's release.

A second report, the Jackson Report on Africanization at Turfloop, was released in tandem with the tabling of the Snyman Report in Parliament. The Jackson Report, which had been commissioned by the University Council in early 1974 but was withheld until the release of the Snyman report, had similar and even further-reaching findings. Led

---

[13] Ibid.
[14] Nkondo, *Turfloop Testimony*, p. 35.
[15] Editorial, *Rand Daily Mail*, 11 February 1976 [HPRA AD1912/258.17].
[16] Ibid.
[17] 'Turfloop: what next?', *Rand Daily Mail*, 19 April 1976.

by Professor Stanley Jackson of the University of the Witwatersrand, it called for improvements to black schooling at the earliest levels, and 'recommended that colleges be established, in close association with the universities which would select and train students of proven capacity for university work'; in addition, it advocated a reversal of apartheid policy in higher education, recommending that 'Black academics be allowed to move freely between White and Black universities'.[18] Though relations between black and white members of the Turfloop community were outside the purview of the Jackson Commission, it noted that 'The university will not function satisfactorily so long as [animosity between the groups] continues.'[19]

On the subject of its commission – Africanization of the university staff and leadership – the commission 'considers that some important preliminary steps should be taken in order to Africanise the university and at the same time maintain its educational standards'.[20] This relatively cautious recommendation was reiterated, 'Africanization must [...] take place at a pace that does not require lowering of standards, either in teaching or management. The high quality of the institution must not be sacrificed to the ideal of Black control.'[21] The Snyman Commission cited the Jackson Report in its own findings on Africanization as well, and also balked at imposing a timeline or other plan for measuring progress towards Africanization, which 'should take place at a pace that will not lower the standards of administration or tuition'.[22]

Though these endorsements may seem less than full-throated, one of the few recommendations that *was* pursued after the release of both the Snyman and Jackson reports was Africanization at the top level of the university. For years students had been calling for a black rector to lead Turfloop. The retirement of Rector Boshoff in October 1976, close on the heels of the release of the reports, which both called for substantive changes in the structure of Turfloop, presented an ideal moment. Ironically Jackson, who had led the commission of inquiry into Africanization, had been considered for the post as an intermediary to black leadership because it was perceived that his politics would make him

---

[18] 'Black education not good enough, says report', *Rand Daily Mail*, 11 February 1976 [HPRA AD1912/258.17].
[19] 'Committee report on Turfloop accepted', *Eastern Province Herald*, 11 February 1976 [HPRA AD1912/258.17].
[20] Ibid.
[21] Ibid.
[22] Snyman Commission Report, p. 100.

sympathetic to the students.[23] However, the recommendations of Jackson's own report, together with Snyman and pressure from both staff and students prevailed. Prior to his own retirement Boshoff announced that his successor would be the first black rector of any university in South Africa: Professor William Kgware.

From the perspective of the University Council, Kgware was an ideal choice for the post. Having arrived there in 1960, he was the most senior black academic at Turfloop, with a long history at the institution. He had demonstrated his authority among his peers, leading them to walk out of the vote on Onkgopotse Tiro's expulsion in 1972,[24] but he also enjoyed a close relationship with the university administration. As early as 1968, Manana Kgware noted in a letter to Colin Collins that her father had been asked to account for her and her brother Bob's activism within the University Christian Movement, but that 'Pop' had diffused the situation because neither she nor Bob had been questioned directly by the Rector.[25] Kgware had resigned his own membership to UCM later in 1968 to avoid conflict with the university, and also later resigned from the Black Academic Staff Association in late 1974, as that organization became more radical.

After the news of his appointment was announced, Kgware himself declared in an interview:

> There is no way that I am going to become a so-called radical in these times. I have been consistent in public life for 40 years and I will not change now, but somewhere a start has to be made to get all our people to regard each other as allies in the greater plan to develop all of South Africa.[26]

That interview, given in August 1976, could hardly have come at a more volatile moment in South African student politics. At pains to reassure a skittish staff, of which two-thirds were white, and to appease a restive and sometimes militant student body, Kgware tried to walk a fine line in his new public role.

---

[23] 'Turfloop move puts ball in Botha's court', *The Star*, 2 April 1976 [HPRA AD1912/258.17].

[24] Author's interview with Percy Mokwele; for a more thorough discussion of this event, see 'The Tiro incident' in Chapter 1 (pp. 47–56).

[25] Letter from M. Kgware to C. Collins, 30 September 1968 [HPRA AD1126/F].

[26] 'New rector is no radical', *Rand Daily Mail*, 11 August 1976 [HPRA AD1912/258.17].

Radicals and 'sell-outs': The polarization of politics at Turfloop

In the aftermath of the Soweto student uprising in June of 1976, Turfloop students took action on their own campus. In late June 1976 the
campus was beset by student protests, which resulted in the destruc-
tion of campus property and some buildings being set on fire; many
students were accused of arson and public violence.[27] At the time there
were rumours of a student plot to hijack a bus of the children of white
university staff on its way to school in Pietersburg, though nothing of
this sort actually transpired.[28] In the aftermath of the unrest Turfloop
fell back on its policy of mass expulsions. However, Professor Kgware,
who was the rector-elect, worked with Rector Boshoff in an attempt to
diffuse tensions between the students, their parents, and the university.
He prevailed on the University Council to readmit 168 expelled students
who had been charged with public violence and/or arson. 'Black parents
have responded wonderfully to this decision to readmit the students, and
the students who stand charged must know that we are sympathetic to
their problems,' he said publicly.[29] This move towards appeasement and
détente proved successful: the accused students returned to campus, and
the university was able to resume functioning normally.

However, circumstances of being the first black rector at an institution like Turfloop did not allow Kgware to tread the line of equivocation
for long. He took office at a time of great polarization between the black
student body and some staff on one side, and many of Turfloop's white
staff on the other. These fissures were broadly along lines of race, even
as figures like Kgware tried to overcome the racial biases inherent in
Turfloop's structure. These two groups found frameworks of support in
the wider political debates between groups like SASO and conservative
supporters of the South African government.

Though there were students, staff, and groups at Turfloop that were
moderate on the political spectrum, tensions at the university pulled
them towards the political extremes. Kgware recognized the challenge
the polarized campus presented:

'I have stood all my life for understanding between Blacks and Whites,
yet I get this appointment at a time when Whites and Blacks across the
country face each other in conflict,' he said [in an interview]. Professor
Kgware knows that there are Blacks who think he is a sell-out, a stooge of

[27] Ibid.
[28] Author's interview with Percy Mokwele.
[29] 'New rector is no radical', *Rand Daily Mail*, 11 August 1976 [HPRA
AD1912/258.17].

the White man's apartheid institution. 'Those people must learn that neither White nor Black can do anything in this country without the other,' he said.[30]

But it would take more than public statements about cooperation, and even changing the most visible university leadership, to address the deep-seated racial inequality and resentment at Turfloop; these struggles would mark the rest of Kgware's time in office and beyond.

Student and staff dissent in Rector Kgware's administration

Less than a year into Kgware's tenure, and in the wake of the Soweto Uprising, student activists across South Africa were rocked by a second major event. On 12 September 1977 Steve Biko was killed in police custody while being detained in Pretoria Central Prison. The news of his death was a major blow to SASO and to its sister Black Consciousness organizations. Though Biko had been banned in 1973 and had been out of the formal SASO executive for even longer, he remained the founder and most prominent advocate of the Black Consciousness Movement in South Africa. His five-day testimony at the trial of the SASO 9 in 1975 had served to reinforce his status in the organization, and it also provided a legal and public platform from which to preach Black Consciousness ideology. In spite of SASO's official tiers of leadership and power, Biko remained the figurehead and face of the movement at the time of his death in 1977. News of his killing hit student activists hard.

September 1977 also marked the mass resignation of Soweto teachers, led by Curtis Nkondo and the Soweto Teacher's Action Committee, and a new round of class boycotts at the University of the North. The Turfloop protest was playing out against a national stage where student boycotts and stay-aways were becoming all too familiar. But it followed even longer trends of such protest at Turfloop itself: in 1969 students had used mass protest when the university refused to allow them to affiliate with the National Union of South African Students (NUSAS). In May of that year more than two-thirds of the student body marched on the Rector's office with a list of grievances including complaints about the affiliation controversy, student suspensions, and being disallowed from speaking to the press.[31] The following year a celebration of the

---

[30] Ibid.
[31] NUSAS local committee report, 'Turfloop Erupts', May 1969 [RUCL MS 18 180/2]; NUSAS open memo regarding 'Demonstration at Turfloop', 14 May 1969 [RUCL MS 18 170/4]; 'Turfloop Students backed by Wits. mass meeting', *Rand Daily Mail*, 14 May 1969 [HPRA AD1912/258.16].

university's 'independence' from UNISA was met with similar protests. By the time of the student strike in September 1977, Turfloop had experienced ten similar, and increasingly serious, student protest actions, including mass boycotts following the expulsion of Onkgopotse Tiro in 1972, the sit-ins and arrests after the Viva-FRELIMO rally in 1974, and the temporary closure of the university after 16 June 1976.

These actions became even more frequent after 1976. The September 1977 strike was preceded by the temporary closure of the university in August, when students 'decided to boycott lectures and stage a hunger strike in protest at the expulsion of a Stofberg theological college student and the quality of hostel food'.[32] Students returned to campus on 12 September by pre-arrangement, but refused to sign a declaration 'that they withdraw all demands made last month; undertake not to take part in unauthorized mass meetings and agree to the revision of the constitution of the Students' Representative Council'.[33] Between their objections to the university's demands, and the news of Biko's death that broke on 13 September, the recently returned students immediately renewed protest to express their grievances. A mass meeting was held for the students who had returned, but during the night some students turned to violence: 'a fire bomb was thrown into the hostel superintendent's bedroom, injuring three children. One student was assaulted and another's room was set alight.'[34]

The following day six students – including the president and vice-president of the SRC – were expelled, and university authorities dissolved the SRC. This precipitated another round of lecture boycotts.[35] These continued for more than two weeks until, on 28 September 1977, approximately 1000 students were asked to leave campus. According to a student spokesman, 'letters of expulsion were handed to [each student] personally yesterday [28 September 1977] requesting them to leave the campus by 2pm. No reasons were given.'[36] In a quick response to this version of events, which was published by the *Rand Daily Mail*, a university spokesman 'denied that students had been expelled from the university. He said a number of students had been refused entrance to

[32] 'Expulsion move set aside by Supreme Court', *Times*, 8 April 1979 [HPRA AD1912/258.17].
[33] 'Students drifting back to Turfloop', *The Star*, 12 September 1977 [HPRA AD1912/258.17].
[34] 'Expulsion move set aside by Supreme Court', *Times*, 8 April 1979 [HPRA AD1912/258.17].
[35] Ibid.
[36] '1000 Turfloop students expelled', *Rand Daily Mail*, 29 September 1977 [HPRA AD1912/258.17].

examinations, however, and had returned home.'[37] He contended that
the move was not political, and had simply been made to allow the
remaining students to prepare for their exams: 'To give those students
who are serious with their studies an opportunity to continue studying
and preparing for the exams which begin on October 24, the university
put the entrance date forward by two weeks.'[38]

In fact, Turfloop had long used eligibility requirements for exams to
exert control over its student body. To be eligible to sit exams, Turfloop
students had to achieve a certain mark for their work during the term.
During the tumultuous years of class boycotts in the 1970s, achieving the
required results was even more difficult. It was a controversial practice
among students, who understood this as a tactic to pre-empt political
activism and often perceived the policy as racist. Harry Nengwekhulu
recalled the practice from his time as a student in 1969 when, he said,
some white staff would permit only 50% of students to sit for exams,
and would pass only 25%.[39]

Student arguments that the procedures were rooted in racial prejudice
were countered by staff who struggled to teach (just as students struggled to learn) in the fraught climate of campus protests throughout the
1970s. But whatever its roots, the practice of excluding students from
campus before and during exams did enable the university administration to exercise a high degree of control over its student body. In 1977
the timing of the decision by the university administrators to move up the
cut-off for exam qualifications was conspicuous, coming as it did in the
midst of student protest, and it was not without backlash. The excluded
students 'agreed among themselves to try to persuade the 100 or so students remaining at the university to return to their homes within two
weeks "or face the consequences of letting the student body down".'[40]
They also exerted pressure on parents at home to recall their children
who had been allowed to remain on campus.[41] The implication that
the student body totalled approximately 1100 students in 1977 is inac-
curate; enrolment data from the time suggests the number was around
1900. The 1000 students who left campus did number more than half

---

[37] 'Turfloop students were not expelled', *Rand Daily Mail*, 30 September 1977
[HPRA AD1912/258.17].
[38] Ibid.
[39] Author's interview with Harry Nengwekhulu (a).
[40] '1000 Turfloop students expelled', *Rand Daily Mail*, 29 September 1977 [HPRA
AD1912/258.17].
[41] Ibid.

of the student body, however.[42] It is also important to note that a high percentage of these students would be returning to homes in Soweto and other urban townships of the Rand when they left campus.[43] In the winter of 1977 most students had been home a matter of weeks before during the August closure of the university, and at the height of resistance and repression in Soweto this fostered strong links between protest in the township and protest on campus.

Less than a year into the job, and after the success of readmitting those students who had been involved in the post-Soweto Uprising protests, Rector Kgware had fallen back on Turfloop's old method of removing protesting students from campus. In addition, the dissolution of the SRC and the expulsion of its leadership recalled the crackdowns of 1972 and 1974, more than the accommodation that Kgware had favoured in 1976. Though it was five years later, and now a black man lived in the Turfloop Rector's mansion, little had changed from the time of Tiro's graduation speech in the way the university dealt with dissent in its student body.

Rather than an isolated incident of punitive action, the rest of Kgware's tenure was marked by similar crackdowns against student protest. In a high-profile example, Ngoako Ramathlodi, a third-year law student at the university and later the first premier of Limpopo Province, was expelled in April 1979, allegedly for organizing and participating in a commemoration of the Sharpeville massacre. The university argued that this contravened the terms of his enrolment, as all students who registered in February 1979 had to sign a pledge (of the type that had been mooted in September 1977) not to participate in any protests. Ramathlodi denied the accusations against him, and argued the case in court. In response, Kgware called for Ramathlodi's case to be dismissed with costs, and 'said that in view of the history of rioting at the university, maintaining discipline there was more important than at other universities in the Republic'.[44] In a blow to the university's authority to impose such bans – and perhaps in contravention of Kgware's argument that maintaining discipline at Turfloop was of primary importance – in July 1979 Justice H.H. Moll of the Pretoria Supreme Court ruled in Ramath-

---

[42] Snyman Commission Report, p. 48; 'Cops at Turfloop', *Post*, 4 May 1979 [HPRA AD1912/258.17].

[43] In 1974 the Snyman Commission noted that approximately 60% of Turfloop students came from urban areas, and the vast majority of these were from the townships around Johannesburg and Pretoria in the southern Transvaal.

[44] 'Court reinstates Ramathlodi', *Rand Daily Mail*, 11 July 1979 [HPRA AD1912/258.17].

lodi's favour, dictating that he be allowed to re-enrol for his final year.[45] This judgment set an important precedent by limiting the university's capacity to use legislation to control its students.

In addition to criticisms of being an apartheid sell-out, Rector Kgware was increasingly accused of merely providing a black face to hide the white power that continued to call the shots at Turfloop. Perhaps no one made this argument more eloquently than respected author Es'kia Mphahlele. Mphahlele had grown up during the 1920s in the rural northern Transvaal outside of Pietersburg, near what is now Lebowakgomo.[46] After joining the ANC in the mid-1950s, he left South Africa in 1957 to teach abroad with the understanding he would not easily be able to return to his home country because of his politics.[47] After spending twenty years in exile and earning a doctorate in the United States, he returned home to South Africa in 1977 to participate in the political turning of the tides that he saw heralded by the student uprisings. He applied to teach English literature at Turfloop, but failed to get the post owing to the 'disapproval of the then Minister of Education and Training'.[48] He went on to take up a post in English literature at the University of the Witwatersrand in Johannesburg, which as a white university was able to exercise a great deal more autonomy over its hiring procedures than a black institution like Turfloop. Years later in his autobiography, Mphahlele wrote of his experience applying to Turfloop:

> Here is an institution that purports to be for Africans, and yet does not reflect the African character; has a Rector who is a mere signature, a megaphone for orders that are issued by whites who are above him. The government imposes its own system of university administration. There is hardly any meaningful control between the University and the African communities in the same district. The people regard it as distinct, inaccessible and alien to their culture and aspirations.[49]

Mphahlele's accusation that Kgware was simply a signature, or megaphone, for whites who were really in charge of what happened at Turfloop was published years after the hiring incident, but similar sentiments circulated among students and staff at the university at the time. In addition to having to answer to ministers in various government departments, it was widely believed that the reviled Academic Registrar of Turfloop, Professor J.C. Steenkamp, wielded more power than

[45] Ibid.
[46] E. Mphahlele, *Down Second Avenue* (London, 1959), pp. 11–14.
[47] Ibid., pp. 209–16.
[48] White, *From Despair to Hope*, p. 126.
[49] E. Mphahlele, *Afrika My Music* (Johannesburg, 1984), p. 182.

Kgware himself. Steenkamp had been a campus figure for many years; in 1974 he had survived a motion by the Black Academic Staff Association calling for his expulsion 'due to alleged racism and mismanagement'.[50] BASA made another call for his resignation years later in 1980, saying that his attitude towards students 'has consistently reflected his arrogance and impatience which borders on contempt and lack of respect for blacks'.[51] According to Dr Ntatho Motlana in 1981, when he was the chairman of the Soweto Committee of Ten[52], '[Steenkamp] has always been the power behind the throne at Turf, the manipulator of people and events. [...] For too long now Turfloop has been under the shadow of domination of rightwing whites, and it is time the situation changed.'[53]

The furore around Mphahlele was not Kgware's only high-profile staffing problem at this time: Gessler Muxe Nkondo, one-time head of the Black Academic Staff Association, had published the text of BASA's joint submission to the Snyman Commission under the title *Turfloop Testimony* in 1976. Nkondo acted as editor of the text and provided a historical preface to it about the founding of the university. Though originally a signatory on BASA's submission before he took up the post of rector, Kgware strongly objected to the publication in his new administrative role. He and the University Council alleged that the book contained 'untrue and/or false statements concerning the university', and required BASA to approve a retraction.[54] In the *UNIN News*, a campus newsletter, the book was called 'a misleading and incorrect reflection of the true state of affairs'.[55] After an emergency meeting in November 1976, BASA reaffirmed its position behind the statement of its submission as represented in *Turfloop Testimony*. BASA was subsequently suspended 'at the university council's pleasure' in March 1977, but by this stage Nkondo was no longer on campus. Shortly after the book's release in early 1976, he took academic leave and went to the United States to pursue a doctorate in English at Yale University. Two years later, on the verge of his return to his post at Turfloop, the university administration under Kgware began disciplinary proceedings against

[50] White, *From Despair to Hope*, p. 107.
[51] 'Turf Prof to go', *Sunday Times*, 20 June 1981 [HPRA AD1912/258.16].
[52] The Soweto Committee of Ten was an early civic group comprised of prominent residents in the township who were convened in 1978, in the aftermath of the 1976 Soweto Uprising and the collapse of the reviled Urban Bantu Council.
[53] Ibid.
[54] 'Turfloop lecturer faces "trial" over book', *Rand Daily Mail*, 19 July 1978 [HPRA AD1912/258.17].
[55] Quoted in White, *From Despair to Hope*, p. 111.

him for the publication of *Turfloop Testimony*. In addition, the administration accused Nkondo of issuing a press statement regarding the university, which neither staff nor students were allowed to do. Nkondo faced a hearing before an all-white disciplinary committee, but refused to attend. After a short return to South Africa, he left Turfloop and took up a teaching post in the United States in 1980.

Conclusion

Even as the Black Consciousness Movement faced repression and decline throughout South Africa – which will be the subject of the next chapter – one of its organizational priorities, Africanization, was achieved (at least nominally) at Turfloop. In 1977 William Kgware became the university's first black rector, thanks to increased pressure after the release of the Snyman and Jackson Commission Reports. But public black leadership did not translate into the political shifts in university administration for which SASO and Black Consciousness activists had hoped. Kgware steered a cautious path in his approach to student dissent: after a brief attempt at conciliation with protesting students in late 1976 (just before his official tenure began) he reverted to Turfloop's more familiar tactic of expulsions and university shutdowns. His administrative problems extended to staffing as well. Public fallouts with Gessler Muxe Nkondo over the publication of *Turfloop Testimony*, and over the failure to appoint Es'kia Mphahlele to a chair in the English department, contributed to suspicions that Kgware was actually just a black figurehead masking the unchanged white power at Turfloop.

These controversies took a personal toll: while Kgware aligned himself with the conservative politics of the university administration, his family continued to be active in anti-apartheid politics. Though his children had graduated and moved away, his wife Winifred remained active in the BPC nationally and in the local Mankweng branch. By the time Kgware had become Rector 'political disagreement [had] broken his marriage and disrupted his family'.[56] These stresses took a deep physical toll and Kgware died in the Rector's mansion in 1980. Rather than the hoped-for political and psychological triumph of Black Consciousness organization, Kgware's time as Rector proved the process of Africanization to be another step in the decline of Black Consciousness politics at Turfloop, and indeed, beyond.

---

[56] Tom Karis trip diary – Visit to Turfloop August 17, 1979 [HPRA A2675/I/14].

4

Black Consciousness in Decline

Student politics in South Africa underwent seismic shifts between 1976 and 1980. In early 1976 the South African Students' Organisation (SASO) remained a major force on black campuses, while its graduates and proponents preached Black Consciousness ideology in schools in some of the country's biggest urban townships. As I argued in Chapter 2, this period marked the height of Black Consciousness' prominence, especially among its student constituency. But, though its impact on South African youth was critical, the student movement was still not considered a central force in liberation politics either by government or by the more established liberation organizations; it represented one element of the resistance against apartheid, alongside the armed struggle, liberation organizations in exile, and trade union movements.

After June 1976 that changed irrevocably. School students in Soweto had shown their country and the world the importance and power of student organization and politics. Protesting against the use of Afrikaans as a classroom medium, they took to the streets of Soweto in tens of thousands. Confronted with armed police, they continued to march until they were fired upon and brutally repressed. The Soweto uprising and its aftermath – when students across the country made their schools and campuses ungovernable – changed the public perception of students in South Africa. It also changed the dynamics of resistance politics in the country. No single liberation organization had been prepared for the scope and scale of the uprising, and the way organizations like SASO and the African National Congress (ANC) dealt with the aftermath would have an important effect on the future shape of student and liberation politics.

Another critical factor impacting this future was government repression, which increased significantly on the organizations that existed under the umbrella of Black Consciousness in the late 1970s. By late 1977 the killing of Steve Biko in a Pretoria jail and mass bannings diminished the capacity of the Black Consciousness Movement (BCM) to influence student politics at the level it had achieved just a year or two earlier. Into the breach, and influenced by all these factors, the multi-racial Charterist politics of the ANC began a resurgence in new student political movements, bringing with it a new wave of student activism for the 1980s.

This chapter explores the shifts away from Black Consciousness and the seeds of Charterism's renewal in student politics that arose in the wake of the Soweto Uprising. One primary focus is the adoption of Charterism by South African students for the first time in a generation. The other is the decline and deterioration of the BCM under pressure from government repression and in exile. The chapter also considers the key role played by political actors from the Northern Transvaal – particularly those coming from and to Turfloop – in influencing these national, and transnational, events.

Ideology in the South African Students' Movement and Soweto, 16 June 1976

The Soweto student uprising of 1976 was arguably the most important event in the history of South African student protests. In previous chapters I have touched briefly on the links between these events and the local developments in student politics at Turfloop, but the events around the uprising and its key actors merit a more focused analysis to consider its subsequent impact on student politics. The grounds for the uprising were laid by the process of conscientization that happened in some key Soweto schools, and Turfloop's student-teacher activists played a leading role in this. The South African Students' Movement was central to this process, particularly in its capacity to engage with diverse ideologies. Of these, Black Consciousness was the most prominent, but the inclusion of other political ideas – notably Charterism – increasingly played a critical role in the trajectory of student politics.

By early 1976 the SASO 9 were on trial for terrorism in Pretoria, but that year was also, as I have argued here, a peak in public recognition and mobilization for the BCM. The trial of the SASO 9 was regularly in national headlines garnering publicity and raising awareness of the movement. Stay-aways, sit-ins, and boycotts at universities like Turfloop were becoming familiar. Until 1976, though, these sorts of actions had been mostly confined to universities and teacher-training colleges; political action had not yet affected secondary schools in a significant way.

In spite of a lack of overt action, political consciousness had been growing among secondary school students, particularly at key Soweto high schools, for some time. With Tiro's death in February 1974 the formal links between SASO and SASM effectively broke down, though other older members of BCM organizations continued to work with

SASM. Aubrey Mokoena, who had been Tiro's contemporary at Turfloop, began to work with SASM, which he described as 'basically a high school student's organization',[1] as a consultant. He participated in a series of planning meetings in the days before 16 June 1976, with members of the Soweto Parents Association (SPA), including Winnie Madikizela-Mandela. Adult organizations like the SPA continued to play a role in the uprising after the events on 16 June, as well. The Soweto Committee of Ten, an organization of prominent Soweto residents led by Dr Ntatho Motlana, was also organized to provide leadership to the community in the turbulent period following the 16 June demonstration, and in the wake of the breakdown of Soweto's Urban Bantu Council (UBC).[2] Support also came from teachers and principals in Soweto schools: in 1977 the Soweto Teachers' Action Committee was formed under the chairmanship of Curtis Nkondo. By late September of that year, this organization led 331 Soweto teachers, including several prominent principals – among them Lekgau Mathabathe, the principal of Morris Isaacson High School who had hired Onkgopotse Tiro – in a mass resignation to protest the inferiority of Bantu Education.[3]

But while adult involvement and support increased markedly after the demonstration, select members of the Soweto Parents Association (like Mokoena and Madikizela-Mandela) were the only ones involved in its planning. This was primarily coordinated by the students of SASM's Action Committee; they planned the demonstration to be a mass march and a one-day class boycott to protest the imposition of Afrikaans as a teaching medium in classes. The Action Committee was composed of student leaders from various Soweto high schools who were members of the SASM executive. The most prominent of these were Tsietsi Mashinini from Morris Isaacson and Tebello Motapanyane from Orlando West. In the aftermath of the uprising, the Action Committee renamed itself the Soweto Students Representative Council (SSRC) as it tried to influence and direct the wave of protest that had begun. Significantly, the rhetoric of these leaders during and after the uprising reflects Black Consciousness ideology. Though the formal links to SASO may have fallen away, the shared philosophy remained, at least in part.

---

[1] Deposition of Aubrey Mokoena taken by Justice of the Peace D.L. Aspelling in Johannesburg. Undated (c. early 1977), p. 20 [HPRA A2953].

[2] E. Zuern, *The Politics of Necessity: Community organizing and democracy in South Africa* (Madison, WI, 2011), p. 25.

[3] 'Top principals join mass resignations', *Rand Daily Mail*, 28 September 1977; '325 Soweto teachers will resign today', *Rand Daily Mail*, 27 September 1977 [GPP].

Mashinini had been a student of Tiro's at Morris Isaacson, and was heavily influenced by his teaching. In an interview given after the uprising in November 1976, Mashinini spoke strongly about the role of the BCM in conscientizing Soweto students, and described SASO as 'the mother body of SASM'.[4]

> The ideology [of SASM and other Black Consciousness Organizations] is the same: to make the Black man more conscious of the evil of the white man, elements of oppression, and so on. The ideology concerned is to peacefully bring about change in the South African social aspect and to bring about the total liberation of the Black man.[5]

In his interview Mashinini privileged the role of the BCM above South Africa's other liberation movements in fostering the student uprising. When asked specifically about SASM's connections with the ANC and PAC he said: 'The ANC and PAC played their part in the South Africa struggle in the 1950s and 1960s. [But now] As far as the students in South Africa are concerned, the ANC and PAC are extinct internally.'[6] But Mashinini's dismissal of the other movements as historical relics, particularly the ANC, was not a position shared by all his fellows in SASM. Black Consciousness was not the only ideological influence on the students of Soweto. Diseko has argued that, in contrast to Mashinini's contentions, by 1975 the ANC was exerting a significant impact on SASM, through local organizers like Joe Gqabi and secretive underground links between SASM members and ANC cells.[7] These activists exposed students to ideologies that countered Black Consciousness and its approach to racialism.

The ANC espoused the principles of the Freedom Charter (hence the term 'Charterist'). The Freedom Charter was drafted and launched at the Congress of the People in Kliptown, near Johannesburg, in 1955. It was a collaborative effort of the ANC, the South African Communist Party, the South African Indian Congress, and other organizations in the congress movement. As described by Tom Lodge, it 'appears a bland enough document. It consists of a list of basic rights and freedoms.'[8] But Lodge rightly points out that protecting these rights and freedoms in the context of 1955 South Africa, when the construction of apartheid legislation was at its peak, had revolutionary potential. In an overt challenge

---

[4] T. Mashinini, 'Behind the Growing Upsurge in South Africa', *Intercontinental Press*, 15 November 1976 [not paginated].
[5] Ibid.
[6] Ibid.
[7] Diseko, 'Origins and Development of SASM', p. 61.
[8] T. Lodge, *Black Politics in South Africa since 1945* (London, 1983), p. 71.

to the racial segregation of apartheid, the Freedom Charter begins with the phrase 'South Africa belongs to all who live in it, black and white.' This multiracialism came to be one of the defining characteristics of all groups under the banner of Charterism – and one that distinguished them from later proponents of uni- or non-racialism, including Black Consciousness and Africanism.

An interview with Tebello Motapanyane, who was the Secretary General of SASM at the time of the uprisings and later became chairman of the Soweto Students' Representative Council (SSRC), by the ANC journal *Sechaba* supports Diseko's contention that Charterism and the ANC had influenced Soweto's students:

> Certainly I would say the ANC was known to the students and its ideas influenced many of them. [...] There were political trials concerning the ANC.
> [...] We would always hear from the papers of ANC activity. [...] From time to time there were ANC pamphlets and journals which we used to get and we saw very little of any underground activity except by the ANC.[9]

Motapanyane's description, while supporting strong ideological links to the ANC, speaks predominantly of an organization that SASM students knew by reputation and myth, rather than one with which they had much concrete interaction. Where interaction did occur it revealed the differing structural priorities of SASM and the ANC. While SASM was conceived by its founders, like Motapanyane, as an above-ground organization that would undertake public mobilization (along the lines of SASO or the BPC), the ANC encouraged it to form underground cells that linked student networks and could operate covertly. This expertise played a key role in the ANC's influence after the uprising, as SASM experienced the full weight of the South African security apparatus.

SASM, then, had a broad ideological scope by 1976 that allowed strong affiliates of the BCM to mobilize under the same umbrella as stalwart ANC supporters. As has been mentioned, Mashinini and Motapanyane were two of the movement's most prominent leaders and they fell on opposite sides of this ideological divide. Perhaps Sibongile Mkhabela (née Mthembu), a SASM leader from Naledi High School during the uprising, captured this ideological diversity best:

> Within SASM there were people who had sympathies for ANC, sympathies for PAC, and all sorts of other sympathies. We'd debate and fight over this, but there would be some consensus. We agreed on certain basic

[9] 'How June 16 demo was planned', interview with T. Motapanyane, *Sechaba*, 11(2), January 1977 [HPRA A2953] (emphasis original).

principles. [...] For me it was a strength [...] within SASM – If you look at Murphy Morobe, he's always been an ANC kind of person. I've always been a BC kind of person. We'd debate and argue [...] but it also did not create enemies as it created enemies later on when we said somebody is PAC, somebody is BC, and got into all these fights.[10]

This ability for opposing ideologies – Charterism, Black Consciousness, and Africanism – to coexist within an organization would not last, as Mkhabela implies. It does, however, mark the first emergence of the ANC's multi-racial, Charterist philosophy in organized student politics among black South Africans since the ANC Youth League had been banned in 1960.[11]

Black Consciousness banned: The turn to exile and AZAPO

Just as Charterism began its incremental return to student politics, in 1977 the BCM was experiencing significant state repression. In September of that year, Steve Biko was arrested for violating his banning order and taken to Pretoria Central Prison, where he was killed in custody on 12 September. Though Biko had long been removed from the formal SASO executive, he remained the figurehead of the movement, a position that was reaffirmed by his five-day testimony at the trial of the SASO 9. His death hit BC activists hard. Only weeks later, on 19 October 1977, SASO, the BPC, and sixteen of their other affiliates were issued banning orders by the government, effectively ending operations of the BCM within South Africa. Eighteen groups in total were banned, including sympathetic organs of the press like The World daily newspaper, and dozens of supporters and leaders of the BCM, who had escaped previous arrest or detention, were detained. Among those affected were two high-profile white activists, and friends of Steve Biko: journalist Donald Woods and cleric Beyers Naudé, as well as eight members of the prominent Soweto Committee of Ten, which had sprung out of the unrest in the wake of the student uprising. In addition, individuals from the Committee of Ten, SASM, the SSRC, and the Soweto Teacher's Action

---

[10] Interview with Sibongile Mkhabela, conducted by the third-year class of African Politics Students at the University of the Witwatersrand, Johannesburg, 13 August 1994 [HPRA A2675/I/23].

[11] NUSAS, the National Union of South African Students, had supported non-racialism since its inclusion of some students from Fort Hare in 1945, but it had also been dominated by white leaders and membership; these two factors contributed to SASO's break with it in 1968, which I discuss in Chapter 2.

Committee were all also banned, drawing further links between these organizations and the BCM.

SASO, the oldest and most developed of the BCM groups, had long been prepared to face banning and repression. October 1977 was not the first time it had faced a heavy loss of leadership. In March 1973 Biko and the first wave of SASO leaders were banned, and a wave of arrests in September and October 1974 had neutralized most of those who were involved in the Viva-FRELIMO rallies. But October 1977 was the first time that all of SASO's affiliates faced the same level of repression, negating them as alternate outlets for continuing its message. SASO had always been designed for above-ground mobilization. Its organizational structure focused on stabling leaders so that when one was banned another could step seamlessly to the fore. But banning the organization itself brought unprecedented challenges. It came at a time when most of the original core of leadership was detained or in prison, like Barney Pityana and Strini Moodley; in exile, like Bokwe Mafuna and Harry Nengwekhulu; or dead, like Steve Biko and Onkgopotse Tiro.

As a result, it fell to the representatives of the BCM who were in exile to transform the movement into one that could operate effectively from outside South Africa. Harry Nengwekhulu had, to some degree, been working towards this since he went into exile in Botswana in 1973, but his efforts had met with little success. Initially Nengwekhulu and the other 1973 exiles relied heavily on the existing network of leadership that still functioned within South Africa, and on the ability of Tiro to move legally into and around South Africa as Permanent Organizer. Essentially, they contributed to the internal movement as much as life in exile permitted, and always through the structures of SASO itself within South Africa. As far as formal structures of the movement in exile went, in the mid-1970s there were none.

By late 1977, even before the October bannings, Nengwekhulu was working to establish links between the BCM and other exiled South African liberation movements: he was in contact with the ANC in Lusaka from early September 1977, trying to arrange a meeting between an ANC delegation to be led by then-party president Oliver Tambo, and a BCM delegation.[12] Arrangements for the meeting were made and subsequently fell through at various times over a period of nearly two years, over which time other BCM activists fled South Africa and moved into exile. Eventually the BCM delegation was also to include Barney

---

[12] Correspondence between Harry Nengwekhulu and Oliver Tambo (2 October 1977 and 26 June 1979), and Harry Nengwekhulu and Thabo Mbeki (10 May 1978 and 3 March 1979) [UFH AZAPO Collection].

Pityana, who had moved to the United Kingdom as a seminarian, and Ben Khoapa, who had become a teacher in the United States. The meeting finally took place in December 1979.[13] Its planning and agenda are important for understanding how the BCM sought to situate itself in exile, and how other liberation organizations like the ANC reacted to it. Anthony Marx has noted that the BCM regarded rapprochement between the liberation movements as a major post-1976 priority, and one that would 'solidify the BC movement's position as the central unifying force in the country'.[14] Indeed, Biko publicly wrote that he 'would like to see groups like ANC, PAC, and Black Consciousness movement deciding to form one liberation group. It is only, I think when black people are so dedicated and so united in their cause that we can effect the greatest results.'[15]

According to Harry Nengwekhulu, one of his primary tasks in exile was to make contact with both the ANC and the PAC structures outside South Africa, and to try to broker unification between the three parties.[16] Logistical challenges of travel and access prevented this plan from ever getting off the ground. Nengwekhulu never met with ANC leadership, in spite of a prolonged correspondence with Tambo's representative, Thabo Mbeki, in which they tried to arrange a meeting in Lusaka.[17] Instead, Pityana, Khoapa, and Jeff Baqwa did meet with ANC leadership in December of 1979, though Nengwekhulu did not attend. Though Nengwekhulu's explanation of the struggle to arrange the meeting of the ANC and BCM in exile points to logistical failure, recent scholarship may suggest other factors as well. Daniel Magaziner has written about the struggle between the ANC in exile and the BCM to claim responsibility for, and control of the narrative around, the aftermath of the Soweto uprisings. He paints a picture of direct competition for influence and support, even as Biko and Nengwekhulu were orchestrating moves toward unity.[18] Indeed, Maaba and Mzamane contend that, though both organizations sought to pursue 'a process of consultation which would lead to unity' through the Lusaka meeting, each side

---

[13] B. Maaba and M.V. Mzamane, 'The Black Consciousness Movement of Azania, 1979–1990' in SADET, *The Road to Democracy in South Africa, Volume 4, Part 2 (1980–1990)* (Pretoria, 2010), 1361–98 (1361).

[14] Marx, *Lessons of Struggle*, p. 82.

[15] Biko, *I Write What I Like*, p. 148.

[16] Author's interview with Harry Nengwekhulu (a).

[17] Correspondence between Harry Nengwekhulu and Oliver Tambo (2 October 1977 and 26 June 1979), and Harry Nengwekhulu and Thabo Mbeki (10 May 1978 and 3 March 1979) [UFH AZAPO Collection].

[18] Magaziner, *The Law and the Prophets*, pp. 155–6.

envisioned that unity happening under its own banner.[19] Stephen Ellis has argued that the ANC feared that Black Consciousness presented a so-called third force that would further divide the anti-apartheid opposition rather than unite them.[20] However, in his recent work on the ANC in exile, Hugh Macmillan has downplayed this concern and points to the organizational efforts of the ANC to help (and recruit) the students of the BCM in the wake of the uprisings.[21] It is likely that the ANC was pragmatically helpful to new Black Consciousness exiles, as Macmillan suggests, in order to capitalize on the organizational momentum that Soweto presented, but also cautious of a new movement with strong and deep political education of its members and an ideology that was in part opposed to theirs. Macmillan notes that one result of the rise of Black Consciousness was that the ANC insisted on compulsory education in exile to combat the 'serious, regrettable political deterioration in our ranks abroad'.[22]

Regardless of the perception of other liberation organizations, this period of communication between the movements suggests important things about the perspective of the BCM. In spite of its failure, the meeting with the ANC and attempt to unify the exiled movements is instructive about how the BCM understood itself in those early exile years. The Soweto uprisings, in which Black Consciousness ideology had played an important role, gave the BCM and its affiliates weight in the collective struggle against apartheid. As I have argued, 1976–7 was the pinnacle of the BCM's political importance in South Africa. At the time its networks and following within the country surpassed those of both the ANC and PAC, both of which had been underground and in exile for nearly two decades. But banning and exile marked the end of this period of success. The leadership was scattered around the world, and with the lack of a dedicated headquarters coordination among them proved an almost insurmountable obstacle to continued activism. Maaba and Mzamane have pointed to fragmentation and in-fighting among exiles, failures of communication and infrastructure, and lack of recognition by

---

[19] Maaba and Mzamane, 'The Black Consciousness Movement of Azania', p. 1363.
[20] S. Ellis, *External Mission: The ANC in exile 1960–1990* (London, 2012), pp. 89–90, 114–15, 307.
[21] H. Macmillan, *The Lusaka Years: The ANC in exile in Zambia* (Johannesburg, 2013), p. 131.
[22] Ibid., p. 107, quoting the proceedings of an ANC Revolutionary Council meeting in Lusaka, July 1971.

international organizations and host states as key factors in the demise of Black Consciousness as a movement in exile.[23]

In addition, the BCM was less successful recruiting the new student exiles than the ANC and even the PAC were. To some degree this too was a failure of logistical coordination, as Black Consciousness had strong ideological links to student activists, many of whom had been politically conscientized by SASO/BCM leaders like Tiro. But the ANC and the PAC had networks and camps in frontline countries, and military structures like *Umkhonto We Sizwe* (MK) and the Azanian People's Liberation Army (APLA) to absorb the flow of new recruits; at the time, the BCM was still organizing itself in exile. In fact, though all the Black Consciousness groups were affiliated, and had sprung from direct or indirect association with SASO, even in 1977 they did not exist under a formally unified banner of the 'Black Consciousness Movement'. Harry Nengwekhulu's correspondence with Thabo Mbeki and Oliver Tambo in Lusaka was all under the auspices of the Black Peoples' Convention, SASO's 'adult' political branch. This suggests that capacity for mobilization was a key component in the success or failure of a particular ideology. Though the students of 1976 arguably had stronger ideological links to Black Consciousness, the ANC's superior organizational capacity in exile meant that it was far more successful in recruiting these new cadres.

A high-profile example of the BCM's failure to absorb exile recruits was Tsietsi Mashinini, whose dismissal of the ANC was discussed above. After a matter of weeks in the role of leader of the Soweto Students' Representative Council (SSRC), Mashinini fled South Africa in August 1976, first to Botswana and later to Europe, America, and eventually to West Africa. Mashinini was an outspoken proponent of Black Consciousness while in exile. He gave many interviews in the international press praising Black Consciousness and criticizing the ANC, accusing it of corruption and of being 'extinct' in South Africa.[24] But after crossing the border to Botswana and arriving in Gaborone in late August 1976, Mashinini did not integrate himself into the Black Consciousness networks that existed there. Professing that he still felt pursued by BOSS (the South African

---

[23] Maaba and Mzamane, 'The Black Consciousness Movement of Azania', pp. 1365–71, 1374–5.

[24] 'Tsietsi trained at Vanessa's Red school', *Sunday Times*, 30 January 1977, and 'Mashinini to head new force', *Sunday Times*, 28 August 1977 [GPP]; transcript of television interview with Tsietsi Mashinini, aired 9 January 1977 in New York City [KGC A2675/I/20]; T. Mashinini, 'Behind the Growing Upsurge in South Africa', *Intercontinental Press*, 15 November 1976 [UFH AZAPO/BCM 14/1].

Bureau of Secret Service), he left Botswana and moved to London in September 1976.[25] Just a month later he was in the United States, giving high-profile interviews about the student situation in South Africa. By early 1977, Mashinini had become the face of South Africa's students in the international press, though his rise to prominence was not without critics. The ANC and some of its allies criticized his aggressive stance in the media, understandably, given the vehement stance Mashinini had taken against the liberation organization.[26]

Perhaps more striking, though, is an open letter to the *Botswana Daily News* from the SRC of the University College of Botswana, criticizing Mashinini for his 'lust for publicity', for being 'a running dog of the white liberal press', and for undermining 'the security of all exiles in Botswana'.[27] Their critique is particularly noteworthy because the language used by the SRC is redolent of Black Consciousness in its castigations of the white liberal press, and an emphasis on black self-sufficiency: 'The Tsietsi cult [...] kills the spirit of self-reliance because of false expectations that the hero will make the first move.'[28]

In spite of his rhetoric, Tsietsi was not incorporated into the BCM in exile. By May 1977 Mashinini moved to Nigeria, where that country's government was attempting to organize a 'new liberation organization' as an alternative force, 'rivaling South Africa's two established liberation organizations [the ANC and the PAC]'.[29] Mashinini became its figurehead. Most of this new group was to be student recruits who sympathized with Black Consciousness, but though the BPC had declared itself responsible for helping 'to organize refugees belonging to the black consciousness movement [and] maintain[ed] a responsibility for the Nigerian students, [they] neither instigated nor approved of the Mashinini initiative'.[30]

The aftermath of the Soweto uprisings and flight into exile by many students presented an additional challenge for leaders of the BCM: how to deal with the issue of violence, and particularly armed struggle. Ideologically SASO and its affiliates had never developed a clear policy with regard to the use of violence in their political struggle; they did not explicitly advocate the tactic of armed struggle, which had been adopted

---

[25] 'Mashinini tells how he got out of SA', *The Star*, 5 October 1976 [GPP].
[26] 'Tsietsi trained at Vanessa's Red school', *Sunday Times*, 30 January 1977; 'Mashinini to head new force', *Sunday Times*, 28 August 1977 [GPP].
[27] 'Mashinini "shut up!"', *Botswana Daily News*, 3 February 1977 [GPP].
[28] Ibid.
[29] 'Mashinini to head new force', *Sunday Times*, 28 August 1977 [GPP].
[30] Ibid.

by both the ANC and PAC in the early 1960s, and never made any moves toward participating in the armed struggle themselves during the first wave of Black Consciousness bannings in 1973. In fact, a group led by Keith Mokoape at the 1972 General Students Coucil who supported adopting armed struggle was shouted down by other delegates because it would jeopardize the position of SASO as an above-ground organization.[31] In 1974, when the Viva-FRELIMO rally at Turfloop pushed student activism into direct conflict with the state, speakers like Tshoni called for violent resistance, paralleling the examples of countries like Mozambique and Kenya. But hers was the most radical and lowest-ranking SASO voice at the rally; the position never gained traction with SASO leadership.

But neither did SASO espouse a policy of *non*violence; indeed, in some of his later writing, Biko explicitly advocated the use of calculated force when confronted with a violent opponent. In an interview a few months before his death in September 1977, Biko gave the (prophetic) example of responding to physical abuse in detention:

> If they want to beat me five times, they can only do so on condition that I allow them to beat me five times. If I react sharply, equally and oppositely, to the first clap, they are not going to be able to systematically count the next four claps, you see. It's a fight. So if they had meant to give me so much of a beating, and not more, my idea is to make them go beyond what they wanted to give me and to give back as much as I can give so that it becomes an uncontrollable thing.[32]

The violence that Biko described here was interpersonal, and the circumstances under which it could occur were when the individual encountered – and was assaulted by – an official of the state. For early Black Consciousness leaders this never translated into pre-emptive or structural violence of the type that armed struggle employed. Gail Gerhart has suggested that SASO's reluctance to engage in such forms of violent resistance lay, not in an ideology of pacifism, but in a pragmatic belief in the importance of patience. Gerhart suggests that for SASO, the experience of the PAC, in particular, was a cautionary tale: 'The PAC's undoing had not been in its ideology but in its reckless rush to confrontation at a time when circumstances did not favour a black victory.'[33] I would add that the affiliates of the BCM lacked the underground and exile structures and capacity to mount an organized campaign of violence,

---

[31] Mzamane, Maaba, and Biko, 'The Black Consciousness Movement', p. 118.

[32] Biko, *I Write What I Like*, p. 153.

[33] Gerhart, *Black Power in South Africa*, pp. 284–5.

and never attempted to develop these while they were able to operate above ground. For SASO, then, the most important questions with regards to violence as a political tool were of timing and situation, not ideology. This facilitated the entry of many young Black Consciousness recruits into the armed wings of the ANC (MK) and the PAC (APLA) in the wake of Soweto 1976. The significance of those events, and the use of violence by the state against thousands of students *en masse*, provided a set of circumstances that permitted the abandonment of patience and the employment of calculated force.

Nozipho Diseko has argued that the ANC's (and to a lesser extent the PAC's) use of armed struggle as a tool attracted the increasingly militant youth of 1976 and 1977.[34] This is persuasive, but not because of disaffection with the nonviolence of Black Consciousness, as she has suggested. Rather, Black Consciousness advocated violent responses to oppression and injustice in particular circumstances, and cautioned patience until such time as these tools could be used successfully. Engagement in armed struggle after the pivotal change in the state's use of violence after June 1976 was not antithetical to the Black Consciousness politics of many young South Africans; it fit neatly into it.

The failure of Black Consciousness figures to successfully organize in exile has been a theme of this chapter, and one that has been largely neglected from the literature on the movement, which generally ends with the death of Steve Biko and the October 1977 bannings.[35] This lacuna neglects an important, albeit unsuccessful, attempt by Black Consciousness exiles to form their own structures as a counterpoint to those of other liberation organizations. One notable exception is Maaba and Mzamane's contribution to *The Road to Democracy in South Africa*, on the founding of the Black Consciousness Movement of Azania; I will extend their discussion of the organization here by looking particularly at its role in incorporating student exiles (or failing to do so).[36]

In 1979 a united Black Consciousness Movement of South Africa (BCMSA) was founded in London by Barney Pityana. Shortly after its founding, in April 1980, the organization held a 'redefinition and

---

[34] Diseko, 'Origins and Development of SASM', pp. 60–1.

[35] Magaziner ends his analysis in the 'quiet' after the BCM bannings, and extends his conclusions to consider the reintegration of Black Consciousness figures into politics in the new, post-apartheid South Africa [Magaziner, *The Law and the Prophets*, pp. 182–90]. Tom Lodge acknowledges the formation of exile structures in passing, but only to note that many of those BC exiles soon joined the ANC [Lodge, *Black Politics in South Africa*, pp. 342–3].

[36] Maaba and Mzamane, 'The Black Consciousness Movement of Azania', pp. 1361–98.

rededication' conference in London, where the name was changed to the Black Consciousness Movement of Azania (BCMA) 'to reflect more truly what the black people feel their country should be called'.[37] This was the first change of name pointing to the rift between racialist politics that had developed among South Africa's various anti-apartheid groups. These included the multiracialism of the ANC, which after the party's 1969 conference at Mogorogoro in Tanzania officially became 'non-racialism';[38] the uniracial Africanism of the PAC; and the nonracialism of Black Consciousness, which constituted itself differently to the ANC's policy of the same name by its inclusion of only those racial groups that were oppressed by apartheid. Black Consciousness had always subscribed to its own brand of Africanism – particularly in their fore-grounding of black cultural identity – and their adoption of 'Azania' in their name reflects this. BCMA suffered from many of the problems that exiled members of the BCM had faced before it; the leadership remained scattered and organizational cohesion was low. At the London confer-ence BCMA's founder Pityana resigned his post as United Kingdom regional chairman owing to 'a procedural disagreement'.[39] The organi-zation was less than a year old, but already it was succumbing to internal divisions. The conference was supposed to 'strengthen and consolidate BCMA's programme for the liberation of Azania through the creation of a unitary structure embodying all exiled activists who were involved internally in organizations such as Saso, BCP, BPC, SASM, Nayo, and others.'[40] But in practice it did little to bridge the gaps in the widely dispersed leadership. As well as Pityana's resignation of his post, Harry Nengwekhulu's role as external director was also phased out. Though BCMA continued to exist in exile for a decade, led by a new cohort of exiles, it was plagued by organizational challenges and failed to unite former BC activists under its banner.

Black Consciousness was – and had always been – primarily about changing the way black South Africans conceived of themselves and their place in their country; in order to do this effectively, it needed to be among the people it was trying to conscientize. SASO's great success had come by effective mobilization techniques through campuses and schools that provided ready access to groups of students. In contrast to the organizational success of SASO, BCMA, having been removed from

---

[37] 'Pityana resigns from post in BC movement', *Sunday Post*, 20 April 1980 [GPP].

[38] D. Everatt, 'Non-racialism in South Africa: Status and prospects', *Politikon*, 39(1) (2012), 5–28.

[39] Ibid.

[40] 'Movement striving for unity', *Rand Daily Mail*, 9 May 1980 [GPP].

its base of operations and from the people it sought to reach, floundered outside South Africa. In particular, it was hurt by its alienation from students and student networks within South Africa, which had always been the great strength of the BCM. Maaba and Mzamane have argued that student life in exile was actually counterproductive to political activism, as scholarships restricted the ability and time of BCMA exiles to politically organize themselves.[41] Universities abroad did not provide the same fertile ground for mobilization that places like Turfloop had.

But the formation of BCMA in exile was only one inheritor of Black Consciousness' mantle; inside South Africa the Azanian People's Organization (AZAPO) was launched in 1978. AZAPO was formed by those SASO/BPC members who had been detained in or before October 1977, but were later released. Lybon Mabasa and Ishmael Mkhabela, two former Turfloop students and former members of the Students' Christian Movement on campus, were the founding members. Mabasa had also been a schoolteacher at Meadowlands High School in Soweto during the uprising and had been one of the first teachers detained in the aftermath.[42] Less than a week after the May 1978 founding of the organization – before its constitution had even been written or its aims publicized – the police once again detained both men. The precedent alarmed observers who described it as 'frightening' and 'alarming'.[43] A professor of law at the University of the Witwatersrand noted that it was the first time an organization had been banned so quickly after it was formed, indicating a new rigour with which the government was prepared to police potentially subversive black organizations.[44]

From the outset, AZAPO faced criticism in the press as well as government repression. White reporters were excluded from its founding conference, leading to accusations of racism and racialism from 'both the liberal and conservative press'.[45] In response, editors of *The Voice*, a black-run weekly paper, argued in an editorial that white reporters had historically given 'prominence to the negative aspects only' of black

---

[41] Maaba and Mzamane, 'The Black Consciousness Movement of Azania', p. 1366.
[42] Deposition of Aubrey Mokoena taken by Justice of the Peace D.L. Aspelling in Johannesburg. Undated (c. early 1977) [HPRA A2953]; author's interview with Lybon Mabasa, Johannesburg, 28 September 2011; Gail Gerhart interview with Lybon Tiyani Mabasa, New York, 7 April 1991 [DISA: http://www.disa.ukzn.ac.za/index.php?option=com_displaydc&recordID=ora19910407.000.009.000].
[43] 'Black Politics at Crossroads', *The Voice*, 2(4), 11–18 May 1978 [GPP].
[44] Ibid.
[45] Editorial, 'We regret…', *The Voice*, 6 May 1978, p. 2 [GPP].

activism.[46] This concern over representations in the press had also been true of SASO activists: white reporters had been condemned for their misreporting and misrepresenting the organization at the 3rd General Students Council meeting in 1972,[47] and Harry Nengwekhulu described a confrontation over representations of blacks in the press with Allister Sparks, editor of the liberal *Rand Daily Mail* in the early days of SASO:

> [The *Rand Daily Mail*] kept on calling us non-whites. I then went there with a friend of mine, and I met [editor Allister Sparks]. And I said, 'Mr. Sparks, [...] why do you continue to call us non-whites? We're not non-whites. You can't be defined in terms of what you are not. [...]' He said, 'No, no. The Institute of Race Relations is looking for a name for you: Africans, Coloureds, and Indians. They have got a name.' I said, 'What is the name?' 'Africolasians.' Africolasians! Africans, Coloureds, Asians. [Laughter] I'll never forget that. [...] The first thing that we did when we had conference at Hammanskraal [in 1972], we didn't invite the *Rand Daily Mail*, which was the most radical newspaper in the country.[48]

AZAPO's policy of no white press was no more racialized than SASO's had been, and in fact it followed neatly on from SASO's contentious relationship with the white media; but by 1979 it faced a great deal more backlash than its predecessor had at the beginning of the decade, reflecting the escalation of internal anti-apartheid politics by the late 1970s. SASO's novelty and separation of races had allowed it space to grow and develop during the late 1960s; a decade later its inheritors were quashed even before they properly began.

It was not until more than a year after its founding that AZAPO held its first congress in October 1979, and elected Curtis Nkondo its first president. Nkondo, whose brother Gessler had caused controversy at Turfloop as the head of BASA and editor of *Turfloop Testimony*, had grown up in the Northern Transvaal near Louis Trichardt and had been a schoolteacher in Soweto before schools there were rocked by the student uprising. Nkondo supported his students, and in the aftermath he became chairman of the Soweto Teachers' Action Committee, which represented Soweto teachers and led more than 300 of them to resign in protest in September 1977. Lybon Mabasa, who became AZAPO's treasurer, and Ishmael Mkhabela, who became chairman, had been released from detention by the time of AZAPO's first congress but were

---

[46] Ibid.
[47] Minutes of the Proceedings of the 3rd General Students Council of the South African Students' Organization, St Peter's Seminary, Hammanskraal, 2–9 July 1972, Resolution 20/72 [SASO A2176/5.2].
[48] Author's interview with Harry Nengwekhulu (a).

unable to attend owing to banning orders.[49] At the congress AZAPO articulated a set of aims and objectives that followed closely on the work of earlier Black Consciousness organizations. They aimed to mobilize black workers 'through the philosophy of black consciousness', as well as to reform the South African educational system so that it better served black students, and to promote a form of liberation theology 'relevant to the black struggle'.[50] These goals bore a great deal of resemblance to those pursued by SASO and the BPC, including the mention of black consciousness, the focus on education, and the echoes of black theology. Yet AZAPO was to have a very different reception on the national scene in South Africa. Far from the unity that had been imagined by some exile leaders, the political parties still active within South Africa during the 1980s would become fierce competitors.

The suspension of Nkondo and AZASO's turn to Charterism

If AZAPO was the ideological heir to SASO and the BPC, it bore much greater structural resemblance to the latter as a political party focused on a broad swathe of the adult population. Not long after its October 1979 congress, 'in November, [...] a conference was held in Johannesburg convened by people who were involved in AZAPO to look into the concept of establishing a student movement, which was seen as a necessity'.[51] This second conference gave rise to the idea of AZASO, the Azanian Students' Organisation, which would be the student wing to AZAPO's more wide-reaching political party. Branches were established at the historically black universities, as well as at one training college; in later years, they expanded among technical and educational colleges, and to black students at the 'open' English-speaking universities, like the University of the Witwatersrand. At Turfloop, the campus branch was established in 1980, with the help of Peter Mokaba, a young firebrand science student, who would go on to become a national youth leader.[52] By AZASO's first official conference in 1981, Turfloop was already something of a stronghold. In an interview discussing the event later, Joe Phaahla, a medical student at the University of Natal who was from Sekhukhuneland in the Northern Transvaal and became a prominent

---

[49] 'Azapo's Blueprint', *Post*, 1 October 1979 [GPP].

[50] Ibid.

[51] 'Student Movement Today' interview with Joe Phaahla and Kate Philip, July 1983, p. 42 [AZASO AG2635/A].

[52] Peter Mokaba Curriculum Vitae, African National Congress Mission to the United States, April 1994 [GPP].

student leader in AZASO, described the Turfloop branch at the 1981 conference as 'the only branch which actually existed' in terms of functioning organizational structures.[53]

At its inception, AZASO espoused the Black Consciousness ideology of AZAPO and its BCM forerunners. It saw itself as the inheritor of SASO's mantle among black university students. Many of its early members, like Mokaba, had been politicized through BC ideology and in the wake of the Soweto uprisings. The links to Black Consciousness were to be short-lived, however. From its very early days there were arguments within AZASO about its political philosophy.[54] These were exacerbated by internal dissent over the suspension of Curtis Nkondo as AZAPO's president. In the role for only a few short months, Nkondo was suspended in early January 1980 for 'violating [AZAPO] principle and policy and not respecting protocol'.[55] His suspension was met with angry condemnation by student groups, like the Congress of South African Students (COSAS) and AZASO itself, by the Writers' Association of South Africa (WASA), and by Winnie Kgware, the first head of the BPC. Mrs Kgware, speaking from Turfloop, said,

> I pledge solidarity with Azaso and Wasa for the stand they have taken on the suspension. Their action is encouraging. [...] We have already noticed trends of selfless leadership in [Nkondo]. To use a black American expression, we say to him: hang in there![56]

The violation of protocol of which Nkondo was accused was variously described as speaking to Helen Suzman, a white politician and member of the Federal Progressive Party, apparently about the whereabouts of his detained brother, Zinjiva Nkondo,[57] and criticizing black trade unions for their 'spineless' avoidance of politics, potentially damaging AZAPO's relationship with the working class.[58] It was considered an open secret, however, that the real cause behind his suspension was that his politics were too sympathetic to the ANC. As Joe Phaahla said, '[S]ome of the people who were in AZAPO thought that why Mr Nkondo really had

---

[53] 'Student Movement Today' interview with Joe Phaahla and Kate Philip, July 1983, p. 43 [HPRA AG2635/A].

[54] Ibid., p. 42; White, *From Despair to Hope*, p. 55.

[55] 'Nkondo Indaba', *Rand Daily Mail*, 19 January 1980 [GPP].

[56] Ibid.

[57] 'Azapo gets a rocket on Nkondo', *Rand Daily Mail*, 17 January 1980 [GPP].

[58] Maaba and Mzamane, 'The Azanian People's Organization', pp. 1299–1360 (1308).

to go was because it was said that he was a "Charterist".'[59] Referring to Nkondo's alleged support for the multi-racial principles of the Freedom Charter, espoused by the ANC, Phaahla was pointing to a key divide in South African liberation politics between Charterism, Africanism, and Black Consciousness.

Up until the mid-1970s Charterism and multiracialism had had little traction in student politics on black campuses. Though in the late 1960s there had been some enthusiasm for affiliating with NUSAS at Fort Hare and Turfloop, the advent of SASO curbed this movement.[60] As noted above, however, the Soweto-based SASM was abandoning its ties to Black Consciousness in favour of cultivating deeper links with the ANC underground by the mid-1970s. Diseko points to frustrations with the racially exclusive doctrine of Black Consciousness and to the BCM's failure to articulate a militant response to state repression (in the mode of armed struggle), and she notes that student activists were cultivating relationships with white activists and sympathizers.[61]

Maaba and Mzamane have pointed to developments in both AZAPO and the BCMA that brought class to the fore of debates in Black Consciousness politics in the 1980s. During the height of the BCM in the 1970s, it had always remained subordinate to the issue of race as the mechanism of oppression and object against which the struggle was waged. But by 1979 and 1980, some activists were adopting a more explicit Marxist class-based analysis of the situation in South Africa; in particular, Neville Alexander, an academic and former Robben Islander, was credited with influencing the adoption of these ideas in AZAPO.[62] As a result, Maaba and Mzamane point to Nkondo's criticism of the unions as another factor in his suspension; it was yet another way that he bucked the trends emerging within his own party.

Following AZAPO's suspension of Nkondo, who was popular with AZASO members, the party's student wing engaged in internal

---

[59] 'Student Movement Today' interview with Joe Phaahla and Kate Philip, July 1983, p. 42 [HPRA AG2635/A].

[60] The most complete account of the attempts of NUSAS to establish a branch and solicit support at Turfloop and other black institutions in the mid-1960s is in a recent thesis by Claire McKay: C. McKay, 'A history of the National Union of South African Students (NUSAS), 1956–1970', unpublished doctoral thesis, University of South Africa (UNISA), 2015. See especially Chapter 7: 'NUSAS and the Ethnic University Colleges', and pp. 296–306: 'The University College of the North (Turfloop)'. For more on NUSAS' turbulent presence at Fort Hare, see Massey, *Under Protest*, especially Chapters 1 and 3.

[61] Diseko, 'Origins and Development of SASM', pp. 59–61.

[62] Maaba and Mzamane, 'The Azanian People's Organization', pp. 1306–8.

discussions of its own political philosophy. In December 1980, the interim committee of AZASO called a summit conference to discuss the issue. According to Joe Phaahla, 'At this conference the deficentcy [sic] of black consciousness philosophy as a rallying point was highlighted by various delegates.' Among these deficiencies delegates noted that the appeal of Black Consciousness had been confined to 'black intellectuals' and that the philosophy had been 'misused by opportunists for their own interests'.[63] The issue was hotly debated at the conference, and one member of the Turfloop delegation even threatened to walk out in protest at the adoption of a new Charterist preamble to the AZASO Constitution.[64] But the majority of student delegates present disagreed, including the rest of the Turfloop delegation: they found that Black Consciousness was too narrow a framework for AZASO and 'that for the organization to play a meaningful role in the liberation struggle, a more broader [sic] but clearer approach to defining issues at stake should be adopted'.

The desire for a broader and clearer approach to political mobilization is noteworthy; from its inception, Black Consciousness had been criticized for being a product of the intellectual elite – born at universities – and this was identified as an impediment to its capacity for mass mobilization. The students of AZASO, though demographically very similar to those of SASO, recognized this limitation. Their calls for multiracialism not only widened their potential pool of recruits, it freed them from the philosophical constraints of Black Consciousness, which had always struggled to find purchase outside its core base of student and intellectual supporters.

This dissension from its ideological roots caused the AZASO delegates to redraft the preamble of their constitution and, importantly, to sever ties with AZAPO and its Black Consciousness ideology. As an expression of autonomy it followed SASO's lead towards student-led protest, if not its ideology. In the 1980s, Black Consciousness in student politics was becoming a thing of the past. It was more than two years before AZAPO formed a new student body to carry its torch, and by the time their Azanian Students Movement (AZASM) was born it lagged behind AZASO in organization and support on the campuses that had once been strongholds of Black Consciousness.

---

[63] SASPU Interview with Joe Phaahla, undated c. mid-1980s [GPP].
[64] Ibid.

Conclusion

The later years of the 1970s brought unparalleled changes in the student politics of South Africa. The Soweto uprisings changed the scale and site of how students articulated grievances with their schools and the state. These owed a debt of ideology and organization to the SASO-affiliated Black Consciousness expelled students from Turfloop in 1972 and 1974. The 'highs' of 1976, as the peak of the BCM's organization and prominence, did not last however. The imprisonment of the SASO 9, Steve Biko's death, and the banning of all the organizations affiliated to the movement dealt a critical blow by late 1977. In exile, Black Consciousness failed to maintain the organizational cohesion and mobilization it had been able to achieve as a movement (rather than a party) within South Africa. Meanwhile, state repression within the country continued to hound its inheritors, and AZAPO faced stiff repression from its outset.

Beyond the organizational dilemmas faced by the BCM and its successors, though, the ANC's nonracial philosophy of Charterism had begun to take root with some student activists as early as 1975. Under the umbrella of the South African Students' Movement, students expressed a variety of political ideologies, from the staunch Africanism of the BCM to the inclusive Charterism of the ANC. In spite of pro-ANC rhetoric from high-profile student activists like Murphy Morobe and Tebello Motapanyane, Charterism remained one ideology among many for the students of 1976.

Both of these ideological positions were influenced by key student and former student activists from the Northern Transvaal. From the role in conscientizing and supporting the students of Soweto played by Turfloop expellees like Onkgopotse Tiro and Aubrey Mokoena, to Harry Nengwekhulu's (failed) attempts to coordinate exile operations for the BCM, to the important sway that Curtis Nkondo exerted on AZASO's shift away from Black Consciousness in favour of Charterism, people who were politicized and mobilized in the region bore significant influence on national trends during this period.

The late 1970s also brought with them the beginning of coordinated student politics on a more local level. The work of SASM and the unexpected student uprisings of Soweto 1976 had shown schools to be a fruitful site for political engagement and action. Though this had been happening incrementally, through politically aware and active teachers, mobilization of politicized students became an important focus in the anti-apartheid movement from 1976 onwards. This renewed focus on students at the most local level – in their schools – would change the face of student resistance.

These two shifts – the turn to Charterism, and the growth of more numerous, local student groups like those that became the first chapters of the Congress of South African Students (COSAS) – would be of paramount importance in shaping the face of student politics in South Africa during the 1980s, and will be a major focus of the next chapter.

5

Congresses and Comrades

The 1983 launch of the United Democratic Front (UDF) in a community hall in Mitchell's Plain on the Cape Flats has come to symbolize the rise of deeply local politics in the anti-apartheid struggle. The UDF was dominated by civics, trade unions, student groups, and women's organizations. Eventually it came to envelop hundreds of these types of local and regional organizations across the country, all under the banner of nonracialism. In a shift from the dominant political ideology among students of the previous decade, when Black Consciousness had advocated racial separation as a necessary precondition for psychological and political freedom, the UDF reclaimed the earlier tradition of the ANC and other Charterist organizations that based their nonracialism on the ethos of the Freedom Charter.

But the birth of the UDF in 1983 was only the latest and most public move to locally root anti-apartheid politics. In this chapter I argue that increasing regionalization in the realm of student politics predates the UDF by several years, and that those early political entities had a profound effect on, and in many cases became, later UDF affiliates. To do so, I will focus particularly on the Congress of South African Students and student and youth congresses of the Northern Transvaal, and the tensions that existed between these local organizations and the national structures to which they affiliated.

The 1979 founding of the Congress of South African Students (COSAS) predated the UDF by four years and marked the first reemergence of Charterism in national politics. It also effectively expanded the student struggle well beyond the crucible of universities, a major centre of 1970s activism, and beyond the schools of Soweto, which had catapulted student protest to international attention in 1976. Tshepo Moloi's study on the Free State town of Kroonstad has suggested that though political activity was slow to start in the area, the activism of school students 'helped shift Maokeng's politics from quiescence to confrontation'.[1] In the Northern Transvaal, Sekibakiba Lekgoathi has

---

[1] T. Moloi, *Place of Thorns: Black political protest in Kroonstad since 1976* (Johannesburg, 2015), p. 104.

pointed to the expansion of Western-style education in rural areas during the 1970s as a key influence on the growth of student organization in the region.[2] COSAS brought the student struggle to remote corners of rural South Africa made newly accessible by the expansion of secondary education that Lekgoathi describes; in the Northern Transvaal its influence was adopted and transformed into youth congresses, which further expanded political engagement to include non-student youth.

In this chapter I consider both students and youth as social and analytical categories; Colin Bundy, in his work on youth in the 1980s Cape Flats, follows Karl Mannheim and argues that the groups share a 'generational consciousness' informed by their shared social and historical circumstances.[3] As Deborah Durham has suggested, youth is a 'historically constructed social category',[4] which gives it a large degree of contextual specificity and flexibility. Though 'student' might be expected to be a more rigid category, defined primarily by school or university affiliation, for South African students and youth in the late 1970s and early 1980s, the distinction was not always so clearly delineated. School boycotts, expulsions, and the detention of school and university students often meant that little time was spent in classrooms, even for those formally enrolled in school or university. In addition, some students remained involved in student structures after they had left school. As Jeremy Seekings has noted, in its early years COSAS was 'dominated by ex-students until 1982'.[5] In spite of having left school, however, most of these former students were not participating in formal work, had maintained connections to their age cohort, and, perhaps most crucially, 'still regarded themselves as students'.[6] As such, they were not only incorporated into COSAS, but they also formed a significant portion of its early leadership.

In addition, the expansion of political activism in secondary schools began to impact young people who were outside the educational networks that broadly encompassed student activists (even those who were no longer technically students). In COSAS there was little room for young people who had no connection to their local school, and whose personal experience did not lend them to politicization over educational issues

---

[2] S. Lekgoathi, 'The United Democratic Front in Lebowa and KwaNdebele during the 1980s' in SADET, *The Road to Democracy in South Africa, Volume 4, Part 1 (1980–1990)* (Pretoria, 2010), 613–67 (630).

[3] Bundy, 'Street Sociology', p. 305.

[4] D. Durham, 'Youth and the Social Imagination in Africa: Introduction to Parts 1 and 2', *Anthropological Quarterly*, 73(3) (2000), 113–20 (114).

[5] J. Seekings, *Heroes or Villains? Youth politics in the 1980s* (Johannesburg, 1993), p. 32.

[6] Ibid., p. 33.

ranging from the cost of books and uniforms to the restrictive, ideological curriculum imposed by Bantu Education. But these rural youth did share Bundy's 'generational consciousness' and many structural grievances with their student counterparts. Together they also formed a political cohort narrower than can be captured by an entire generation. Most obviously, both were subject to oppression by the apartheid state, and by the mid-1980s an economic slump and rising unemployment harshly confronted both those with school matric certificates and those without them. This differentiated them from youth counterparts even less than a decade earlier, when school enrolment had been lower and economic prospects had been better; by the mid-1980s black school leavers in rural villages could likely expect to be unemployed, and would join a growing portion of their generation outside formal employment.

Part of this cohort's generational consciousness, differentiating them from their parents, was a rejection of traditional rural economic, or agrarian, activities.[7] Emphasis was rather placed on extending formal education, and the achievement of bureaucratic jobs in the Bantustan governments, or as teachers, for those who could get them. Even for students who came out of the politically radical environment of Turfloop, these jobs, offering security and stability, were desirable. However, those who gained such employment were a very lucky few. Looking specifically at the context in the Northern Transvaal, Sello Mathabatha has written of the accelerated deterioration that schools in Lebowa experienced during this period owing to 'poorly planned and poorly resourced expansion', and its deleterious effect on students.[8] In the face of such dismal prospects, fuelled by shared generational consciousness and grievances, by the mid-1980s the student political movement broadened to include structures for non-student youth.

Another hallmark of protest politics in the 1980s was the increased violence that was both experienced and expressed by student and youth activists. In rural villages across the Northern Transvaal young 'comrades' led violent witch-purges in efforts to cleanse their communities of evil, adapting a traditional discourse of witchcraft with contemporary political language and accusations. Meanwhile, student activists at

---

[7] For a more complete discussion of the importance of the land, livestock, and agrarian lifestyle during the mid-twentieth century in Sekhukhuneland and its decline, see Delius, *A Lion Amongst the Cattle*, particularly Chapters 4 and 5 (pp. 108–71).

[8] S. Mathabatha, 'Missionary Schools, Student Uprisings in Lebowa and the Sekhukhuneland Students' Revolts, 1983–1986', *African Studies*, 64(2) (2005), 263–84 (265).

Turfloop experienced heightened degrees of violence in their relationships to the university administration, to the police and South African
Defence Force (SADF) who had garrisoned troops on campus, and even
between student groups of opposing politics. The increased regionalization and localization of politics during this period, and the inclusion of
non-student youth in the realm of what had previously been student
politics, meant that organizations sometimes struggled to exert control
over their rank and file – the cases of witch killings in parts of Lebowa,
Gazankulu, and Venda that I discuss in this chapter is an example of
this. Further, spiralling violence as a mode of political expression mirrors the situation in other areas of South Africa, acting as a point of
common political expression between comrades in the rural north, on
university campuses, and in the townships of the country's major cities.

COSAS, the Resurgence of Charterism, and the expansion of politics in schools

The Congress of South African Students (or COSAS) was founded in
1979; it was the first 'congress' organization in South Africa since the
banning of the African National Congress in 1960. The founding of
COSAS marked a major change in the shape of South African student
politics. Previously Black Consciousness organizations had dominated
student politics during the 1970s, but COSAS heralded a return to the
nonracial politics of the ANC and its Freedom Charter. COSAS was the
first such organization to make this shift, preceding the formation of
the UDF (of which it would become an affiliate) by four years.

COSAS was founded after a three-day conference at Wilgespruit Fellowship Centre in Roodepoort, outside Johannesburg. It was attended
by delegates from across the country, and informed by deliberations
among a mix of actors. Students who had been involved in the uprisings around the country in 1976–7 were the core of COSAS' early
leadership, and they were supported by ANC cells underground within
South Africa. Joe Gqabi, who had been involved in the aftermath of
the Soweto uprisings, was perhaps the most prominent of these links
between the student movement and the ANC. Lynda Schuster has written of Gqabi's influence on the politically important Mashinini family,
and his conversion of Mpho Mashinini (brother of Tsietsi, who publicly
supported Black Consciousness and scorned the ANC) to Charterism.[9]

---

[9] L. Schuster, *A Burning Hunger: One family's struggle against Apartheid* (London, 2004), pp. 153–4; for further discussion of Tsietsi Mashinini's political
ideology, see Schuster's Chapter 4, 'Black Consciousness Banned: The turn to
exile and AZAPO' (pp. 168–81).

Through the work of such activists, Charterism was already making deeper incursions into the student movement following the uprisings of 1976, as Black Consciousness foundered under the weight of state repression and organizational failures in exile.

Badat has suggested that the increased visibility of Charterist organizations during the early 1980s influenced the renewed interest of students in Charterism and nonracial ideology; in particular, he points to increased activity by *Umkhonto we Sizwe*, especially the high-profile bombing of SASOL oil refineries on the night of 31 May 1980, and to the launch of the Release Mandela Committee that same year, which raised the profile of Nelson Mandela and, by proxy, other ANC political prisoners who had been in prison for nearly two decades.[10] Seekings has pointed to this period as the moment when 'a Charterist movement began to cohere inside the country'.[11] Also in 1980 the *Sunday Post* printed a copy of the Freedom Charter alongside an article on the history of the document; they also ran a Free-Mandela petition campaign.[12] With the founding and growth of COSAS, the ideological shift of AZASO, and increasing visibility and adoption of the Freedom Charter, 1980 was the year that Charterism – if not necessarily the banned movements that had championed it – came out from underground.

Meanwhile prison, always a critical site of conscientization for adult political activists, now became the crucible for a new group of inmates: many of the students involved in the Soweto Uprisings had been detained in the wake of 1976–7, and prisons – particularly Modderbee Prison on the East Rand – became a site of regrouping and planning.[13] According to Super Moloi, one detained student, the idea for COSAS arose from discussions that he and others who were detained at Modderbee under

---

[10] Badat, *Black Student Politics*, pp. 213–16.

[11] Seekings, *The UDF*, p. 36.

[12] Badat, *Black Student Politics*, p. 216; Seekings, *The UDF*, p. 36.

[13] There is a rich biographical literature on the role of political education within South Africa's prisons during apartheid, centring predominantly on Robben Island; in particular see A. Kathrada, *Memoirs* (Cape Town, 2004), pp. 214–18 on the importance of access to study materials and news for increasing consciousness among prisoners; N. Alexander, *Robben Island Dossier, 1964–1974* (Cape Town, 1994), pp. 47–65, on the challenges political prisoners faced in pursuing education, including censorship of materials and restrictions on courses deemed too political; M. Maharaj (ed.), *Reflections in Prison* (Cape Town, 2001), especially Nelson Mandela's reflection 'Whither the Black Consciousness Movement?' for a discussion of competition among the political ideologies represented on Robben Island; also see Marx, *Lessons of Struggle*, pp. 97–9, for a brief discussion of the influx of Black Consciousness prisoners into Robben Island and its effect on political education.

section 10 had had in 1977.[14] According to Tshediso Matona, a COSAS executive member in the 1980s, in his honours thesis on the subject, the push for COSAS to be an educational, rather than overtly political, organization came from ANC advisers to student leaders. Gqabi, in particular, was concerned that COSAS not be repressed before it had a chance to develop, and discouraged the new organization from having too political a platform and explicit ties to the ANC.[15]

In April 1979 the idea that had been fostered in prison came to fruition at COSAS' founding conference. Delegates were drawn from student bodies across the country, as well as student activists whose formal schooling had stopped in 1976 and 1977. Within this body there were delegates of diverse political ideologies: most prominently Charterists in the mould of the ANC were represented, but there were also delegates adhering to Black Consciousness, members of the Azanian People's Organization (AZAPO) and other groups. This led to some debate over the direction that the new organization would take in forming its ideological platform. 'On the question of a name, ANC sympathisers insisted that it should include the word "congress", while BC supporters proposed the Venda name *"Khuvhangano"* (Union) or alternatively, a name including "Azania".'[16] The latter would clearly have aligned the new organization with AZAPO, which had inherited the mantle of Black Consciousness and adhered to a racially separatist philosophy. Selecting *Khuvhangano* would not have tied the new organization as clearly to either Black Consciousness or Charterist ideology, but it celebrated African heritage above nonracialism. In the end, the Charterists triumphed in the naming debate, and the Congress of South African Students was born.

In spite of this debate and its conclusion in the Charterists' favour, COSAS' goals as laid out at that first conference did not explicitly reference Charterism as its political philosophy. At this stage, the new organization was feeling its way through the political landscape of late 1970s South Africa, and it aimed to provide space for its Charterist, Black Consciousness, and Africanist members to coexist, much as the SSRC had in the aftermath of the Soweto Uprising a few years earlier. The late 1970s were a period of flux and uncertainty for both movements so soon after the repression of Black Consciousness organizations and

---

[14] Nozipho Diseko's interview with Super Moloi, quoted in Matona, 'Student Organization and Political Resistance', p. 42.

[15] Matona, 'Student Organization and Political Resistance', p. 43; Seekings, *Heroes or Villains*, pp. 35–6.

[16] Matona, 'Student Organization and Political Resistance', p. 45.

the founding of AZAPO, and in the midst of Charterism's reemergence in above-ground politics. For a period COSAS provided space for both ideologies. The decision not to form a political party aided this position. In its earliest programmes COSAS strove to focus primarily on educational concerns.

With an explicit educational focus, COSAS' five main objectives located their role in the struggle firmly within secondary schools, from which they were eventually able to organize throughout the country. They aimed to 'normalize' student and teacher relationships, and to strive for 'dynamic, free and compulsory education for the advancement of society'.[17] At the time of the UDF's 1983 founding, COSAS was its largest student affiliate.[18] Matona and Seekings argue that COSAS' early stronghold was in the Southern Transvaal Pretoria–Witwatersrand–Vereeniging (PWV) area. Both authors focus on the role of urban organization (and, in the case of Matona, some specific branches in the Eastern Cape), and their analysis neglects an important part of COSAS' national growth in rural areas, particularly in the Northern Transvaal.

At their first conference, COSAS delegates elected Ephraim Mogale, a young man from the small town of Settlers in the Northern Transvaal as their president. It is noteworthy that Mogale came from outside the core of detained student activists who had helped conceive of the new organization. However, he appealed to a majority of delegates because he had successfully organized several youth clubs in his home area. Mogale had a Charterist political background; his family supported the ANC underground, and in the late 1970s he was involved in recruiting for the ANC. His election marked another victory of Charterism over Black Consciousness in COSAS' political development. In contrast to the space that had existed within SASM for Charterism to exist alongside Black Consciousness, for COSAS Charterism was its foundational ideal. COSAS was the first 'congress' organization in South Africa since the banning of the African National Congress in 1960. Names were important signifiers of ideology and affiliation; COSAS' name associated it from the outset with the ANC, the congress movement, and its multi-racial ideals. It was directed at pre-university students, the first such body since the Soweto Students Representative Council (SSRC) had been banned along with BCM organizations in October 1977.

In its early days, COSAS sought to establish links with other anti-apartheid groups, reaching out beyond student-specific issues to support issues like rent and shop boycotts, the Release Mandela Campaign, and

[17] 'New student body formed', *Rand Daily Mail*, 6 April 1979 [GPP].
[18] Seekings, *The UDF*, p. 59.

to create ties with workers' organizations.[19] But by the mid-1980s it maintained a primary focus on educational issues, a divergence from SASO's broad political approach but with similarity to SASM before 16 June 1976. As self-described in a 1984 pamphlet, COSAS aimed to educate students and organize them around school-based issues like corporal punishment, poor resources, and unqualified teachers. They also 'saw the need to unite all students throughout the country, Africans, Indians and Coloureds'.[20]

Racially inclusive language like that in the pamphlet marked COSAS clearly as a Charterist organization (though it is worth noting that the groups they sought to unite – Africans, coloureds, and Indians – were the same that SASO had grouped under the banner of black). More covertly, COSAS' early leadership was suspected of having links to the ANC underground.

Between 1977 and 1979 Mogale and his friend Thabo Makunyane, a student at Turfloop and son of the President of the Lebowa Chamber of Commerce, had organized local youth clubs around Potgietersrus, south of the region's largest town of Pietersburg. At these groups they distributed ANC literature like the exile journal *Mayibuye*, and other banned materials including political tracts called 'Being Black in South Africa Today' and 'Declaration of War'. These early youth groups were designed to 'provide social facilities and communal services' to local youth and students, but were not explicitly situated in schools. As discussed above, young people who were no longer students but maintained affiliation to student networks were some of the key leaders of student groups in the early 1980s – indeed both Makunyane and Mogale had left school by the time they set up these youth groups; Mogale was 20 in 1977, and Makunyane was 21.[21]

Eventually the two young men were accused, tried, and convicted of using these youth clubs to 'promote unrest'.[22] After a frequently postponed trial, a Pietersburg court convicted them both of offences under the Terrorism Act. They were each sentenced to eight years in prison. The evidence brought before them in court detailed links with the ANC,

---

[19] COSAS flyer, 'Workers, workers, build support for the students struggle in the schools', c. 1982 [HPRA AD1790]; van Kessel, *Beyond Our Wildest Dreams*.

[20] COSAS Potchefstroom pamphlet, 'We Remember June 16: A Nation Mourns', 1984 [HPRA AD1790].

[21] 'Students guilty of aid to ANC', *Rand Daily Mail*, 3 September 1980 [GPP].

[22] 'Terror Trial is postponed once more', *Rand Daily Mail*, 26 August 1980 [GPP]; 'Student leader in court again', *Rand Daily Mail*, 25 June 1980 [GPP]. Their treason trial, conducted months after Mogale had become COSAS president, resulted in each man being sentenced to eight years in prison.

including distributing banned literature and recruiting for the organization.[23] The presiding judge, Justice W.G.M. van Zyl, found that 'the aim of the accused was to galvanize the black youth so that they would identify with unrest and uprisings when they occurred'.[24] In addition to links with the ANC, the judge's decision reveals the scope of Mogale's organization in the Northern Transvaal, which was spreading across the region. Mogale's contact with local groups of students stretched from southern Sekhukhuneland, to Venda in the far north, to Potchefstroom in the Western Transvaal.[25] These local organizations in the small towns and townships of the Transvaal would become the forerunners of the youth congress movement that swept the country in the mid-1980s.

When Mogale became COSAS President in 1979 he built upon his earlier experience with youth groups; the new organization focused on students and rooted itself in secondary schools. Previously, the youth clubs had flourished especially well in Moutse district, near southern Sekhukhuneland, because they were organized around the personal networks of Mogale and Makunyane themselves, but COSAS transcended this. It made concerted efforts to shape itself as a national student movement, in contrast to the locally rooted Soweto Students Representative Council of 1976–7 and other predecessors.[26] But arguably even more critical to its success was its mode of organizing through schools themselves. The model of establishing branches in schools offered COSAS a point of entry into every town and village with a secondary school. This enabled them to organize students with a degree of freedom. As Ineke van Kessel has noted, '[A]lthough school grounds and university campuses became major battlefields during the 1980s, during at least the first half of the decade they were preserves of relative freedom.'[27]

In addition to more freedom to organize, operating from schools afforded COSAS access to equipment like photocopiers and meeting space, as well as to students themselves, who were the most critical resource to expanding its base. Schools also directly shaped COSAS's political engagement. Even when COSAS strove to reach out beyond the student community to engage with other groups in the struggle, they still sought to orient this engagement around education. A 1982 campaign to

---

[23] 'Student leader in court again', *Rand Daily Mail*, 25 June 1980 [GPP].
[24] Pietersburg Regional Court, Decision Against Thabo Makunyane (24) and Ephraim Mogale (23), 17 October 1980 [GPP].
[25] Ibid.
[26] Matona, 'Student Organization and Political Resistance', p. 44.
[27] van Kessel, *Beyond Our Wildest Dreams*, p. 20.

engage workers used slogans like 'Workers, workers, build support for the students' struggle in the schools', and further declared:

> Like you workers: we want democratic committees under our control (SRCs) to fight for our needs. Like you workers: we students are prepared to fight all and every dismissal from our schools. Like you workers: we defend older students from being thrown out of our schools, just like you defend old workers from being thrown out of the factories. Like you workers demand free overalls and boots, so we students demand free books and schooling. And students don't pay for books and schools IT IS THE WORKERS WHO PAY. Just as the workers fight assaults against the workers in the factory so we students fight against the beatings we get at school.[28]

These appeals not only raised the profile of educational issues, but also aimed to tie the plight of the students to that of workers by articulating that the struggle of workers and the struggle of students were deeply intertwined. This was a critical linkage for COSAS to make, because the relatively privileged concerns of students sometimes failed to attract outside support. Such criticism had been a challenge for earlier groups, like the South African Students' Organisation (SASO). SASO had been based primarily on university campuses, and its members were sometimes criticized by parents and elders for being too liberal regarding things like sex and drugs, for being idle, and for wasting the privilege of being at university by neglecting their studies for politics.[29]

To overcome these sorts of preconceptions about students in politics and to build solidarity across the anti-apartheid struggle, COSAS sought to draw familial and communal links between themselves and other groups: 'Workers, you are our fathers and mothers, you are our brothers and sisters. Our struggle in the schools is your struggle in the factories. We fight against the same bosses [sic] government, we fight the same enemy.'[30] There is little evidence that these overtures went beyond the rhetorical, though. COSAS did not develop any direct alliances with unions in its early years. Perhaps consequentially, this linking had limited success, and within a few years they had returned to targeting their outreach primarily at students themselves.

This shift back to students owed a debt to the founding of the UDF in 1983, which enabled COSAS to be officially linked to other local

---

[28] COSAS flyer, 'Workers, workers, build support for the students' struggle in the schools' (emphasis original) [HPRA AD1790].

[29] Author's interview with Lybon Mabasa.

[30] COSAS flyer, 'Workers, workers, build support for the students' struggle in the schools', c. 1982 [HPRA AD1790].

non-students' organizations like civics, parents' associations, and even unions. No longer did they have to legitimate student concerns as part of the larger struggle. Instead they could focus on expanding COSAS branches to new schools, which is where they gained organizational prominence. As a UDF affiliate they were part of a much broader network than solely student politics. Perhaps ironically, that breadth allowed them to focus more narrowly on student concerns and to flourish by doing so. The tension between the politics of UDF affiliates being deeply local, and the national profile that it also offered, is important. Once student politics began to move outside of schools in the Northern Transvaal in the mid-1980s contention emerged between local forms of political expression and regional and national leadership.

By 1984, shortly after the founding of the UDF, COSAS had reoriented its slogans and campaigns to target students: 'Each One, Teach One', and 'COSAS support students' demands' spoke primarily of solidarity within the student community during a time of growing unrest in schools. Walk-outs in Pretoria and Cradock, and the expulsion of five students from Hwiti High School in Mankweng, just outside the gates of Turfloop, called attention to the escalation of tensions within schools. In Mankweng, tensions between students and the school administration reached the breaking point when students boycotted in protest at being televised on the state-run South African Broadcasting Corporation on the occasion of the anniversary of Bantu Education. Protest over the use of press on campus – both not being allowed to speak to journalists, and being used to publicize university affairs – had long been a source of conflict and protest at nearby Turfloop. Now similar tactics were being employed in schools. According to the newsletter of COSAS' Mankweng branch, students felt the publicity violated their political principle 'of non-collaboration with the oppressor and institution created by the racist regime'.[31]

In response to the boycott, school authorities expelled five students, thought to be some of the most politically active in the student body, including three members of the Student Representative Council. COSAS rallied around these students, calling for regional and national solidarity. The Mankweng branch declared, 'We view the expulsion of our colleagues as part of the dirty tactics used by the white minority racist settlers regime and its collaborators to silence those who are opposed to it [...].'[32]

---

[31] COSAS Mankweng Branch Newsletter, August 1984 [HPRA AD1790].
[32] Ibid.

The students of the 1980s were products of a restrictive system of Bantu Education, but – perhaps more importantly – as the quotes above demonstrate, they were also products of the generation of 1976 that had come before and claimed schools as a site of political struggle. As one of the founders of the UDF, Rev. Alan Boesak, said, despite apartheid's attempts to 'brainwash' them, these students were 'the most politically conscious generation of young people, determined to struggle for a better future'.[33]

The shift to multiracialism and the reintroduction of Charterism in student politics that was led by COSAS reached full fruition when AZASO and COSAS collaborated with NUSAS, the white liberal students' union, and the National Education Union of South Africa (NEUSA) on the Education Charter Campaign. Launched in 1985, to correspond with the International Year of Youth, this initiative had been in the works for more than a year previously. When it announced itself in April 1985, the Education Charter Campaign had drafted a list of grievances and demands relating to education in South Africa, which was formed on the model of the Freedom Charter. It was frequently printed under the banner heading, 'The doors of learning and culture shall be opened!',[34] which is a direct quote from the Freedom Charter itself. The Education Charter pledged 'to interlink the struggles in education with the broader struggle for a united, free, democratic and non-racial South Africa'.[35] The language within the Charter itself, of a united and nonracial South Africa, the format of the document and its heading, and, perhaps most visibly, the united front presented by multi-racial groups like AZASO, COSAS, and NUSAS represented the full conversion of major African student organizations to multi-racial Charterism, and of its ascendancy in student politics.

The development of youth congresses

Youth involvement in the anti-apartheid struggle was growing outside classrooms, as well. The growth of youth congresses catering to non-student youth in the mid-1980s acted as a supplement or counterweight to COSAS' organization in schools. Although in its early years, COSAS had included many non-student youth in its membership, these were

[33] COSAS flyer, 'COSAS Support Students' Demands Solidarity', c. August 1984 [HPRA AD1790].
[34] 'The Doors of Learning and Culture Shall be Opened', Education Charter Campaign pamphlet, 1985 [HPRA A2635/A].
[35] Education Charter, April 1985 [HPRA A2635/A].

mostly former students who had finished school, but had not yet moved into other formal structures for activism like civics, unions, or the armed struggle. According to Seekings, 'The history of COSAS thus straddles the period [1979–82] in which the category of youth was reconstructed to embrace former student activists.'[36] As Seekings suggests, and as I argued in my introduction to this chapter, the categories of youth and students fluctuated and sometimes overlapped to accommodate various political actors. For instance, COSAS' early leadership was drawn from a cohort that, though they associated themselves with school networks, were no longer enrolled students. But by 1984 COSAS had reoriented itself around school-specific issues, and it no longer provided as relevant a space for the concerns of non-student youth. To fill this gap, local youth congresses began to arise around the country.

Chisholm dates the national rise of youth congresses to 1982, growing out of a base of unemployed youth in urban areas.[37] In Cape Town, Durban, and Johannesburg these structures grew in tandem with COSAS and the student movement in schools. But in the rural Northern Transvaal, youth congresses were slower to take hold. Lekgoathi has argued that, in Lebowa, they emerged first in the urban or peri-urban pockets of the Bantustan (particularly Seshego and Mankweng) before expanding to rural areas.[38] Schools provided a natural centre for organization, and, as has been noted, students shared a set of concerns that facilitated their politicization. Local unemployed youth were less organized as a group and were not typically engaged in the social and criminal groupings that gangs provided their urban counterparts. COSAS had already established itself as a national and local fixture in schools when, in rural Sekhukhuneland students inspired by COSAS' organization and rhetoric took the struggle out of their schools and formed village-based youth groups.

The first of these, the Sekhukhune Youth Committee, which later changed its name to the Sekhukhune Youth Organization (SEYO), was formed in late 1984 or early 1985 in the neighbouring villages of Apel and GaNkoane. The group, led by local students but open to all village youth, took inspiration from COSAS in nearby schools and from AZASO at the University of the North, where some local activists

---

[36] Seekings, *Heroes or Villains*, p. 31.

[37] L. Chisholm, 'From a revolt to a search for alternatives', *Work in* Progress, 42 (1986), 14–19 (17).

[38] Lekgoathi, 'The United Democractic Front in Lebowa and KwaNdebele', p. 623.

had family enrolled as students.[39] For its part, the Turfloop branch of AZASO actively worked to build the capacity and political consciousness of such local youth groups. Mpho Nchabeleng, a Turfloop student and AZASO member, recalls that it was an explicit policy of AZASO to try to mobilize students in schools and training colleges.[40] To do so, they engaged with the structures in schools where COSAS had laid the foundation for political mobilization; Richard Sekonya, another SEYO founding member, was initially politicized through the SRC in his secondary school, Tompi Seleka College of Agriculture.[41] SEYO quickly transcended the impact of local branches of COSAS and other student formations, though, and brought together students from various schools together with non-student youth. As one activist described, 'When SEYO came then COSAS activity died. Because SEYO was our own organization. People now pursued the same issues in SEYO, and it were [sic] mostly the same people who were involved.'[42]

The new youth group was centred in Apel on the Nchabeleng household. Patriarch Peter Nchabeleng was a former political prisoner on Robben Island and the UDF's regional president in the Northern Transvaal at the time. He had been banned to the remote village in 1972, and the banning order was renewed after he was tried and released as one of the 'Pretoria 12' in the trial of the *State* v. *Sexwale* in 1977.[43] Richard Sekonya, one of SEYO's founders, remembers Peter Nchabeleng's role in guiding the organization:

> He was a well-known political figure at the time. He had been in prison for a number of years. Then we decided, there is this old man – let's go and see, probably he will give us a very good guide on what it is that we can do to establish youth formation, people that we can contact. [...] We then started knowing the old man, he guided us. We then established the Youth Formation of SEYO here at home.[44]

Most of Nchabeleng's sons also became involved in political organization; Luthuli, the eldest, left the country for military training with

---

[39] van Kessel, *Beyond Our Wildest* Dreams, pp. 102–3; author's interviews with Maurice Nchabeleng, Polokwane, 13 October 2011(a) and 6 September 2012(b), and Mpho Nchabeleng, Pretoria, 22 October 2011.

[40] Author's interview with Mpho Nchabeleng (a).

[41] Author's interview with Richard Sekonya, Apel, Sekhukhuneland, 18 November 2011.

[42] Quoted in van Kessel, *Beyond Our Wildest Dreams*, p. 104.

[43] *State* v. *Sexwale*, Statement of Petrus Mampogoane Nchabeleng, Accused No. 8 – Detained 2 January 1977, p. 1 [GPP]; 'Nchabeleng combatant and patriot', 'SASPU Nation', April/May 1986 [GPP].

[44] Author's interview with Richard Sekonya.

Umkhonto we Sizwe, while Elleck, the second son, recruited for the ANC and spent six years on Robben Island. After his release Elleck settled in Johannesburg and worked for the Community Resource Information Centre (CRIC). The younger sons participated in student politics locally: Mpho, a law student at the University of the North became an active member of AZASO on campus and worked to mobilize Sekhukhune youth through that organization, while his younger brother Maurice (along with Sekonya, quoted above) became a founding member of the Sekhukhune Youth Committee in Apel.[45]

Maurice Nchabeleng was a student at Magong High School when the Sekhukhune Youth Committee was formed around 1984. He had been politicized at home, part of a family of activists, but found that owing to the activities of COSAS-affiliated SRCs in schools many of his fellow students, both at Magong and at his previous school, Madithame High School, were also politically aware and that many were receptive to the idea of a political youth formation. This climate influenced the success of the nascent youth committee. After COSAS was banned in August 1985 the Sekhukhune Youth Committee became the most significant youth organization in the region. As Ineke van Kessel has argued, in the Northern Transvaal youth organization preceded other forms of political activism during the 1980s; every village that had a civic organization already had a youth congress first.[46] In 1986 the Sekhukhune Youth Committee changed its name to the Sekhukhune Youth Organisation (SEYO), in line with other UDF-affiliated youth congresses around the country, like the similarly named SOYO (Soweto Youth Organisation). One of the features of the new youth group that contrasted the structures of student organizations before it was the crosscutting nature of its membership and leadership. As Maurice Nchabeleng describes the make-up of the group, '[I]t was mostly constituted of students, of course with unemployed people. But students were coming from high schools and from the University of the North. [...] And those [university students] were the people who had been also to give political education.'[47] SEYO drew its members from a variety of local schools and training colleges, as well as support from Turfloop students, who, as both Maurice and Mpho, above, note, were instrumental in the political education of younger, and particularly non-student, youth.

SEYO made conscious efforts to unite the youth of Apel and neighbouring GaNkoane. The two villages had been involved in historic land

[45] Author's interviews with Maurice Nchabeleng (a) and Mpho Nchabeleng.
[46] van Kessel, *Beyond Our Wildest Dreams*, p. 98.
[47] Author's interview with Maurice Nchabeleng (a).

disputes, which led to factionalized fighting. These disputes originated in conflict over land rights between the two villages: the people of Apel claimed that, as the first settlers in the area they had primary rights to local land and that the people of GaNkoane were encroaching on this space. This mirrors patterns of access to and conflict over land, based on longevity of tenure, that Delius has noted across Sekhukhuneland.[48] Apel existed as a village in the early twentieth century, while GaNkoane was likely part of a rapid expansion of betterment villages and settlements set up by the South African Native Trust in the 1950s and 1960s. The people of GaNkoane, however, 'maintained that the original settlers [of Apel] did not establish themselves in the present village of Apel', thus invalidating their claim to land rights based on longevity.[49] The dispute was contested both in court and in physical conflict over decades in the middle of the twentieth century. 'In the 1970s, Peter Nchabeleng's father was killed in one such armed invasion from GaNkoane.'[50] But by the mid-1980s the youth of the area were keen to overcome this historic dispute. As Maurice Nchabeleng describes it:

> [A]s youth, we decided to say 'to neutralize this faction fight, we need to form one organization that encompasses the two villages'. We then established a branch called Apel-GaNkoane Branch of SEYO.[51]

Richard Sekonya, an early SEYO leader from GaNkoane, concurs with this description of local youth overcoming old grievances:

> [...] GaNkoane and Apel [...] belong to two different tribal authorities, but we [the founders of SEYO] decided that it was time that we should actually cross the tribal barriers and mobilize all young people around the area.[52]

SEYO's emphasis on overcoming the 'tribal barriers' of their parents' and grandparents' generations is noteworthy. The UDF leadership in the Northern Transvaal had encouraged organizations to work across ethnic lines. In some areas of the region, particularly in the east where Lebowa and Gazankulu territories were in close proximity, this was a real concern.[53] But both Apel and GaNkoane were BaPedi villages, and had no

---

[48] Delius, *A Lion Amongst the Cattle*, pp. 144–5.
[49] van Kessel, *Beyond Our Wildest Dreams*, p. 124.
[50] Ibid., p.124.
[51] Author's interview with Maurice Nchabeleng (a).
[52] Author's interview with Richard Sekonya.
[53] Gazankulu, in particular, had seen an influx of Mozambican refugees from that country's civil war between FRELIMO and RENAMO, beginning in the early 1980s. By 1987 there were an estimated 30,000 Mozambican refugees

close proximity to other ethnic groups; Sekonya's use of the term 'tribal' indicates something other than ethnic difference between the two. Each fell under the jurisdiction of a different chief, and it is this authority that the youth of Apel–GaNkoane identified as the root of the old conflict. In an adaptation of UDF policy, they decided to 'cross the tribal barriers' that separated them; though these were not ethnic disputes, it was recognized that they could easily distract from the business of fighting apartheid and the Bantustan system.

SEYO's early membership comprised students from both Apel and GaNkoane. They were also predominantly boys and young men. This was less a distinct shift than an exacerbation of the male domination that existed in the ranks of student organization. Educational organizations like COSAS and AZASO provided a forum for young women to participate, though broadly leadership was dominated by men. Recent work by Emily Bridger on young women's political activism in Soweto during the 1980s has highlighted the critical role that COSAS played as an entry-point to politics for these activists.[54] In contrast youth congresses, which existed outside the networks of education, had much less female representation. In SEYO, one of the only female members, Sauwe Maditsi, became involved through her interest in politics developed at Madithame High School where she was a member of the SRC: 'And it was so strange, because you find yourself the only woman among men. [...] When we started I was the only woman within the group, and then later on I also recruited my friend and then she joined.' But these young women remained notable exceptions in a realm of youth politics dominated by their male counterparts. Part of this gender bias can be explained by significant social pressure on young girls in rural Sekhukhuneland. Maditsi noted that her involvement in politics caused concern among her family and the community as a whole, particularly over her gender:

---

in Gazankulu. These refugees, ethnically similar to the Tsonga/Shangaan of Gazankulu, sometimes experienced attacks from local South Africans, though these were likely due to increased competition for scarce resources as opposed to ethnically motivated tensions [Susan Pleming, 'SA sends back thousands of war refugees', *The Star*, 9 December 1986; and 'Mozambican refugees get "identity cards"', *Weekly Mail*, 20–26 February 1987]. In fact there were many efforts by locals to aid the refugees in Gazankulu, in spite of competition for work and resources [Peter Goldsmid, 'Those who have so little welcome those with nothing', *Weekly Mail*, 20–26 February 1987] [SAHA ANCYL AL2451].

[54] E. Bridger, 'South Africa's Female Comrades: Gender, identity, and student resistance to Apartheid in Soweto, 1984–1994' (unpublished PhD thesis, University of Exeter, 2016).

[My family] also used to fight with me in terms of attending meetings. By then it was not easy to host the meeting during the day; we have to do it at night and I'm a woman, and I have to get out of the house at night, you see? [...] It was [difficult] because as I'm telling you – especially in terms of our culture, you also have to cook, and fetch wood, and fetch water. And you also have the other commitments. [...] And if you aligned yourself with men, the community will think of you somehow –not necessarily that you want to achieve a certain goal, they will think that you are having relationship with more than five men, because you are the only woman within that group.[55]

In spite of the pressures she faced to stay out of politics, Maditsi recalls being invigorated by the discussion-oriented format of SEYO meetings, which were often held at the Nchabeleng household. The father, Peter, and older brother, Elleck, provided ideological direction for these discussions. According to Maurice,

So [Elleck] used to come [from the Community Resource Information Centre] with material, reading material and the Freedom Charter. [...] so we will have somebody coming from Johannesburg, or coming from the same organization to come and take us through the Charter, so that we understand what are we doing, the demands that were on the Freedom Charter.[56]

This adherence to and study of the Freedom Charter as a document locates SEYO firmly in the Charterist political camp, in a more profound than nominal way. Acquaintance with the contents of the Charter itself was at the fore of SEYO's politicization methods. Richard Sekonya describes the focus on the Charter itself, and its relationship to other political tracts:

[Elleck] would give us the literature, we would read this literature. And from our readings we would organize workshops, saying this person would talk about the Freedom Charter – what the Freedom Charter says – this person would read... you know from very foundation politics up to hardcore Marxist literature. [...] But the ones that link [SEYO to the urban areas of the Rand] – you see people like Elleck would get the literature and bring it here at home.[57]

1985 had marked the thirtieth anniversary of the Freedom Charter, and that year brought a push from within the ranks of the ANC and UDF affiliates to commemorate the signing and reinforce the continued

---

[55] Author's interview with Sauwe Maditsi, Polokwane, 18 April 2012.
[56] Author's interview with Maurice Nchabeleng (a).
[57] Author's interview with Richard Sekonya.

relevance of the document. Raymond Suttner and Jeremy Cronin published an edited volume with chapters on all aspects of the Charter and its importance for South Africans in the mid-1980s.[58] This text was designed to guide the sort of conversations groups like SEYO were having. It addressed issues ranging from education and gender to land and workers. As Maurice Nchabeleng and Richard Sekonya describe above, SEYO members would discuss the contents of the Freedom Charter, and its implications for understanding political theories like Marxism. In this way SEYO sought to establish a strong political ideology within its ranks. They would often be led in their discussions by Elleck Nchabeleng or another activist who had come from Johannesburg, and often from the Community Resource Information Centre (CRIC).

CRIC, which had been founded by white activists from NUSAS, formed an important link between the urban centres of Johannesburg and Pretoria that produced and distributed political literature and the rural villages of the Northern Transvaal. As Sekonya notes, '[T]hrough organizational efforts like CRIC I think that's where [SEYO] found [...] that linkage.'[59] Using go-betweens like Elleck Nchabeleng and on-the-ground youth groups like SEYO, CRIC disseminated ANC/Charterist literature across large rural areas. It became an important centre for student activists to access organizational and political materials, and attracted prominent activists. Deacon Mathe, who went on to play an important role in the development of the South African Youth Congress (SAYCO), which is discussed in Chapter 6, was one of Elleck's colleagues at CRIC.[60] They worked with COSAS in schools, as well. Mpho Nchabeleng recalls that CRIC partnered with Ephraim Mogale, the first president of COSAS and, by this time, a high-profile student leader:

> [CRIC] started to interact with the youth movement of the organizations in Moutse District, which already had powerful people who were involved, like Ephraim Mogale and Jabu Mahlapo. They spent almost all their time there.[61]

In addition, CRIC helped to fund SEYO's outreach to other schools and villages, fostering the growth of youth congresses across Sekhukhuneland. Members worked through personal networks and through schools, particularly SRCs, to create interest in forming new groups.

---

[58] R. Suttner and J. Cronin, *30 Years of the Freedom Charter* (Johannesburg, 1985).
[59] Author's interview with Richard Sekonya.
[60] Ibid.
[61] Author's interview with Mpho Nchabeleng (a).

We would actually have planning meetings and say, 'Who in the next village do we know? Who are the most relevant guys we can start speaking
to on an interim basis?' [...] and you know we would actually sit with
them so they would bring other guys that might be of importance. Picking
various SRCs from various high schools; I think that's how we identified
our target guys.[62]

As well as SEYO's links to groups like CRIC, and branches of COSAS,
the organization maintained links to the branch of AZASO at the University of the North, where Mpho Nchabeleng was a member. Turfloop's
branch of AZASO was heavily involved in outreach throughout the
region, connecting with other student and youth groups.

That was actually AZASO's strategy at that time, to go to high schools, to
mobilize high schools and even training colleges. [...] So we just became
part of it, and with us we were concentrating on our area, with mobilizing youth around Sekhukhuneland, because we held these side meetings
[...] to concentrate on Sekhukhuneland youth. Youth generally – whether
students or youth, we concentrated on them.[63]

Following such concerted efforts at politicization throughout the villages and towns of the Northern Transvaal, groups like SEYO quickly
multiplied, and by 1986 youth congresses were a common feature in
villages throughout Sekhukhuneland and other parts of the region. They
attracted politically active students who were members of COSAS or
AZASO, or involved in local SRCs. But in an important shift, which
Mpho Nchabeleng alludes to above, they also began to attract non-
student, unemployed youth. Historically these young men had been
alternately neglected by or at odds with their student counterparts who
were involved in the struggle. Clive Glaser has written about the adversarial and sometimes violent relationship that existed between students
and young *tsotsis* on the streets of Soweto in the 1960s and 1970s. The
middle of the 1980s marked a shift in the adversarial nature of the relationship between students and youth: in urban areas Franziska Rueedi
has written about the recruitment of a new cohort of unemployed youth
during and after the Vaal Triangle uprising of 1984, and that strategies
of violence in the townships of the Vaal emerged from the intersection of
local conflicts and broader ideologies.[64] As I have argued here, the rise of

---

[62] Author's interview with Richard Sekonya.
[63] Author's interview with Mpho Nchabeleng.
[64] F. Rueedi, 'Political Mobilisation, Violence and Control in the Townships of the
Vaal Triangle, South Africa, c.1976–1986' (University of Oxford, DPhil, 2013);
'Siyayinyova! Patterns of violence in the African townships of the Vaal Triangle,
South Africa, 1980–86', *Africa*, 85(3) (2015), 395–416.

groups like the Sekhukhune Youth Organization also changed that relationship in the villages where it had branches and brought unemployed youth into the fold of student politics.

Violence

Violence came to be a key characteristic in political expression for youth during the 1980s. From the campus of Turfloop to rural villages throughout the Northern Transvaal, heightened aggression and physical confrontation were frequent occurrences. In the comrade movement that swept rural villages from Sekhukhuneland to Venda, young men used violence to enforce new social parameters within their communities, policing domestic relationships, schools, and eradicating accused witches. As I will explore in a subsequent section, at Turfloop violence between students and staff in confrontations with the army (which was garrisoned on campus), and even between rival political groups, sent many people to hospital, and even left some students dead. In part this reflects the ungovernability that was sweeping South Africa in the mid-1980s; violent techniques used in witch-hunts in the Northern Transvaal reflected the tactics that comrades in the townships used to deal with state informers and collaborators. The importation of the violent necklacing technique, whereby a tyre doused in petrol was put around the shoulders of an accused witch and set alight, was borrowed from townships where it had been used on suspected state informants.

Youth congresses also struggled to create ideological diffusion through their ranks, and consequently had to grapple with the use of generally uncontrolled violence as a form of political expression. Though these groups were affiliates of the UDF, and associated themselves with the ANC, the national organizations failed to exert control over the local youth congresses; this became especially evident during the witch-hunts of the late 1980s.

The turn to violent revolt marked a change in the way that youth were confronting state repression – a similar though more dramatic shift towards confrontation than the 1974 Viva-FRELIMO rallies – but also in the way they were confronting other social structures and the world around them. As noted above, in the Northern Transvaal it drew on techniques and methods from the urban areas of the Rand, where the 1984 Township Revolt, sparked in the Vaal Triangle, had catapulted violent resistance to the fore of a rent boycott. In her study about the rhetoric around contemporary violence on the Rand, Monique Marks has pinpointed, among other justifications, that youth believed that the root of the violence they used 'lay in the direct and structural violence of the apartheid state' and that youth, as defenders of their communities 'should be involved in public acts of violence'; they also 'perceived themselves as having responded in the mid-eighties to the call of the ANC in taking up armed struggle as a strategy for change'.[65] This call was the summons to ungovernability, which had become the watchword of youth activism after the ANC in exile called for the country to be made 'ungovernable'.[66]

In 1984 and 1985, Oliver Tambo, the exiled president of the ANC, who was based in Lusaka, Zambia, made calls on the party's Radio Freedom network for the youth inside the country to make South Africa ungovernable. This was echoed in the UDF's platform for 1986: 'From governability to ungovernability'.[67] Young people throughout the country enthusiastically pursued their own understandings of that strategy. The appeal of inverting existing power structures – both political and generational – and the release of embracing a type of chaos in the face of strict legal and, in rural areas, social constraints may help explain the appeal of ungovernability for young comrades. In this section I will analyze the ways in which ungovernability manifested itself in several villages in the Northern Transvaal – through witch-hunts and generational inversions of power – and will consider issues of violence and its inverse relationship to ideology, the appeal of ungovernability, and the creation of moral communities.

Comrades and witch-hunts

In spite of strides made by COSAS and later youth congresses, the inclusion of non-student youths in congresses that had essentially risen out of student politics was not a smooth process. There were often struggles within the congresses over ideology and appropriate forms of political expression, and generational divides were emerging among activists. By early 1986 the youth of Sekhukhuneland were articulating generational grievances that put them in opposition to chiefs, parents, and village elders, and no longer just the apartheid state. By February 1986 this discontent had erupted into the Sekhukhune Youth Revolt.

---

[65] M. Marks, '"We are fighting for the liberation of our people": Justifications of youth violence by activist youth in Diepkloof, Soweto', *Temps Modernes*, 585 (1995), 133–58 (134).

[66] 'Make South Africa Ungovernable', Broadcast on Radio Freedom by O.R. Tambo, 10 October 1984 [http://www.anc.org.za/show.php?id=4457] and 'Address by Oliver Tambo to the Nation on Radio Freedom', 22 July 1985 [http://www.anc.org.za/show.php?id=4470] Accessed 6 September 2013.

[67] van Kessel, *Beyond Our Wildest Dreams*, p. 118.

As youth across South Africa answered calls for ungovernability with violence, and 'liberated zones' were established in some townships, the situation grew increasingly tense, and parts of the country fell under a state of emergency imposed in July 1985. In rural Sekhukhune, the nascent SEYO began to recruit all local youth into membership. Parents alleged that their tactics involved cooptation and forced recruitment. 'In 1986, the youth invaded our houses to take our children. They said all children must come; they were forced.'[68] Isak Niehaus has described similar coercion by the comrades of Bushbuckridge, nearly 200 kilometres to the east of Sekhukhuneland. One of his informants, Henry Mohale, 'claimed that marshals regularly forced youths to attend political meetings at night. Before adjourning, the marshals whipped all "non-liberated" boys who did not come to the meetings voluntarily [...].'[69] Such tactics were just one facet of a larger blurring between politics and crime. According to Ineke van Kessel, in Sekhukhuneland

> shops were raided, cars hijacked, and money extorted in the name of the 'struggle'. Since all youth were considered members of the youth movement it could be difficult for the politically motivated comrades to disassociate themselves from the thugs.[70]

This dichotomy between activist and thug is at the heart of the struggle to define what exactly SEYO was. Van Kessel's statement suggests these categories were distinct (if not easily distinguished by outsiders): the student political activists were adhering to a UDF-led agenda, while the youth thugs brought criminal elements into the movement. But these categories could be and often were entangled. Political leader Maurice Nchabeleng also chaired a meeting to determine why a young activist had been struck and killed by lightning, an event frequently attributed to witchcraft and which usually received swift and violent retribution.[71] And violence and coercion were used by 'thugs' in the name of the struggle, as Van Kessel notes. As I will argue in this section, anti-apartheid politics provided motivation and justification for youth comrades to undertake unusual and unsanctioned activities, sometimes outside an overtly political scope. Though young activists interpreted their actions as political, often the broader community did not, and sometimes even SEYO's leadership struggled to exert control over its members. This

---

[68] M.W. Makgaleng, quoted in van Kessel, *Beyond Our Wildest Dreams*, p. 119.

[69] Niehaus, *Witchcraft and a Life*, p. 66. This treatment and other violent confrontations with the ANC-aligned Charterist comrades eventually prompted Henry to join the rival Pan Africanist Congress.

[70] van Kessel, *Beyond Our Wildest Dreams*, p. 122.

[71] Ibid., p. 126.

tension – over what was appropriately political and what was not – is one of the core issues addressed in this section.

At its heart SEYO was an ideological movement, but it struggled to create deep ideological diffusion throughout its ranks, in spite of the political education that was organized through the networks cascading out from activist households and despite its relationship with CRIC. SEYO's ideology was shaped by local beliefs as well as the political doctrine of the Freedom Charter and the UDF. Its activists were primarily concerned about the struggle against the apartheid system, but within that struggle they articulated grievances against their parents' politically 'timid' generation, and the existence of what they perceived as evil within their communities, typically expressed in the form of witches.

For a period of two months in 1986, the youth of Sekhukhuneland asserted themselves in opposition to the authority of their parents' generation, articulating a range of grievances, some of which fell outside the political agenda of the UDF. They protested against traditional rites of initiation, favouring, as van Kessel has argued, the groupings of their own age sets through the youth movement.[72] This recalls the shared generational consciousness that Bundy argued characterized young people in the townships of the Cape Flats, and which I contend linked student and youth activists across the Northern Transvaal. The youth of Sekhukhuneland also appropriated social and communal functions previously organized by more senior members of the community – particularly chiefs or heads of households. Among these, 'people's courts' – often mass meetings led by a core group of youth – were set up to arbitrate in domestic and communal disputes in order to 're-establish harmony and to effect reconciliation'.[73] This they typically accomplished at the end of a *sjambok* (whip). In Bushbuckridge, Niehaus has even described three youth comrades taking over a local high school, usurping the function of the principal, suspending school rules, and disciplining teachers: 'Comrades whipped one teacher who had sexual relations with a married student, and they left him for dead.'[74]

Yet in addition to this intergenerational conflict, the Sekhukhune Youth Revolt and comrade movements in other parts of the Northern Transvaal did succeed in making large parts of the region ungovernable by the South African state, and by the Bantustans of Lebowa, Venda, and Gazankulu. The young comrades employed the language of political liberation, even within their efforts at social restructuring. In an

---

[72] van Kessel, *Beyond Our Wildest Dreams*, pp. 107–8.
[73] SEYO activists, quoted in ibid., p. 143.
[74] Niehaus, *Witchcraft and a Life*, p. 64.

interview in 1986 Peter Mokaba, who had helped establish the AZASO branch at Turfloop and was now a prominent regional youth leader and member of the UDF's Northern Transvaal executive, said,

> We intend removing tribal chiefs as soon as possible. We have called on them to resign. Our ultimate intention is to allow the people to govern themselves. We have already established people's courts in some areas and are in the process of forming our own militia which will carry out the orders of the courts.[75]

Mokaba's position as a high-profile youth activist involved in the UDF, and his invocation of a language of self-governance by the people, both tie the liberation struggle to the generational upheaval that parts of Sekhukhuneland were experiencing. The struggle against the chiefs and the struggle against the state became intertwined in youth rhetoric, and in this they were at least partially supported by UDF policy: chiefs and tribal authorities were often 'equated with Bantustan structures', and the National Working Committee of the UDF resolved in 1986 that they 'should be replaced with democratic organizations'.[76] The youth were successful, at least temporarily, in displacing the old authorities. Apel and GaNkoane, the centre of SEYO activity and once heavily policed by both Lebowan and South African police, became no-go areas for law enforcement during the revolt.

But in early April 1986 the uprising came to an end, after a rash of witch-killings over the course of one week. In Apel and GaNkoane alone, thirty-two people were burned alive.[77] Usurping traditional mechanisms of arbitration, the youth dispensed with consulting *dingaka*[78] about witches' guilt, and instead adopted a sort of mob justice to purge the villages of Sekhukhune of the perceived evil. They used the necklacing method, which had been adopted from the urban township revolts where it was a common tactic for punishing suspected *impimpis*, informers or collaborators with the apartheid state. There was sometimes confla-tion between these political accusations (which were rarely specific) and

[75] *Sunday Times*, 11 May 1986, quoted in van Kessel, *Beyond Our Wildest Dreams*, p. 116.
[76] van Kessel, *Beyond Our Wildest Dreams*, p. 80.
[77] Ibid; Niehaus, *Witchcraft, Power, and Politics*; author's interview with Maurice Nchabeleng (a).
[78] *Dingaka* is the plural of *ngaka*, the BaPedi/Northern SeSotho word for a diviner or 'witch doctor', a person who employs techniques like bone throwing and 'medicine' to identify witches and performs other social functions in mediating the unknown realm in which witches are perceived to exist. It is analogous to the Zulu *sangoma*, and the TshiVenda *vhangome*.

the more traditional activities of witches (which were much more often specific): bewitching people and enchanting zombies for economic gain and prosperity, for example. In Venda, suspected witches were often accused of selling traditional medicine, or *muthi*, as a form of protection to members of the homeland government.

Van Kessel has argued that in Sekhukhuneland witch-hunting represented an attempt to 'construct a new moral community' and to supplant the failures of traditional structures and older generations. Though the youth may have perceived their innovations as building a new moral community, their legitimacy did not extend beyond the group itself. I contend the new moral community was a hybrid of principles gleaned from the liberation struggle and local systems of belief, but that it gained the broad legitimacy of neither. As with the people's courts and coerced political activism, which parents and elders saw as a usurping of social power, the youth were overlaying their social activism with political justifications. The new 'moral community' of youth prized education and activism over age and status, but it also remained deeply concerned about the power of evil within communities. Similar attacks spread throughout the Northern Transvaal, to Gazankulu and Venda, as well as to other parts of Lebowa.[79]

Just after the killings in Sekhukhuneland, in April and May 1986 similar purges began to take hold of the villages around Bushbuckridge. Young comrades, led by the Brooklyn Youth Organisation, 'attacked more than 150 suspected witches in Mapulaneng [a district of the Bushbuckridge area near the Lebowa–Gazankulu border] killing at least 36'.[80] Niehaus has noted that in the majority of these cases, though young men did the actual witch-hunting, adults had often made the accusations beforehand. Many of the targeted victims of the hunts had previously been accused or suspected of being witches. In one case, one of those executed had previously been accused at the local chief's *kgoro* (court) of bewitching children, but had been acquitted. The retrial, of sorts, of such previous accusations is another example of young comrades usurping the social function of village elders. It also echoes youth frustrations with older generations' failure to combat evil in their midst: this associated and sometimes conflated their inability to excise witches from their communities with their cooperation with or impotence in the face of apartheid repression. Interestingly, Niehaus points out that this

---

[79] N.V. Ralushai *et al.*, *Report of the Commission of Inquiry into Witchcraft Violence and Ritual Murders in the Northern Province of South Africa* (Pretoria, 1996).

[80] Niehaus, *Witchcraft, Power and Politics*, p. 149.

power may not have been taken from adults entirely unwillingly: 'By delegating this responsibility [of witch hunting] to youth, adults could sustain anonymity and preserve their moral integrity.'[81] But for youths in Bushbuckridge, as for the comrades of Sekhukhuneland who ran people's courts, appropriating these social functions actually enhanced their own legitimacy as arbiters and enforcers of moral good in their communities, at least in their own self-perception.

In Venda, in the far north-east of the Northern Transvaal, witch-hunts began later – around 1990 – but they followed remarkably similar patterns to what had happened in Sekhukhuneland and Bushbuckridge. Young comrades who identified themselves with the liberation struggle and the ANC through the vehicle of local youth congresses had undertaken to purge their communities of witches, and in February 1990 the villages of Venda experienced attacks very much like those four years earlier in Apel–GaNkoane, Sekhukhuneland, and Mapulaneng, Bushbuckridge. Large groups of villagers were led predominantly by young men; in one trial of thirteen defendants, who had pursued and attacked three accused witches in the village of Ha-Maduwa, most were in their late teens.[82] They were inspired and mobilized by the change sweeping through South Africa, by the campaign for ungovernability in the townships, and by the liberation movements, to whom they were self-referential, singing freedom songs and often claiming membership of Charterist youth congresses. These youth were moved by generational power shifts, and by the legal and social marginalization of traditional authorities (both chiefs and *vhangome* or diviners).

Witch-beliefs were a dynamic and mutable, if violent and divisive, analysis of local authority and expression of political mobilization.[83] The Venda witch-hunts represented a melding of old and new similar to those experienced in other parts of the Northern Transvaal; they arose from the culmination of increasing social and political pressure in South Africa at a particular moment in the last years of apartheid.[84] They articulated disaffection with traditional authorities, particularly concern over corruption among chiefs, and concern over the local economic situation, which was a failing agricultural economy with a youth bulge (due to rapid increases in population over the previous two decades and the increasing restrictions on recruitment for mining and industrial work).

---

[81] Niehaus, *Witchcraft, Power and Politics*, p. 149.
[82] A. Heffernan, 'The Ralushai Commission and a South African Witch-hunt in Legal and Historical Perspective' (University of Oxford, MSc, 2008), p. 31.
[83] Ibid., pp. 33–4.
[84] Ibid.

Unemployment escalated at this period. Moreover, the chronological proximity to Nelson Mandela's release from prison recalled the political change marking all aspects of contemporary South African life, and the use of necklacing associated the comrades with those taking part in township revolts and their 'witch' victims with *impimpi* collaborators. By articulating such contemporary issues through a rhetoric of witch-finding, the young comrades of Venda demonstrated their own version of radical politics and their own search for a new moral order.

The witchcraft accusations in Venda during the early 1990s marked a distinct departure from the traditional use of diviners, *dingaka* and *vhangome*, to adjudicate on matters of witchcraft. These practices had become constrained by restrictive witchcraft laws and their enforcement by the middle of the twentieth century. But they were also predicated on trust in the structures of chiefly rule by the people, which had been deeply damaged – in the eyes of the youth, at least – by association with the homeland government. Delius and Lekgoathi point to similar erosion of trust in chiefs over the first half of the twentieth century in other areas of the Northern Transvaal: Sekhukhuneland and Zebediela, respectively.[85]

In an application for amnesty to the Truth and Reconciliation Commission Samuel Magoro, one of the perpetrators of a fatally violent witch-hunt in Ha-Maduwa village in Venda, drew a direct line between witchcraft and the Venda homeland government: 'those witches take medicine and give it to the people in the highest office in the [Venda] government so that they could remain intact, their place, and then they cannot be removed'.[86] He further complained that structures of the chieftaincy were collaborating with the government and preventing 'the people' (led by the Maduwa Youth Congress) from addressing the problem presented by witches. Similarly, in her own amnesty hearing, Mmabatho Mulaudzi, a youth activist from the nearby village of Shinga, accused the Venda government of committing ritual murder:

> Because something had to be done with that government, I started engaging myself in a campaign to explain to the youth about the situation at the time, [...] I indicated to them as to how the then government was oppressing us, the manner in which they were engaged in ritual killings, nepotism,

---

[85] Delius, *A Lion Amongst the Cattle*, pp. 71–2, 115–17, 218; Lekgoathi, 'The United Democratic Front in Lebowa and KwaNdebele', p. 631.

[86] Truth and Reconciliation Commission Amnesty Hearings, Mutshutshu Samuel Magoro, Thohoyandou, 10 May 2000, Case AM2714/96 [SAHA SABC TRC].

killings of the comrades who were in support of politics and also the perpetual detention of those who used to give us political advise [sic].[87]

Magoro and Mulaudzi both associate the homeland government with the use of forms of *vhuloi* – *muthi* and ritual murder – but they also, as Mulaudzi's statement makes clear, associated these transgressions with the very specific political circumstances of the time. In the perception of youth activists, the government used witchcraft to oppress political expression in intangible ways.

But while some youth in the Northern Transvaal were fashioning a 'new moral community' and reshaping traditional practices, the organizations to which they publicly associated themselves were scrambling to address this perceived atavistic embarrassment. Both the UDF and ANC structures in the province spoke out against the witch killings as un-modern, and as unacceptable in relation to the political struggle. During the Sekhukhune Youth Revolt of 1986 Peter Nchabeleng held a meeting with SEYO youth to try to convince them to stop attacking accused witches. Richard Sekonya, a leading member of SEYO at the time, described the struggle of the leadership to control these elements within the youth groups. He alleged that the police were linking the witch burning to the comrades of SEYO:

> But you see what the police at the time did was try to link the political struggle with this isolated incident of witch-burning. As a result they harassed everybody, they arrested local people, they tried to link this burning of people with the organization at the time. And we totally rejected that, because it wasn't anything that was discussed at the formal meetings of the youth formation at the time. I think after it went loose we called communities, we said no, no, no – this is not a programme of the ANC. This has nothing to do with the ANC.[88]

Though Sekonya acknowledged that the violence was perpetrated by members of SEYO (whom he described as 'certain quarters of young men'), he was also at pains to note that it was not sanctioned by the leadership of the group. In fact the SEYO leadership struggled, and largely failed, to quash the streak of witch-hunting in their midst – although it abated in particular locations after reaching a crescendo.

In Venda as well, formal political structures struggled to control the reactions of the young comrades. Godfried Dederen, an ANC supporter and lecturer at the University of Venda at the time, recalls:

[87] Truth and Reconciliation Commission Amnesty Hearings, Mmabatho Popular Mulaudzi, Thohoyandou, 10 May 2000, Case AM3280/96 [SAHA SABC TRC].
[88] Author's interview with Richard Sekonya.

They [the ANC's armed wing, *Umkhonto we Sizwe*] couldn't stop it. That was terrible, man. A really depressing time, 1990. The one hand, you know it's [liberation is] done – it's just a matter of a few years – and on the other hand now they're really spoiling it completely, tarnishing the whole liberation thing by burning [witches].[89]

In the cases of Venda, Bushbuckridge, and Sekhukhuneland, the outbreaks of witch-hunting stopped when the police and army cracked down and reasserted control over the areas. In Sekhukhuneland, where the youth had achieved some degree of success in establishing 'liberated zones' this was a major political setback. The security police arrested much of the SEYO leadership: Peter Nchabeleng was taken on the night of 11 April 1986. He died in police custody twelve hours later in the Schoonoord Police Station, having been severely beaten. The police interventions also ended the reign of youth in Sekhukhuneland and SEYO as an organization. The leadership who had avoided arrest fled into hiding in the nearby mountains and even on campus at Turfloop.[90] Maurice Nchabeleng and SEYO's vice chair, Silas Mabotha, were eventually arrested at Turfloop in June 1986.

The sweeping arrests and crackdowns accomplished what neither Nchabeleng and the UDF leadership, nor the ANC and MK, had been able to do: by and large witch killings in the Sekhukhuneland area subsided, though of course witch-beliefs persisted and the pattern of killings erupted a few years later in Venda. Niehaus has argued that witchcraft beliefs are rooted in the poverty, marginality, and insecurity of life in rural South Africa.[91] They are also most often articulated in local, personal situations. Witchcraft is a phenomenon rooted in the complex maze of human relationships, and the crimes that witches are accused of committing are most often crimes of familiarity; accused witches and their victims are rarely strangers – they are family, friends, and neighbours. As such, it is a phenomenon that has most currency in the social networks of tightly knit communities. Ashforth argues persuasively that these communities need not be rural, though this has typically been a bias in the literature on witchcraft,[92] but whether in Soweto or Sekhukhuneland, accusations of witchcraft almost always arise in the context of local, personal relationships and communal stress. This, perhaps, is one reason that it found political currency in villages at the same time

---

[89] Author's interview with Godfried Dederen, Thohoyandou, 4 September 2012.
[90] van Kessel, *Beyond Our Wildest Dreams*, p. 129.
[91] Niehaus, 'Witchcraft in the New South Africa', p. 193.
[92] Ashforth, *Witchcraft, Violence, and Democracy*, pp. 20–1.

that politics in the Northern Transvaal became more locally rooted and moved beyond institutions like Turfloop.

Factional violence: AZASO v. AZASM, and Turfloop in the 1980s

The violence experienced during the comrade movements in the rural villages of the Transvaal was not isolated. As has been mentioned, in its form and language it sometimes mimicked the violence that was sweeping South Africa's urban townships during the township revolts. It also found a counterpoint nearer to home, on campus at Turfloop where violent confrontations between students and the police, and between differing student groups, were becoming more frequent and more severe. As I argued in Chapter 2, the 1974 Viva-FRELIMO rally on campus marked an important turning point in Turfloop students' confrontation with both their administration and with the security police. Prior protests, though tense, had never resulted in physical violence, and the willingness of the police to use force against protesting students – and of the students to return it by throwing rocks and bottles – brought unprecedented aggression to the relationship between the two groups. A decade later, the situation had changed drastically.

By the mid-1980s Turfloop was under the administration of its second black rector, Professor P.C. Mokgokong. His selection, after the sudden death of Rector William Kgware in 1980, came after an outcry from the student body and black academic staff when it was mooted that the 'controversial [white] rightwing academic registrar' Professor J.C. Steenkamp might take over as rector.[93] In protest at the very suggestion, 'the entire black academic staff threatened to resign' and insisted Kgware be replaced by a new black rector.[94] Mokgokong, a senior member of Kgware's administration, got the post. He inherited a campus in conflict, and faced early challenges with the student body over the detention of two female students in late 1980 and during celebrations of Republic Day in 1981.

On-campus protest had become a hallmark of life at Turfloop, and this continued through the late 1970s and early 1980s, but by 1985 life on campus was coloured by a marked increase in violent forms of expression. Early that August 'a heavy police contingent arrived on campus and conducted a three-hour raid', which resulted in the detention of three students.[95] Within days more raids, arrests, and confiscation of

---

[93] 'Turf Prof to Go', *Sunday Times*, 20 June c. 1982 [HPRA AD1912/258.16].
[94] Ibid.
[95] 'Students flee boycott campus', *Weekly Mail and Guardian*, 27 September 1985 [HPRA AD1912/258.17].

documents followed. '"The whole campus was surrounded by Lebowa police while the SAP [South African Police] and members of the Security Police searched the residences," the SRC said.'[96] One of the raids left one student in hospital, fearing he might lose the sight of one eye; another was injured in a police assault allegedly over a poster of a 'semi-naked white model' in his room, and a third sustained a fractured ankle 'after jumping from his third floor room'.[97] Nine more students were detained. A week after the raids, a student was shot and killed on campus, leading to student protests over the inability of controversial and unwanted security guards to ensure student safety while at the university.[98] Less than two weeks later, five students were charged in court with 'pouring acid over a Law lecturer'.[99]

These events speak to the violence that was becoming ever more commonplace on Turfloop's campus in the mid-1980s, most prominently in confrontations between students and police, but also in interpersonal relationships between students (as with Nash Mogane, the student who was shot) and between students and university staff.

Violence also erupted between on-campus political groups in 1985. In late April the student wing of AZAPO, the Azanian Students' Movement (AZASM), held a meeting at Turfloop to discuss its upcoming national convention. The meeting was interrupted when 'a group of students shouting support for the Freedom Charter marched into the hall' carrying an assortment of weapons and 'a fracas broke out'.[100] In the fray several members of AZASM and AZAPO, including the latter's former president (and former Turfloop student and Black Consciousness activist) Lybon Mabasa, were assaulted and later hospitalized. As Mabasa described the incident:

> Thami [Mcerwa, AZASM's vice-president] and I were caught in the toilets. I saw the students chopping and stabbing him. They knocked Thami unconscious and then came for me. They said I had been confusing a lot of people with the Black Consciousness philosophy and socialism. They beat me up with hammers and stones. I received a knife wound in the arm when I tried to block the attack. They told me to chant 'Mandela'. I refused and they beat me up until I lost consciousness.[101]

---

[96] 'Students flee boycott campus', *Weekly Mail and Guardian*, 27 September 1985 [HPRA AD1912/258.17].
[97] Ibid.
[98] Ibid.
[99] Ibid.
[100] 'Students beat up ex-Azapo leader', Paper unknown, 22 April 1985 [GPP].
[101] Ibid.

The attackers, who were 'shouting support for the Freedom Charter' and sought to make Mabasa chant support for imprisoned ANC leader Nelson Mandela, were members of AZASM's on-campus rival, the Azanian Students' Organisation. As discussed in Chapter 4, AZASO had been AZAPO's original student wing until its ideological split from the parent party in 1980. Conflicts between members of AZASM and AZASO were increasingly frequent by the middle of the decade, and even dissuaded some students from joining either group for fear of the violence. Jimmy Mohale, a Turfloop student in 1985 and 1986, later recalled in an interview with Isak Niehaus:

> The big rivals were AZASO and AZASM. There was no tolerance. At one stage all the AZASM students had to leave our residence because their lives were being threatened. There were about six of them. AZASM then tried to kill my floor-mate – Andrew Dipela – who was a member of AZASO. The ASAZM members came one night to attack Andrew. They broke his door and he had to flee. I did not understand this in-fighting. That is why I never wore a T-shirt of any organization.[102]

Violent confrontations between supporters of Charterist organizations, like AZASO and the UDF, and supporters of Black Consciousness ones like AZAPO were becoming prevalent beyond Turfloop, as well.[103] A month before the attack on Mabasa and Mcerwa at Turfloop, a UDF affiliate, the Port Elizabeth Youth Congress (PEYCO), had forcibly barred local AZAPO members from attending a mass funeral for victims of unrest in Uitenhage, in the Eastern Cape.[104] In the wake of this, '[t]here were attacks and counter attacks, hostages were taken and houses burnt out, and there were assassination attempts on local leaders'.[105] In September of 1985 prominent clergy, including Bishop Desmond Tutu, intervened to start 'peace talks' between AZAPO and the UDF.[106]

The situation at Turfloop was to become even more tense during the following academic year. In June 1986 the South African government issued a state of emergency, granting itself expanded powers. Around 2 o'clock in the morning on 12 June, the first day of the state of emergency,

---

[102] Jimmy Mohale, quoted in Niehaus, *Witchcraft and a Life*, p. 58.
[103] Seekings, *The UDF*, p. 146.
[104] 'AZAPO flays UDF action', *Sowetan*, 15 March 1985 [GPP]; it was later revealed that the AZAPO–UDF clashes were sometimes instigated and even framed by the security police [Truth and Reconciliation Commission Amnesty Hearings, Johan Martin Van Zyl, Port Elizabeth, 23 February 1998, Case 5637/96 [SAHA SABC TRC]].
[105] Seekings, *The UDF*, p. 146.
[106] 'AZAPO smoke peace pipe', *Sowetan*, 5 September 1985 [GPP].

Turfloop students were awakened by 'the police accompanied by a large contingent of soldiers' conducting raids on student rooms in the hostels and confiscating 'subversive' materials, including the SRC constitution. They also arrested people who were using Turfloop as a haven from the police, hiding among the students. Among those arrested were Maurice Nchabeleng and Silas Mabotha, two of the SEYO leadership. In the course of these raids, '[s]ome students were *sjambokked* and others were bitten by dogs'.[107] According to some reports as many as 200 students were initially detained, while the majority of other students left campus.[108] Several days later the university was officially closed.[109] When Turfloop reopened weeks later in late July, however, the situation had not improved. Police and soldiers remained on campus, and students boycotted the first four days of lectures in protest, demanding the unconditional release of those students who were still in detention, and the removal of security forces from campus.

Rather than concede these demands, however, the university administration, under Rector P. Mokgokong, seems to have devolved more authority to the police and army. Security forces were brought to oversee registration for the following semester. Students who successfully registered were issued with an ID bearing the emblems of the South African Police, the Lebowan Police, and the South African Defence Force, which had to be produced on demand when on campus.[110] One student group even alleged that the university authorities had so little control over the process that the army and police 'were further given powers to determine who must be admitted or not',[111] though I have been unable to verify this. Another student from Atteridgeville, near Pretoria, told a reporter,

> [A]uthorities here are an extension of the government. They do as the government tells them and ask no questions. There is no university

---

[107]'The situation at the University of the North', undated memo to the South African Council of Churches, c. late September 1986 [HPRA AC623/31.16].

[108] 'Lips are shut tight at Turfloop', *Sowetan*, 5 March 1987 [HPRA AD1912/258.17].

[109] 'The situation at the University of the North', undated memo to the South African Council of Churches, c. late September 1986; also 'The Army Occupation of the University of the North (Turfloop) 1986', memo by the Concerned Democratic Students – Turfloop, c. June 1988 [HPRA AC623/31.16].

[110] 'The situation at the University of the North', undated memo to the South African Council of Churches, c. late September 1986 [HPRA AC623/31.16].

[111] 'The Army Occupation of the University of the North (Turfloop) 1986', memo by the Concerned Democratic Students – Turfloop, c. June 1988 [HPRA AC623/31.16].

autonomy; the Sadafs [South African Defence Force] and Lebowa police run the campus, not the constituted staff.'[112]

It is clear in any case that the national state of emergency had the by-product of effectively bringing Turfloop under control of the security forces, either through the complicity or impotence of the university administration. Beginning around September 1986, and lasting through 1989, South African Defence Force (SADF) troops were garrisoned on Turfloop's campus, and played roles in corralling students and ushering them to class, as well as raiding rooms, confiscating banned materials, and disrupting gatherings.

For some students, particularly those who were not overtly political, the presence of the police presented a dilemma. Jimmy Mohale, who recalled the clashes between AZASO and AZASM but was not affiliated to either organization, greeted the arrival of troops positively:

> [The army] protected us and escorted us to class. The army even sent us 'Good Luck for the Exams' cards, and the soldiers monitored the exams. There was ambiguity. I wanted them there because I wanted my degree. I wanted them to protect us.[113]

But though Mohale initially saw the soldiers and police as providing protection from the violence that had swept through campus, he also objected to their use of violence against the students, and came to decide that the occupation actually caused more insecurity than it prevented:

> The police caused more shit and they added fuel to the fire. They came onto campus to shoot people, not to police crime. The situation was almost like a concentration camp. [...] The police once dispersed a gathering of students and randomly started firing at the students. They shot and killed one student as he was mounting the fire escape steps of our residence. [...] When he died I wondered why the life of a black person should be so cheap. I could not understand why the campus security allowed the police onto our campus.[114]

As Mohale alludes, the university had allowed the police and soldiers onto the campus; in fact, Rector Mokgokong had enlisted them to control student protests over registration in the winter of 1986. But in doing so, the university administration had, perhaps, gotten more than it bargained for. By abdicating power and responsibility over some of the daily running of the university – registration, issuing IDs, controlling

---

[112] 'The alternative university', *Sunday Times*, 8 November 1987 [HPRA AD1912/258.16].
[113] Jimmy Mohale quoted in Niehaus, *Witchcraft and a Life*, p. 61.
[114] Ibid.

students' class attendance, and even monitoring exams – the administration helped to enshrine a kind of aggressive force into those procedures, making overt violence not only common but permissible on Turfloop's campus. Students describe being 'stormed' by police if they gathered in the open square between buildings,[115] and individual instances of violence like those described above continued to be the norm on campus through to the end of the decade.

Conclusion

In this chapter it has been argued that the period of the early 1980s marked an unprecedented regional expansion of student and youth politics, as well as an ideological shift back to Charterism, and that critical groups in these models arose in the rural Northern Transvaal.

With the advent of COSAS, in 1979 Charterism once again became the founding ideology of a student group in South Africa, the first time it had been so since the banning of the ANC Youth League in 1960. This ideological shift coalesced around the breakaway of AZASO from AZAPO, and finally can be seen to have reached fruition in the Education Charter Campaign, in which COSAS and AZASO collaborated with white liberal organs to campaign for education reforms based on the ANC's Freedom Charter. The trend to Charterism was more than the result of a single factor – it happened incrementally, spurred by the presence of some ANC organizers like Joe Gqabi in Soweto, and by the ANC's superior exile organization and ability to absorb new recruits, but it did not fully begin to take hold until the Black Consciousness Movement had been crippled by state repression and its own failures of organization, both within South Africa and in exile. The growth of Charterism in student politics was a combination of germinating ideas planted by ANC activists, and the space that the absence of the fully fledged BCM provided for those ideas to flourish.

The founding of COSAS in 1979 marked a shift back towards Charterism after a decade of student politics dominated by Black Consciousness, but it also brought the struggle more effectively to the local village level than any of its predecessors had previously done. No longer was Turfloop the only centre of resistance in the Northern Transvaal. Ephraim Mogale's work organizing youth groups and politicizing existing student bodies across the region culminated in the founding of the Congress of South African Students, and his later imprisonment. COSAS became a

[115] 'The alternative university', *Sunday Times*, 8 November 1987 [HPRA AD1912/258.16].

major force in national student politics, bringing the struggle to class-rooms across South Africa. What is more, its model inspired the incor-poration of non-student youths into the political struggle through the establishment of youth organizations in villages throughout the region in the mid 1980s. Analysis of these organizations, like the Sekhukhune Youth Organisation and others, demonstrates some of the difficulties that this expansion of youth politics faced – notably in establishing dis-cipline over ideology and political practices among members. Political violence became enmeshed with generational disputes, economic discon-tent, and close social relationships, erupting in witch-hunts by young men in Sekhukhuneland, Bushbuckridge, and Venda. But nonetheless youth congresses like SEYO brought the anti-apartheid struggle to a generation of rural students and youths who would have been largely neglected by political organizations just a decade earlier. The period from 1979 to 1986 marks the most significant period of expansionism for local student politics of the anti-apartheid struggle.

But the latter part of the 1980s also brought about widespread vio-lence, often as a by-product of the increased regionalization – and weak-ened hierarchy – of student and youth politics. The witch-hunts that swept Sekhukhuneland, Bushbuckridge, and Venda, are examples of the way that politically couched violence was used to reorient social systems in many villages and districts. At Turfloop violence came to define the way that students interacted with staff, with the security forces, and with one another. With the garrisoning of troops on campus, aggressive force became routine at the University of the North during the last years of the 1980s.

Increased localization, then, brought about greater variety in the expression of political activism among youth and students – incorporat-ing cosmology like witchcraft – and brought new actors to the struggle, but it also failed to exert organizational discipline over its new comrades, which would continue to be a challenge for youth political organizers into the next decade.

6

Populism and the New Youth League

In 1987 activists still languished under the state of emergency that had facilitated nationwide crackdowns the previous year, including the one that halted the Sekhukhuneland youth revolt.[1] The UDF and its allies found themselves in a 'holding operation', trying to weather the detention of thousands of local and national activists, while maintaining a public profile.[2] Its chief success in this regard came in the formation of a new organization: the South African Youth Congress (SAYCO) was created to unite all the Charterist youth groups under a single banner. It aimed to bring together the disparate local congresses discussed in Chapter 5. Though many of these had been allied through their mutual affiliation to the UDF, SAYCO provided the first opportunity for them to organize around the common identity of youth.

Meanwhile, on university campuses like Turfloop, Charterism was quickly becoming the dominant political ideology among student activists. The Azanian Students' Organisation (AZASO) was consolidating its position against its Africanist and Black Consciousness-adherent competitors, most notably the Azanian Students' Movement (AZASM). As Saleem Badat and Shaun Johnson have each argued, by 1986 AZASO was characterized by high levels of 'organizational confidence'[3] and a renewed impulse towards ideological purity.[4] By late 1986 AZASO leaders took the decision to change their organization's name to the South African National Students' Congress (SANSCO) in order to bring it more firmly into the Charterist fold by including congress in the name,

---

[1] The nationwide state of emergency that had been declared by P.W. Botha on 12 June 1986, in fact, would not be lifted until negotiations to end apartheid were under way. F.W. de Klerk lifted the state of emergency for all provinces except Natal on 7 June 1986.

[2] Valli Moosa, quoted in Seekings, *The UDF*, pp. 226–7.

[3] S. Johnson, '"The Soldiers of Luthuli": Youth in the politics of resistance in South Africa' in S. Johnson (ed.), *South Africa: No turning back* (Basingstoke, 1988), pp. 109–10.

[4] S. Badat, *Black Student Politics: Higher education and Apartheid from SASO to SANSCO, 1968–1990* (Pretoria, 1999), p. 261.

and to jettison the last nominal tie to their Black Consciousness roots: the use of 'Azania' rather than 'South Africa'. As we have seen in the debates around the naming of COSAS, naming was an important aspect for any youth organization, and it was the first and most public declaration of a group's political affiliations. In the case of AZASO, the renaming to SANSCO sought to do just that, but it did not signify any changes in policy. These had already been consolidated after its break with AZAPO in 1980. In fact, the change was explicitly in name only. AZASO had been a firmly Charterist organization since its break with AZAPO; now its name finally reflected those affiliations.[5] That the decision to change its name came so long after their shift in ideology is interesting. By late 1986 AZASO was the senior Charterist student organization in the country; and after the 1985 banning of COSAS, it was also the most prominent. Its change of name came at a time when it was consolidating this position and its role on university campuses. But a great deal of student and youth organization continued to exist outside AZASO's scope: among younger students and non-student youth. As discussed in the previous chapter, these young people were frequently mobilized through local youth congresses. When the matter of uniting them arose, it was to be the new SAYCO, rather than its student-run counterparts, that took the lead.

This chapter will consider the role played by the South African Youth Congress in uniting disparate Charterist youth organizations under one, sometimes contentious, banner, and the ways in which that structure became critical to the early formation of the ANC Youth League in 1990. In particular, it considers the impact of Peter Mokaba as president, and of regional structures in the northern Transvaal on the SAYCO–ANC Youth League transition.

Peter Mokaba: SAYCO's founding father, and Mankweng's son

As groups like AZASO and COSAS gained traction with students and young people, they began to experience harsh government repression under the states of emergency in 1985 and 1986. COSAS was banned outright in 1985, and other groups and leaders were increasingly harassed by the security forces. Despite this repression, overall the period from 1985 to 1987 was one of important growth and development for Charterist youth political structures. In March 1987, perhaps the most significant change yet affected youth congresses across the country: the

---

[5] For a complete discussion of this break, see Chapter 4.

South African Youth Congress (SAYCO) was launched. As its president Peter Mokaba said days after the launch,

> We have been able to launch Sayco despite numerous roadblocks, police harassment and the use of the vigilantes. That is because Sayco is a direct product of long suffering – politically, socially and economically.[6]

It was also the product of the broad network of local and regional youth congresses across South Africa: SAYCO operated primarily as a coordinating body for these disparate youth congresses that had emerged during the 1980s. It adopted the ideals of the Freedom Charter, aligned itself with the ANC (even seeking the approval of the party in exile before its launch), and worked to unite the local congresses that had come to characterize youth politics across the country. In this SAYCO was different from the student and youth movements that had preceded it: it gathered together a vast constituency that had already organized itself into units. With this foundation, SAYCO started from a position of demographic strength: initially it comprised ten regions with '1200 affiliates, over half a million signed-up members, and a support base of two million', according to Jeremy Seekings.[7] Estimates of SAYCO's size vary widely, owing to the lack of consistent record-keeping and disparate membership requirements among its affiliates, but even the smallest estimates put its numbers in the hundreds of thousands. Uniting this vast base around a common ideology and exerting organizational cohesion and discipline was to be the primary challenge for SAYCO's new executive committee.

Peter Mokaba, a former Robben Island prisoner from the Northern Transvaal, who had been politicized during the 1976 uprising, led the new organization. Mokaba was born in Pietersburg in January 1958, but soon after his birth his family was forced to move 30 kilometres away to the peri-rural township of Mankweng, when their township of New Look Location was declared a black spot in a whites-only area. Shortly after they moved, construction began on the farm adjoining Mankweng that would give its name to the university built on the site: Turfloop. The Mokabas lived in the poorest area of Mankweng. In Peter Mokaba's own words, 'In Mankweng we lived as squatters in shacks, and moved from one yard to the next in the township.'[8]

---

[6] Peter Mokaba, quoted in 'A toughened prison veteran at just 25', *Weekly Mail*, 3 April 1987 [GPP].

[7] Seekings, *The UDF*, p. 210.

[8] K. Mamaila, 'Mokaba's deathbed memories', *The Star*, 13 June 2002 [GPP].

Mokaba attended a variety of primary schools before graduating into Mankweng's Hwiti High School in the early 1970s.[9] It was at Hwiti that he first became involved in politics. The school had a history of political involvement linked to its close proximity to the University of the North. It was not unusual for activists from the university to influence and politicize Hwiti students through political schools and programmes both on and off campus. While a teacher there in the 1960s and 1970s, Winifred Kgware, the first president of the Black People's Convention, exposed her students to anti-apartheid politics through her links to the University Christian Movement and SASO. Years after Kgware's tenure, political involvement remained a key facet of the school.

During the 1976 student protests that began in Soweto and spread across the country, Mokaba became one of the local leaders of the student movement and helped organize school boycotts in the Northern Transvaal, until police pressure during the uprising forced him into hiding.[10] During this period, Mokaba was inspired primarily by Black Consciousness leaders. In a biographical article written shortly before his death in 2002, he identified 'Onkgopotse Tiro and various black consciousness poets as [his] role models'.[11] He was finally arrested on charges of public violence in November 1977, but was acquitted when all twenty-eight state witnesses refused to testify against him.[12] Following this incident, both the South African government and the government of Lebowa refused to allow him to enrol again in school, and Mokaba completed his final year of school at home in 1978.[13] In 1980 he enrolled at the University of the North, and participated in founding the campus branch of AZASO (which was still affiliated to AZAPO and Black Consciousness at the time), but before the year was out he was expelled for political activities and forced to leave campus after police raids.

Equally interesting are the tales of Mokaba's life that may be at least partially myth. In 1976 and 1977 he infamously fled into the mountains of Lebowa where he hid in the bush and evaded arrest for nearly eighteen months. Residents in Mankweng tell stories of SADF helicopters scouring the area looking for the local hero. In addition, two years separate

[9] African National Congress Mission to the United States (April 1994), Peter R. Mokaba Biography [GPP].

[10] Ibid.

[11] T. N'wa Mhangwana and J. Arenstein, 'The guerilla who loved a good waltz', *Mail and Guardian*, 25 June 2004 [GPP].

[12] 'Tussle for leader of the youth', *Weekly Mail*, 12 June 1991 [GPP]; Mhangwana and Arenstein, 'The guerilla who loved a good waltz' [GPP].

[13] African National Congress Mission to the United States (April 1994), Peter R. Mokaba Biography [GPP].

the end of Mokaba's university career and his next arrest in 1982: he claims to have gone into military training with the ANC's armed wing, *Umkhonto we Sizwe* (MK), in Angola and Mozambique. This is likely to be true: when he returned to South Africa he was arrested on charges of terrorism, membership of MK, attempting to recruit for the ANC, and having undergone military training.[14] While each of these stories is rooted in truth, they have been expanded and exaggerated, contributing to the myth of Mokaba as another 'Black Pimpernel', the name attributed to Nelson Mandela when he was on the run before his arrest in 1962.

After returning to South Africa, in 1982 Mokaba was detained under section 6 of the Terrorism Act, and was tried and convicted of furthering the aims of the ANC. He was sent to Robben Island to begin serving a six-year sentence. After a successful appeal and retrial in 1984 reduced his sentence to three years suspended for five years, Mokaba returned home to the Northern Transvaal in March 1985.

By this time the predominant ideological force in student politics had shifted from Black Consciousness to Charterism. AZASO, with which Mokaba had been involved at Turfloop in 1980, had severed its ties with the BC-affiliated AZAPO and dedicated itself to Charterism in 1981. Mokaba's own military training with the ANC prepared him to reenter a political arena dominated by the ideals of the Freedom Charter. He quickly became involved in the nascent structures of the UDF locally. He also continued to clash with the security police, and was detained three separate times after his return home from Robben Island.[15]

Within days of his release from one such detention on a suspended sentence for being in possession of a Marakov pistol, Mokaba attended the March 1985 conference of the UDF at the University of the North.[16] Here the decision was taken to form a regional branch of the UDF that would separate UDF administration of the Northern Transvaal from the urban areas to the south. Peter Nchabeleng, a Robben Islander himself and the patron of the Sekhukhune Youth Organisation, became the regional president of the UDF in the Northern Transvaal, and Mokaba joined the interim regional organizing structure, along with Turfloop staff members: librarian Joyce Mabudafhazi, and lecturer Louis Mnguni. Mokaba went on to become patron of the Mankweng Youth Congress,

---

[14] African National Congress Mission to the United States (April 1994), Peter R. Mokaba Biography [GPP].

[15] Ibid.

[16] S. Gastrow, *Who's Who in South African Politics*, 5th edn (Johannesburg, 1995), p. 194.

helped to set up the Mankweng Civic Association, and eventually became the regional publicity secretary for the UDF. In 1986, he became the Education Officer of the Northern Transvaal Youth Congress, SAYCO's largest affiliate with reportedly more than 200,000 members by 1988.[17] From late 1986 until its launch in March 1987 he was instrumental in the founding of SAYCO, and became its first president.

Founding SAYCO

Talks of founding a national youth organization began as early as 1985, but the wheels of motion were more fully engaged in mid-1986, when Mokaba and Deacon Mathe, another youth leader (who had been involved with CRIC as a colleague of Elleck Nchabeleng), travelled outside South Africa to meet with the ANC leadership in exile to discuss the plans for the new youth body.[18] In Harare, Zimbabwe they discussed direction and political content of the new organization with the ANC leadership there. Hugh Macmillan has noted that this was a period of unprecedented contact between the ANC in exile and groups within South Africa.[19] Nevertheless, this level of cooperation and consultation linked SAYCO more directly to the ANC than any youth organization had been since the ANC Youth League, which became defunct after the state banned the ANC as a whole in 1960.

The ANC's support may have been motivated by the need to keep South Africa's youth onside and under a semblance of control, as well as by the desire to unite groups under the Freedom Charter. The violence that became a key characteristic of the political expression in the mid-1980s is discussed in some depth in the previous chapter. In 1986, under the state of emergency, youth in South Africa's townships and rural villages were rioting to make the country ungovernable. Hugh Macmillan has noted that the ANC in exile had long been concerned about harnessing the political potential of the youth inside South Africa, particularly in the wake of the Soweto Uprising. A 1979 presidential report worried that 'we will fritter away the considerable talent of our youth and lose it to reactionary politics and wasting life styles'.[20] Their support for building a national structure to organize youth under a Charterist banner demonstrates that this was still a priority a decade after 1976.

---

[17] 'SAYCO Refuses to Surrender', *South*, 7 April 1988 [GPP].
[18] Gastrow, *Who's Who*, p. 193.
[19] Macmillan, *The Lusaka Years*, p. 217
[20] 'President's draft report', May 1979 (ANCL 1/149/58), quoted in Macmillan, *The Lusaka Years*, p. 136.

Later in 1986 Mokaba, Mathe, and other youth leaders inside South Africa participated in a series of planning meetings for SAYCO: in July 1986, Mokaba became education officer of the interim National Youth Organisation (NYO) at a consultative youth conference in Cape Town. In late October, he organized a workshop in Pretoria under the auspices of the NYO, which then organized the consultative conference that eventually drafted the SAYCO constitution.[21] The extended process of these consultations was, in part, due to heavy state repression that made it difficult for representatives from the various youth organizations to attend, but Seekings notes that 'the ANC's backing seems to have facilitated progress'.[22] SAYCO's first conference in 1987 was held under quiet, if not precisely secret, conditions. Approximately 250 delegates attended the launch in Cape Town on 28 March. There, Mokaba was unanimously elected president with Rapu Molekane as vice-president, and Ephraim Nkwe as education officer.

The new organization took an aggressive and sometimes militant line from the outset in their struggle against apartheid. The slogan 'Freedom or death: victory is certain!', which Mokaba claimed to have coined,[23] clearly set out SAYCO's political stance. In this it followed a pattern of increasingly militant protest epitomized by the use of violence under the states of emergency, discussed in Chapter 5. Whereas COSAS had sheltered, to some degree, under the cover of student and educational issues, SAYCO took its attack to the heart of apartheid politics, challenging policies of detention and execution, and vocally supporting *Umkhonto we Sizwe*.[24] It engaged directly with the ANC in exile, as well as being one of the UDF's largest affiliates.

Though the ANC was not explicitly mentioned in any of SAYCO's founding documents – it was still banned in 1987 and public affiliation would have been dangerous – its imprint is evident on SAYCO's constitution, which advocates adherence to the Freedom Charter and the Mass Democratic Movement (the alliance between the UDF and COSATU (the Congress of South African Trade Unions)). In their preamble, SAYCO's founders declared themselves dedicated to the creation of 'a free, unitary, non-racial and democratic South African culture'.[25]

---

[21] Gastrow, *Who's Who*, p. 195.

[22] Seekings, *The UDF*, p. 210.

[23] M. Gevisser, 'Of politics and hairdressing', *The Weekly Mail*, undated, c. 1995 [GPP]; Mokaba adapted this phrase for SAYCO's slogan, but did not coin it. It was popular among both the MPLA in Angola and FRELIMO in Mozambique, where it was used in Portuguese: '*Liberte o morte: Victoria e certeza!*'

[24] SAYCO pamphlets, c. September 1987 [SAHA ANCYL AL2451].

[25] SAYCO Constitution, 1.1 Preamble [SAHA Collection AL2457 J7.3.2].

But SAYCO was also deeply concerned with asserting its independence amid the swell of liberation organizations of the late 1980s. As I will argue, its emphasis on the nonracialism espoused in the Freedom Charter was mostly nominal; in its demographics and its emphasis on African self-reliance, SAYCO exhibited a streak of Africanism at odds with its declared ethos of Charterism. This marks an important reintegration of Africanism into the mainstream of liberation politics, which had been sidelined in the youth and student movements since the split between AZAPO and AZASO in 1980. The focus on self-reliance can been seen in SAYCO's founding documents. A great deal of its constitution is devoted to spelling out the new organization's autonomy, stressing that 'The central administration of SAYCO rests in its own decision making structures alone [...]',[26] even while affirming SAYCO's connection to other 'fraternal organizations' with which it shared membership, including, in particular, the United Democratic Front (UDF) and the Mass Democratic Movement (MDM).[27] The tension between SAYCO's autonomy and its place among a wide array of movements pushing for democratic change in South Africa shaped the movement. It straddled a constant dilemma between independence and belonging, something that its progeny, the ANC Youth League, would come to inherit.

Loyalty, autonomy, and SAYCO's relationship to the UDF

Autonomy at all levels, offset by an emphasis on organizational adherence, was an early priority for SAYCO: the youth congresses that affiliated to it retained their autonomy and names at the local level (so, for instance, local branches of the Sekhukhune Youth Organisation, like the one in Apel–GaNkoane, retained that name). However, zonal, regional, and national structures were branded with SAYCO titles and programmes (so the Sekhukhune Youth Organisation as a regional coordinating structure ceased to exist). In an interview with the ANC's journal *Sechaba*, Joe Nkuna, a member of the SAYCO executive in 1987, said of organization at the local level:

> The [SAYCO] street committees are where democracy is exercised fully. We take decisions in the street committees, where everyone is participating. Then to the area structures and to regional structures where those decisions are implemented or are reviewed. But the people who are very

---

[26] SAYCO Constitution, 2.4 Independence [SAHA Collection AL2457 J7.3.2].
[27] SAYCO Constitution, 2.3 Rights and Duties of Members [SAHA Collection AL2457 J7.3.2].

important and are playing a leading role are the masses, who are participating from the street committees to the highest levels.[28]

Faye Reagon, another member, agreed about the importance of being
connected to the grassroots level:

> SAYCO is not structures 'up there'. SAYCO is not leaders 'up there'.
> SAYCO is street committees and defence committees. In fact the top lead-
> ers are streetwise, they are in community organizations; these leaders are
> in our communities.[29]

The local congresses were expected to support SAYCO's national
and regional structures insofar as 'the National Political Education Programme, National Mass Campaigns, Finance and accounting policy and
general political ideology, policies, and programmes are concerned'.[30]
But as Nkuna and Reagon imply above, they also 'retain[ed] their
autonomy in as far as local campaigns and administration are concerned, respecting the principles of democratic decentralization which
allows creativity, initiative, ingenuity and imagination in furtherance
and pursuance of SAYCO's Aims and Objectives'.[31] These conflicting
imperatives would have real implications for SAYCO's organizational
coherence from the national to the local level, and would also influence
the trajectory of national youth politics after unbanning in the 1990s.

Though SAYCO protected the autonomy of its Youth Congress affiliates to act in their own local areas, as discussed above, it also began
to pursue a national agenda. This focused in part on youths already in
detention or prison. In late 1987 they launched their 'Save the South
African patriots' campaign, and attempted to pressure the state to release
young political prisoners who were on death row.[32] They also collaborated with other organizations, including with COSATU on a rally com-
memorating the 16 June Soweto Uprising.[33] They were more successful
than COSAS had been at forming an alliance with workers (and organized labour in particular). Several factors likely contributed to this; as a
youth organization SAYCO was less hampered by some of the prejudices

---

[28] 'SAYCO Has Shattered the Dream of the Apartheid Regime', *Sechaba*, September 1987, p. 7 [HPRA AK2117/G3.8.1.2].

[29] Ibid.

[30] SAYCO Constitution, 2.3 Rights and Duties of Members [SAHA AL2457
J7.3.2].

[31] Ibid.

[32] 'Save the 32 South African Patriots', SAYCO flyer, undated c. 1987 [SAHA
AL2451].

[33] 'Umhla Ka – June 16 Usuku Lwethu', undated c. June 1988 or June 1989 [SAHA
AL2446].

against 'elite' students than its student counterparts. Working youths even formed a part (though a smaller one than unemployed youths) of its membership. The organization was also explicitly employing Marxist philosophy, which led it to sympathize with workers and to ally with organized labour. COSAS' primarily educational focus had narrowed the scope for such common interest, though the UDF helped to bridge that gap, as discussed previously. SAYCO also played a crucial role as one of the UDF's most significant affiliates. A UDF National Working Committee in 1987 described SAYCO as 'inspiration, not only to the hundreds of youth congresses around the country, but to the Front as a whole'.[34]

But the relationship between the UDF's organizing body and one of its largest affiliates did not remain so close for long. The UDF had been dogged by criticisms of being controlled by an internal cabal of activists who dominated resources and decision-making during the middle of the 1980s, particularly during the states of emergency in 1985 and 1986.[35] According to Steve Tswhete, a UDF chairman from the Border Region of what is now the Eastern Cape, 'They use what is known as CM (control and manipulation) strategy. Because the cabal has resources at its disposal which people in townships do not have, it is easy for them to use these advantages to control organizations.'[36] Along with Tshwete, other high-profile figures within the UDF also criticized the cabal, among them Peter Mokaba. Their criticisms were implicitly tinged by race, as the prominence of Indian leaders like Azhar Cachalia and Valli Moosa in the UDF reinforced the idea of a cabal that marginalized African leaders, who were its most vocal opponents. For these leaders the ideal of multiracialism was increasingly supplanted by the continued reality of African marginalization, even within the liberation organizations that were meant to defeat the racism of apartheid. Regionalism was at issue as well; the alleged cabal was based in the regional structures of the UDF in Natal. It also reflected the complicated internal politics within the UDF, which encompassed a wide breadth of ideologies among its activists and organizations, from socialist to capitalist, to Africanist. Increasingly, SAYCO was falling into this last category; though it paid lip service to nonracialism, it was deeply enmeshed in the racialized politics of the UDF, with its leadership firmly in the Africanist camp.

---

[34] UDF National Working Committee 1987 Secretary's Report, quoted in Seekings, *The UDF*, p. 210.

[35] Seekings, *The UDF*, p. 219; van Kessel, *Beyond Our Wildest Dreams*, pp. 63–5.

[36] Quoted in 'Inside the UDF's secret society', *City Press*, 25 November 1990 [GPP].

The most vocal critic of the UDF's leadership was Aubrey Mokoena, the former Black Consciousness activist who had become politicized through SASO while at Turfloop. After the Black Consciousness bannings of 1977 Mokoena was detained several times in the late 1970s; in the 1980s he shifted his political allegiances to Charterism and assumed leadership of the Release Mandela Campaign in 1983. Jeremy Seekings has argued that the Release Mandela Campaign acted as 'a base for Charterists who were critical of the UDF's moderation, its reticence about openly championing the Charterist cause, and the prominent role of TIC [Transvaal Indian Congress] and NIC [Natal Indian Congress] activists'.[37] Mokoena personified this frustration within the UDF. He had been a prominent leader in the organization and member of the National Executive Committee for most of the 1980s, but he was also part of a fringe within the Front advocating a more aggressively nationalist platform. Seekings has said that Mokoena even initiated plans 'to build a national Charterist network outside and alternative to the UDF'.[38]

Shortly after the ANC was unbanned in February 1990, Mokoena's break with the UDF was essentially complete. In an open letter to the ANC in June 1990, he criticized the UDF for becoming an organization in itself, rather than a front for other organizations. He strongly advocated for the UDF's dissolution in light of the ANC's unbanning, feeling that the newly unbanned movement could better lead the Charterist cause.[39] But he also addressed some very specific concerns about the so-called cabal within UDF leadership. Mokoena's letter was actually in response to an internal UDF document, which 'allegedly set out the cabal's position on negotiations [to dismantle apartheid], [and which said] Popo Molefe, Terror Lekota, and [Peter] Mokaba had to "be isolated as soon as possible"'.[40] All three of these were prominent African (and in Mokaba's case, increasingly Africanist[41]) leaders in the UDF, and Mokaba in particular had ruffled feathers among the UDF's more moderate leadership with his fiery populist rhetoric at the helm of SAYCO.

By 1990, at the time of Mokoena's letter, SAYCO was the most significant youth structure within South Africa. Though its organizational cohesion had been tested by the pull between national and local

---

[37] Seekings, *The UDF*, p. 75.
[38] Ibid., p. 249.
[39] Ibid., p. 269.
[40] 'Inside the UDF's secret society', *City Press*, 25 November 1990 [GPP].
[41] For more on Mokaba's shifting ideology within Charterism, see A. Heffernan, 'Blurred Lines and Ideological Divisions in South African Youth Politics', *African Affairs*, 115(461) (2016), 664–87.

priorities, it boasted mass membership and representation in all corners of the country. It had achieved this feat in spite of state repression that made mass meetings so difficult that, after its initial conference in March 1987, SAYCO did not have a national conference again until April 1990. That second conference also marked the first time that SAYCO's national executive, a group of leaders under close government surveillance, had all met publicly.[42] It was, according to Peter Mokaba in his presidential address, 'a victory congress'.[43] And indeed, 1990 was a victorious year for SAYCO. Not only had the South African government begun the process of unbanning activists like Nelson Mandela and organizations like the ANC, SAYCO had also triumphed in its internal conflict within the UDF.

One such indication of SAYCO's successful sidelining of the UDF was in its cultivation of a relationship with Winnie Madikizela-Mandela in the late 1980s. Upon the February 1990 release of Nelson Mandela, this positioned them close to the first couple and leadership of the ANC. South African papers reported that the couple were guarded by 'fierce Sayco youths': '[Mandela's] personal bodyguard of suited "young lions" prowl about public events, assessing crowd situations, and appear to be armed. They are also much in evidence at the ANC leader's home.'[44] In addition, reports said that 'members of the Mandela household have since been directing media queries to Sayco general-secretary, Rapu Molekane, for comment'.[45] This involvement with the Mandelas generated tension between SAYCO and the MDM's National Reception Committee over who would manage the Mandela press campaign, and even raised questions about the youth organization's ability to challenge the policies of the MDM and the UDF. This position had not come about by chance: SAYCO had allied itself closely to Winnie Madikizela-Mandela before her husband's release from prison. Mokaba, in particular, was a political protégé of hers, and the two frequently appeared at public events together. SAYCO as an organization defended Winnie against criticism from various quarters during the early 1990s.

Mokaba and Madikizela-Mandela shared a close and mutually politically beneficial relationship: later, in the wake of the break-up of her marriage to ANC President Nelson Mandela, with allegations of abuse and kidnapping against her, and her removal from leadership positions

---

[42] P. Mokaba, SAYCO National Congress Presidential Address, 1990 [SAHA AL2425].

[43] Ibid., p. 2.

[44] 'Fierce Sayco youths guard Mandelas', The Star, 17 February 1990 [GPP].

[45] Ibid.

within the ANC, Mokaba said of Winnie, 'We are going to confound those who are biting behind her back. She has the support of all those who support me.'[46] This was true, broadly speaking: the two shared a constituency among South Africa's militant youth, for whom Mokaba was their leader and 'Ma Winnie' was a mother figure. Her biographer, Emma Keller, has pointed out that this was not unusual for the woman who came to be known as the mother of the nation: speaking of Madiki-zela-Mandela's banishment to the Free State in the late 1970s, Keller writes, 'As always, Winnie's popularity base was with those younger than herself.'[47]

SAYCO's increasing autonomy from the UDF and proximity to the ANC proved strategic. The ANC overtook the UDF at the forefront of the anti-apartheid struggle once it was unbanned. Though many UDF members straddled allegiances to the Front and the ANC, others, like Aubrey Mokoena, shifted their membership entirely. Positions in ANC leadership were key to maintaining influence as apartheid was dismantled. As Seekings has noted, criticism of the cabal by Mokoena and others affected ANC leadership choices, particularly at the regional level in Natal. '[T]he ANC's new REC [Regional Executive Committee] included many ex-[Robben] Islanders, and key "cabalists" [...] failed to gain election.'[48]

(Re)Building the ANC Youth League

Meanwhile, SAYCO was making the most of the relative freedom that unbanning had given them to operate, and was preparing for the ANC to lead South Africans into a post-apartheid era. The pressing task of the April 1990 conference was to define SAYCO's role in this future. In his presidential address, Mokaba lauded the unbanning of the ANC and its allies as 'undoubtedly the most significant development in the history of the liberation struggle'.[49] He was quick to point out the role that above-ground organizations like SAYCO still had to play, however: 'As a victory we ourselves have won in all-round struggle, we must then be responsible for taking it forward.'[50] The clear way to take it for-

[46] E.G. Keller, *The Lady: The life and times of Winnie Mandela* (London, 1993), p. 285.
[47] Ibid., p. 123.
[48] Seekings, *The UDF*, p. 270.
[49] P. Mokaba, SAYCO National Congress Presidential Address, 1990 [SAHA AL2425].
[50] Ibid.

ward, as far as Mokaba and other youth leaders both inside and outside the country were concerned, was to reconstitute the moribund ANC Youth League (ANCYL). SAYCO was keen to be at the forefront of this initiative. Mokaba said that SAYCO had experience of organizing under government repression that the new ANC Youth League 'cannot do without'.[51] He further exhorted the SAYCO members,

> Although the ANC has still to take a decision as to how best we can found the ANC Youth League, we must not wait for formal contact. Make preparations for the undertaking of this task.[52]

The urgency with which Mokaba pushed SAYCO towards organizing for the new ANC Youth League is revealing on several counts. It indicates the degree to which SAYCO had distanced itself from the UDF by 1990. Mokaba makes no mention of the Front, or even the MDM in his speech, though both are clearly mentioned in the SAYCO constitution. Instead he pays considerable attention to the ANC and its alliance partners, the SACP and the newly merged union bodies SACTU (South African Congress of Trade Unions) and COSATU (Congress of South African Trade Unions) *outside* their role in the MDM. In a very public display of support, Nelson and Winnie Mandela attended SAYCO's April 1990 congress, underscoring the close relationship of the ANC and SAYCO, as well as the importance of youth as a constituency for the ANC.

But Mokaba's expediency also hints at the politics behind the reformation of the ANC Youth League itself. Though SAYCO was by far the largest youth movement within South Africa, it was going to have to merge with other internal Charterist youth groups, and with the ANC's Youth Section, which had managed youth issues for the party while in exile, in order to form the ANC's new youth wing. Jackie Selebi, the head of the ANC's Youth Section in Lusaka, was also the chairman of its repatriation committee, and was organizing the return of young exiles, many of whom were MK cadres.[53] A resolution adopted at the 1990 congress endorsed pursuit of such a merger. 'The unbanning of the ANC has made it important that we consider merging with the movement's youth section in order to have one strong Youth League,' Mokaba told a reporter in attendance.[54] What he did not say was that the merger

---

[51] P. Mokaba, SAYCO National Congress Presidential Address, 1990 [SAHA AL2425].

[52] Ibid.

[53] Macmillan, *The Lusaka Years*, p. 269.

[54] 'Sayco will merge with ANC for new Youth League', *Weekly Mail*, 20 April 1990 [GPP].

would posit the ideological and structural priorities of these two groups against one another. Competing for influence in this process was going to require political machinations, and Mokaba knew it. To get SAYCO engaged in the process early, particularly with such dominant numbers, was a savvy move.

Unlike the more narrowly defined COSAS and SANSCO, SAYCO's membership stretched across the breadth of youth including students, young workers, and unemployed youth. The ANC Youth League sought to emulate this catholicism in its launching manifesto, addressing an array of specific constituencies including young workers, unemployed youth, young women, religious youth, young traditional leaders, and many others.[55] They called for all of these groups to unite:

> In our classrooms and campuses; on the factory floor and in our communities; through our actions as caders [sic] of Umkhonto we Sizwe, the People's Army; on the sportsfield and and [sic] through our creative works we have earned ourselves a place of honour in the fight for national democracy.[56]

Mokaba's gambit to leverage SAYCO early into the formation of the Youth League paid off. COSAS and SANSCO had elected to remain independent and retain their focus on educational issues, leaving SAYCO and the ANC Youth Section to vie for position within the new organization. In the negotiations and plans surrounding the October 1990 launch of the Youth League, SAYCO was able to dominate the formation of a league with real political weight in the ANC, while the ANC's Youth Section, which advocated a much more limited youth desk, was sidelined.[57] These positions reflect the situations of both organizations – SAYCO had been a major national force for three years, with a great deal of autonomy from and criticism of the UDF, in spite of its affiliation to the Front. The Youth Section had been a small corner of the ANC's exile machine, and acted very much in the service of the main party. In addition, though there were young people in exile awaiting return to South Africa, they were a small fraction of the size of the SAYCO membership, and the repatriation process – especially for rank and file – was a remarkably slow one. Most would not be back in South Africa

---

[55] Launching Manifesto of the ANC Youth League, 27 October 1990 [SAHA AL2451].

[56] Ibid.

[57] C. Glaser, *A Jacana Pocket History: The ANC Youth League* (Johannesburg, 2012), p. 100.

in time for the ANCYL's preliminary launch in October 1990.[58] Aware of its relatively strong position, SAYCO did not disband until 1991, a full year after that launch, when it was clear that the new Youth League would follow its precedent.[59]

As a consequence of these factors, the ANC Youth League that emerged from the negotiations resembled SAYCO far more than it did the Youth Section, and that similarity made a natural transition for its hundreds of thousands of members. This was implicitly referenced in the launching manifesto, which noted that 'the present situation places an even greater responsibility on the youth. It demands of us: the building of organizations throughout our country which are deeply rooted amongst the people [...].'[60] In this SAYCO's advantage was clear – it *was* rooted among the people throughout South Africa. It had structures and leadership in place from the village to the national level, and it had loyalty among its mass base.

Mokaba, in particular, inspired great devotion among the youth of SAYCO throughout the country. After unbanning and SAYCO's first public congress he became a highly sought-after speaker for youth congresses across the country, from the Western Cape to the Northern Transvaal. In his old home province Mokaba was especially in demand: letters from SAYCO branches in Sekhukhuneland, Phalaborwa, and at the University of the North came in asking him to speak on the current political situation in South Africa, to preside over the launch of new branches, and, in the case of the philosophical society at Turfloop, to address 'Transformation – Turning internal organs of apartheid (Bush Colleges) into Mass weapons for peoples Power' [sic].[61] His was the acknowledged voice of South Africa's youth on a wide array of topics.

For the youth in the rural Northern Transvaal, the connection was even deeper: Mokaba was their famous son, a local freedom fighter who had risen to national standing. Rural areas had often been overlooked or neglected by national leadership, sometimes simply owing to practicalities of access, and the rush of groups in the Northern Transvaal to claim ownership of Mokaba reflects this feeling. In September 1990 the Apel–GaNkoane Youth Congress, the reformed remains of the local branch of

[58] For discussion of the process and speed of repatriations, particularly for the ANC community in Lusaka, Zambia, see Macmillan, *The Lusaka Years*, pp. 268–71.
[59] Glaser, *The ANC Youth League*, p. 100.
[60] Launching Manifesto of the ANC Youth League, 27 October 1990 [SAHA AL2451].
[61] Correspondence from the University of the North Philosophy Society 'Crito' to the SAYCO Head Office, September 1990; and from Namkgawe SAYCO Branch to the Secretary, SAYCO NEC, 25 September 1990 [SAHA AL2425].

SEYO (discussed in Chapter 5), which had affiliated to SAYCO, wrote to invite Mokaba to speak at the launch of a new local civic organization. The chairman, Lucas Mokgalaka, wrote that

> Members of the SAYCO in this area have been longing for the moment when they will be listening to the voice of their leader Comrade Peter Mokaba [...] Comrades in the rural areas have always lost the benefit of being addressed by their leadership due mainly to the lack of resources to reach places like FNB [the stadium on the edge of Soweto where the new ANC Youth League was launched in 1990].[62]

Here Mokgalaka makes a special claim to Mokaba's leadership as a representative of a neglected rural area. (Perhaps to ensure that Mokaba would come, Mokgalaka also announced in his letter of invitation that he would go ahead and advertise the visit among local SAYCO members, and he warned that they would be very disappointed if their leader failed to turn up.) The enthusiasm, even 'longing', of the youth congress' membership that he describes reflects the depth of feeling for Mokaba in SAYCO's varied and far-flung youth congresses, particularly in the hard-to-reach corners of the Northern Transvaal. It was a dedication that also helped bridge the transition of youth politics from SAYCO to the ANC Youth League; Mokaba became a transformational figure, bringing the constituency of SAYCO into the fold of the ANC.

As much as Mokaba was the undisputed leader of the youth, he was also a deeply controversial figure, among the white politicians and farmers offended by his singing of the *Dubul 'ibhunu* ('Shoot the Boer') struggle song, but also within the ANC itself. An editorial in the *Weekly Mail and Guardian* reported that members of the ANC intelligence community were investigating accusations that Mokaba had been an informant to the security police, and that they tried to persuade members of the National Youth Section to marginalize him during the negotiations between SAYCO and the Youth Section over the shape of the new Youth League.[63] They were unsuccessful, and Mokaba was elected first president of the new ANCYL. He achieved this victory against opposition from the Youth Section, and even from within SAYCO itself: Mokaba's vice-president, Rapu Molekane, was expected to contest the ANC Youth League presidency, but 'failed to receive the necessary one-third support

---

[62] Correspondence from the Apel–Nkoane Youth Congress to the National Secretary of SAYCO, 18 September 1990 [SAHA AL2425].

[63] 'Why can't the ANC get rid of Mokaba? He's too powerful', *Weekly Mail and Guardian*, 20 August 1993 [GPP].

from the house to make his candidacy possible' in the first round of nominations.[64] In the end Mokaba ran unopposed.

One point of contention during the merging and creation of the Youth League in which SAYCO was victorious was the age limit of members: the ANC argued that membership for the Youth League should be from 12 to 30 years of age, while SAYCO advocated for a wider cohort including ages 14 to 35.[65] Many SAYCO members, and most of its leadership, were over 30 at the time of negotiations. 'Mokaba said practical conditions on the ground had shown that some people just above 30 years were still suitably placed in youth congresses.'[66] He was 32 at the time of the conference. In the end, membership age limits were set from 14 to 35, giving the Youth League access to a larger pool of the general population, and reinforcing SAYCO's dominance in the negotiations. The age cap of 35 also gave the Youth League influence over a greater share of the ANC general membership. The older members also became members of the ANC itself: the Youth League accepted members from the ages of 14 to 35, but all Youth League members automatically also became members of the ANC at 18. Mpho Nchabeleng, who had been a law student and AZASO member at Turfloop, remembers the importance of this transition for the youth:

> SEYO, what actually became SEYO became branches of the Youth League and the ANC. And [the] majority of those people were no longer the youth, like me. We were actually transcending this thing of being youth to become members of the ANC.[67]

This dual membership technique enabled a seamless flow of young members directly into the ANC, while maintaining the primacy of the Youth League for inducting members below 18. But from the beginning, the Youth League was an important vehicle for its older members, as well. Mokaba was elected president of the ANCYL in 1990, a post he held until he 'aged out' of it, turning 35 in 1994. Even at this early stage the Youth League was already becoming a platform by which ambitious young members might rise through the ranks and position themselves for leadership positions in the party proper when the time came. At the end of his tenure as president, Mokaba was at the head of the Youth League's list of nominees for inclusion as ANC candidates in the 1994

[64] 'Tussle for leader of the youth', *Weekly Mail*, 12 June 1991 [GPP].
[65] 'Sayco will merge with ANC for new Youth League', *Weekly Mail*, 20 April 1990 [GPP].
[66] Ibid.
[67] Author's interview with Mpho Nchabeleng.

election, and then went on to become a member of parliament and a government minister.[68] This platform for upward mobility was to be an important facet of the post-apartheid Youth League, and is discussed further in the next chapter.

Roaring Young Lions: Peter Mokaba's rhetoric during the political transition

In spite of Mokaba's remarkable success bridging the transition from SAYCO to the ANC Youth League, that process was neither smooth nor uncontroversial. Mokaba was a firebrand who quickly acquired a reputation for inflammatory rhetoric during the delicate process of negotiations between the ANC, the National Party, and other political stakeholders in the final years of apartheid. The early 1990s, during which negotiations under CODESA (Conference for a Democratic South Africa) were taking place, were a period of intensified violence and conflict. The Inkatha Freedom Party (IFP) engaged in a bloody struggle, primarily against the ANC, for control of KwaZulu and Natal, which spilled into urban areas on the Rand. In addition, there were accusations and suspicion of a 'third force' who were undermining the negotiation process on the side of the government.[69] High-profile massacres in 1992 at Boipatong, near Vereeniging, and at Bisho in the Eastern Cape, as well as the April 1993 assassination of *Umkhonto we Sizwe* commander Chris Hani, set the country on the edge of what many watching thought could be full-blown civil war.

As Glaser has noted, 'much of SAYCO's constituency was immersed in [the] culture of township violence and militarized defence'[70] that characterized the mid-to-late 1980s and early 1990s. In this tense atmosphere, Peter Mokaba rallied his constituents with fiery speeches and sometimes violent language. In August 1993, he was rebuked by ANC President Nelson Mandela and censured by the party for a controversial speech he made at a Tembisa funeral, in which Mokaba called on mourners to demolish hostels 'brick by brick' and to 'direct (their) bullets against (President) De Klerk'.[71] The ANC and its ally, COSATU,

---

[68] 'Youth League puts up 22 for ANC poll list', *The Star*, 23 November 1993 [GPP].

[69] S. Ellis, 'The Historical Significance of South Africa's Third Force', *Journal of Southern African Studies*, 24(2) (1998), 261–99.

[70] Glaser, *The ANC Youth League*, p. 104.

[71] E. Waugh, 'Mokaba: A-G set to make decision', *The Star*, 16 August 1993 [GPP]; 'Mokaba is read riot act by ANC', *The Star*, 14 August 1993 [GPP].

were both quick to distance themselves from the statements, saying that '[The ANC] completely distanced itself from any statement, or alleged statement, that may indicate that we will condone attacks on President De Klerk or any other person.'[72] COSATU said that Mokaba's words 'played into the hands of those who orchestrated the present violence, [and that] it also gives carte blanche to those who are using the hostel dwellers to wage war'.[73] In the early 1990s hostels were a key site of the bloody conflict between ANC supporters, and supporters of the ethnically Zulu Inkatha Freedom Party. Mokaba also vocally opposed amnesty for those in the apartheid state, and declared he hated De Klerk. He became well known for singing the inflammatory struggle song, *Dubul' iBhunu* or 'Shoot the Boer' (and was censured for it by the ANC in May 1993[74]), and for leading crowds in the protest dance, *toyi-toyi*.

In a period of unprecedented tension, Mokaba's heated words to a loyal and impressionable youth base had the power to ignite further violence. He walked a fine line, making incendiary statements and following later with coerced apologies. A *Weekly Mail* editorial after the Tembisa funeral noted, 'Mokaba's retraction this week of the remarks he made at a funeral in Tembisa is more likely the product of tactical consideration than genuine repentance.'[75] Even Mokaba's more moderate statements sometimes had an ominous edge, managing to satisfy militant youths, without crossing party lines. Of the negotiations process he said, 'The implementation of one method should not exclude other methods. When the ANC adopted armed struggle, we did not say it should abandon mass struggle. Our position is clear that we will always opt for the shortest possible route to freedom.'[76] Mokaba's implication that even as it was embarking on negotiations (of which he had been highly critical), the ANC should not – and the Youth League perhaps *would* not – abandon armed struggle flouted the party's authority and Nelson Mandela's new agenda of national forgiveness, but it appealed to his youth base.

Despite the quick back-pedalling from both the ANC and COSATU after the Tembisa funeral speech, and other examples of the ANC leadership's exasperation with their hot-headed youth leader, Raphaël Botiveau

---

[72] 'Mokaba is read riot act by ANC', *The Star*, 14 August 1993 [GPP].
[73] Ibid.
[74] P. Mokaba, '"Kill the Boer" is merely a chant', *The Star*, 15 May 1993 [GPP].
[75] 'Why can't the ANC get rid of Mokaba? He's too powerful', *Weekly Mail and Guardian*, 20 August 1993 [GPP].
[76] 'Sayco will merge with ANC for new Youth League', *Weekly Mail*, 20 April 1990 [GPP].

has argued that Mokaba's incendiary rhetoric was actually useful to the party:

> By going 'too far' Mokaba served the will of the ANC not to negotiate in a completely peaceful climate: it was a question of renouncing the use of armed struggle while simultaneously showing the government that the population remained mobilised.[77]

The ANC was able to cast itself as a 'reasonable alternative' to the radicalism espoused by the Youth League, in spite of the fact that the Youth League was a constitutive part of the ANC itself.[78] This highlights the high level of autonomy that the Youth League maintained under Mokaba, extending to the ability to articulate policy differences from the main party, and even to flout clear party directives about public statements. Clive Glaser has noted that this autonomy was a key feature of the newly formed Youth League, and has argued that it was, in part due to a failure to resolve 'the extent to which the League could step out of line publicly with ANC policy'.[79]

This failure opened the door for a politician like Mokaba. His rhetoric and political manoeuvring during the negotiations period established a precedent of public autonomy and rebelliousness in the Youth League's relationship to the ANC. For both the ANC and the Youth League this situation was advantageous, but also somewhat precarious. As Botiveau has argued, the ANC benefited from the perspective of moderation that its more fractious youth arm cast on the main body; and the Youth League retained a good deal of power to chart its own course in terms of rhetoric, if not necessarily policy, that its branches had had under SAYCO. But it was equally critical to present a united front during the negotiations, to ensure that the ANC kept both the militant youth, and more moderate sections of the South African public onside. Deborah Posel has pointed to this legacy of autonomy in the ANCYL as a key factor in opening 'a space of ideological and political unruliness [...] within the ANC' that has endured well beyond the period of negotiations.[80] The breadth of its appeal to different constituencies is a key aspect of the post-apartheid ANC. It is often called a 'broad church', signifying the number of divergent groups and perspectives within its

---

[77] R. Botiveau, 'The ANC Youth League, or the Invention of a South African Youth Political Organization', *Les Nouveaux Cahiers de l'IFAS (Institut Français d'Afrique du Sud)*, 2007, p. 52.

[78] Glaser, *The ANC Youth League*, p. 107.

[79] Ibid., p. 101.

[80] D. Posel, 'The ANC Youth League and the Politicization of Race', *Thesis Eleven*, 115(58) (2013), 58–76 (64).

scope. This room within the party for dissent and opposition, but the imprecation for unity in the face of division, was a hallmark of the ANC's relationship to the Youth League in the early 1990s.

In *The Idea of the ANC*, Anthony Butler has discussed unity as a key organizational motif for the party: 'The ANC has developed a complex system of alliances that allow diverse class, ideological, gender, and generational differences to be expressed and yet at the same time remain incorporated into a wider project.'[81] The Youth League of the early 1990s, much like the ANCYL of 2012–13, when Butler was writing, represented a distinct set of generational issues within the ANC. In some cases, as with its tacit dismissal of negotiations and a tendency towards violence, the Youth League found itself outside the pale of party support. But always before such strains could become breaks, the Youth League and the ANC would come together again, united in their shared cause. In this vein, in an op-ed sent to *The Star* newspaper in the wake of the controversy over his singing of 'Shoot the Boer, Kill the Farmer', Peter Mokaba said an ANC meeting to clarify the issue of the song 'resolved that the ANC and the Youth League will always and everywhere present a united front in order to defeat the aim of the regime to depict us as a divided house – which we are not'.[82]

[81] Butler, *The Idea of the ANC*, p. 70.
[82] P. Mokaba, '"Kill the Boer" is merely a chant', *The Star*, 15 May 1993 [GPP].

7

Julius Malema and Youth Politics in the New Limpopo

A tale of two leaders

The Northern Transvaal, now Limpopo Province, has not typically been renowned for famous daughters and sons, or for its contributions to the anti-apartheid struggle. Some activists from the area have been overshadowed by peers from other areas, written out of struggle history, or have come to prominence after migrating to the urban centres on the Rand, disassociating their legacies from their roots in the north. Many of these activists have been discussed in the preceding chapters, in an attempt to highlight their contributions, and the contribution of Limpopo, to the history of student and youth politics in South Africa. It is instructive to consider their omissions from regional struggle history – the way in which prominent national figures like Cyril Ramaphosa and Frank Chikane are now mostly divorced from their political roots at Turfloop in popular memory – but it is equally important to consider who *is* remembered in association with their regional roots.

Two men have been intimately linked with the politics of youth in Limpopo Province, as well as on a national scale in post-apartheid South Africa, and it is instructive to consider them both here. One, Peter Mokaba, founder of SAYCO and the first president of the 1991 Youth League, has already been discussed in some detail. The other, Julius Malema, who eventually succeeded Mokaba as the head of the Youth League, has not yet been mentioned. These two youth activists, separated by a generation, bear a good deal of comparison. Both came from poor townships near Pietersburg, were politicized relatively young through school structures, and rose to national prominence through immense populist appeal among their youth constituency. Both occupied a rhetorically radical space within the ANC, eliciting rebukes and censure from the main party, while exciting their base. The production of such leaders, and what they share with earlier activists from the province, has important implications for understanding youth politics in Limpopo, and its impact on youth politics nationally.

When we left Peter Mokaba in the previous chapter, he was a fire-brand, immensely popular with his constituents, but notoriously difficult for party structures – both those of the UDF and of the ANC – to control. It is a measure of his political weight among a vast constituency of young South Africans that he weathered and survived not just charges of insubordination, but of disloyalty. In the early 1990s rumours flew that Mokaba had been an informant for the security police. An investigative report in the *Weekly Mail* alleged this had been discovered in interrogation by the ANC in Lusaka in 1989. Hugh Macmillan has written in detail about the unruly and often violent behaviour of the ANC's National Intelligence and Security Directorate (NAT) in Lusaka during the late 1980s. Alleged to participate in the kidnapping and torture of suspected 'agents' of the apartheid state, the organization underwent restructuring in 1987 to address accusations of corruption, embezzlement and theft, and 'its reputation for being extremely repressive and brutal'.[1] As Macmillan notes, 'It is an open question whether there was any significant improvement in the performance of NAT after the change of management in 1987.'[2] But though Mokaba is purported to have admitted to informing to the security police during his NAT interrogation, ANC President Oliver Tambo made the decision to 'allow him to return home on condition he cut all links with the security police [because] O.R. felt it would be very disillusioning for the youth, for whom he was a hero'.[3] Put more bluntly in a 1993 editorial, 'South Africa's youth, representing the majority of the ANC's support, is Mokaba's stamping ground. He is one of the few ANC leaders who have the unreserved respect of township militants.'[4] The implication here is that, during the turbulent early 1990s, the ANC needed Mokaba to keep the youth in line.

Gavin Evans, who was an operative for the South African Communist Party and involved in internal ANC politics at the time, suggests there may have been more machinations behind the scenes, beyond Tambo's intervention, to keep Mokaba in the fold of the ANC. Evans alleges that a faction of 'several prominent anti-Zuma communists' helped keep Mokaba on the National Executive Council, and 'with Winnie Madikizela-Mandela's muscle, he hung on as youth leader'.[5] But this last point, at least, does Mokaba a disservice. As evidenced in Mokaba's ability to

---

[1] Macmillan, *The Lusaka Years*, p. 232.
[2] Ibid., p. 232.
[3] 'Mokaba issue still on the boil', *Weekly Mail*, 30 May 1991 [GPP].
[4] 'Why can't the ANC get rid of Mokaba? He's too powerful', *Weekly Mail and Guardian*, 20 August 1993 [GPP].
[5] G. Evans, 'Two faces of Mokaba', *Mail and Guardian*, 14 June 2002 [GPP].

sway the founding of the Youth League to the advantage of SAYCO over the Youth Section, and his unanimous election to the presidency when no other candidate even secured a place on the ballot, his popularity among the youth was unparalleled, and not simply a result of Winnie Madikizela-Mandela's popularity, or coercion. He had political muscle of his own.

Indeed, Mokaba and Madikizela-Mandela shared a close and mutually politically beneficial relationship, as discussed in the previous chapter. They also both fell foul of prominent factions in the ANC. And like Peter Mokaba, Winnie Madikizela-Mandela was also rumoured to have been a police informant, though journalist-turned-spy Gordon Winter has attested that, at least in the 1970s, the Bureau of State Security planted false rumours against her.[6]

Mokaba himself unfailingly denied the charges that he had collaborated with the security police, and publicly considered suing the state in 1992 following disclosures that Military Intelligence may have aimed to discredit him by fuelling speculation around the allegations, as they had done with Madikizela-Mandela.[7] This was a common tactic employed by the security services to sow distrust inside the liberation movements.[8] Evans, though, citing sources within the ANC including Jacob Zuma and Joe Nhlanhla, insists the allegations are true. For its part, the ANC's defence of their youth leader was somewhat ambiguous; their Publicity and Information Department said, 'With regard to Comrade Peter Mokaba, the ANC places on record that we regard him as a fully-fledged member of the ANC, in good standing. The ANC does not doubt the bona fides of Comrade Peter Mokaba.'[9] Given the conflicting evidence, and the use of violence, torture, and misinformation employed by both the South African Secret Service, and the ANC's National Intelligence and Security Directorate, it is difficult to say whether the allegations against Mokaba were true. In a newspaper profile of Mokaba published some years after the scandal, Mark Gevisser concluded, '[T]he only thing of lasting significance about these allegations is that, while they have never been conclusively denied by the ANC, they have not even slightly dented Mokaba's ambitions.'[10]

The allegations did not dent Mokaba's ambitions, nor his subsequent achievements; once he was too old to lead the ANC Youth League any

---

[6] G. Winter, *Inside BOSS* (London, 1981), p. 237.

[7] 'Mokaba considers lawsuit', Paper unknown, 19 November 1992 [GPP].

[8] 'Mokaba issue still on the boil', *Weekly Mail*, 30 May 1991 [GPP].

[9] Ibid.

[10] 'Peter Mokaba, Deputy Minister of Environmental Affairs and Tourism in the Mark Gevisser Profile', c. 1995 [GPP].

longer, he ran with the support of the League on the ANC's ticket for parliament, became an MP and the deputy minister for Environmental Affairs and Tourism. He remained a popular figure in his home province, leading political rallies there as late as 2000, and he was rumoured to be challenging Ngoako Ramathlodi, a fellow Turfloop alumnus, for the provincial premiership in 1998, though in the end he did not.[11] In 1999 he was given extended medical leave from parliament to address an unspecified respiratory illness. At the time there was substantial speculation in the press that he was suffering from complications of HIV/ AIDS, though Mokaba, a prominent AIDS denialist, firmly denied this. He remained officially in government until he became too ill to continue working, in 2002. He returned to Mankweng and he died in June of that year.

Two years after his death, Limpopo unveiled its first major public memorial, on the site of Mokaba's grave in Mankweng cemetery. The black granite tower is decorated with an ANC flag and topped by a defiant clenched fist. It looms over everything else in the otherwise sedate and unremarkable graveyard. At its erection on Youth Day 2004, the new provincial secretary of the ANC Youth League in Limpopo spoke of the importance of Mokaba and his legacy in the province: 'The tombstone and planned museum are both the first of their kind in Limpopo. The tombstone is also meant to be the biggest yet for a struggle hero,' said Julius Malema, at the unveiling. 'The fist will remind us all that the person below died fighting.'[12]

According to his biographer, Fiona Forde,

> If there was anyone Julius Malema wanted to be like, it was the late Peter Mokaba, who led the ANCYL after it was unbanned in 1990. [...] It was his defiance that Malema loved him for. It was Mokaba who turned the struggle song 'Shoot the Boer' on its head when he changed its words to chants of 'Kill the Boer, Kill the farmer' at the same time as his party leadership was trying to negotiate an end to apartheid with the white regime. When Mokaba sang it, millions sang with him, and when Malema trotted it out in its less radical form twenty years later, it was a curtain raiser all over again.[13]

---

[11] 'Livening things up with populist humour', *Sunday Times*, 23 July 2000; 'Hold your horses – I'm back in the saddle', *Sunday Times*, 1 July 2001; and 'Ramathlodi in all-out battle to regain top ANC post in Northern Province', *The Star*, 23 June 1998 [GPP].

[12] T. N'wa Mhangwana and J. Arenstein, 'The guerilla who loved a good waltz', *Mail and Guardian*, 25 June 2004 [GPP].

[13] F. Forde, *An Inconvenient Youth: Julius Malema and the 'New' ANC*, 2nd edn (London, 2012), p. 60.

This passage from Malema's biography, *An Inconvenient Youth*, hints at the political common ground between Julius Malema and Peter Mokaba. But there are some important biographical similarities as well. Malema also grew up very poor, in the Masakaneng section of Seshego, the sprawling African township on the north-western outskirts of Pietersburg (now Polokwane), not far from Mokaba's birthplace in New Look Location. Malema was born in 1981 and first became involved in politics in the early 1990s, during South Africa's tense transition period from apartheid to democracy. Perhaps as early as 1990, but more likely at the age of 12 in 1993, he became involved with the local ANC, running errands and doing small jobs for more senior members of the local party branches. Thabo Makunyane, who had helped Ephraim Mogale found COSAS and was imprisoned on Robben Island (see Chapter 5) had been released from prison in 1989, and became the ANC's coordinating figure in the region around Pietersburg. In the preparations for the 1994 elections, Makunyane remembers the young Malema as being practically ubiquitous: 'By then we all knew him. [...] He was everywhere. And he was a popular youth.'[14] He hung posters, helped with registration, and did odd jobs. He also began to make a name for himself with local leaders in the ANC. As Forde described it,

> From a fairly hellish life and humdrum township upbringing, Julius Malema woke up one morning to find himself in the thick of a liberation movement that was no longer outlawed, a political party that was the talk of the country, and which was on a steady march towards victory in the elections of 1994. It couldn't get much better than this in the young boy's mind. And there was no going back.[15]

Here I think Forde overstates the suddenness of Malema's political engagement, while perhaps underplaying his uniqueness. Rather than a sudden awakening, he became involved in politics unusually young, the only one of his cohort to do so, gradually ingratiating himself to older party members and working his way into the ANC fold. As Forde indicates, he did so at a pivotal moment in South Africa's political history, when the country was moving steadily towards a democratic transition, and the ANC was leading the charge. Malema associated himself with the party at this critical time, and went on to join its youth and student structures. He became further involved in politics, joining COSAS as a young high school student at Mohlakaneng High School, and officially joining the ANC Youth League as soon as he turned 14 in 1995.

---

[14] Forde, *An Inconvenient Youth*, p. 70.
[15] Ibid., pp. 71–2.

With the advent of democracy in 1994, the four provinces of apartheid South Africa were dissolved, the ten Bantustans reincorporated, and the country was divided into nine new provinces.[16] For the first time ever, the Northern Transvaal became a unified political entity, rather than the rural outlier of its southern, urban heart. Initially it was named the Northern Province, but after a process of public consultation in 2003 it became Limpopo Province.

This was the new country – and province – in which Julius Malema was coming of age. Though apartheid was officially over, the student movements that had been founded to combat it remained, and many continued what they saw as the struggle legacy: COSAS continued to advocate for the creation of Student Representative Councils and better learning environments for school students. Malema became the provincial chairperson of COSAS in Northern Province in 1997, following his growing prominence in his own school and around Seshego as an advocate for students. Thomas Namathe, a teacher at Mohlakaneng at the time, recalls: 'Malema would never allow anyone else to speak in his name or in the name of the students. If the media came to cover a story and we, as the staff, tried to give our point of view, he would be the first to speak up on the side of the learners.'[17] His ascension to the COSAS regional executive in 1997 gave him a much broader platform than he had previously had, and led to higher ambitions. In 2000 he contested the COSAS presidency, but after a disbanded conference he was forced to renew his quest the following year. He was successful, and became COSAS' national president in 2001 at the age of 20.

The circumstances surrounding the June 2000 conference of COSAS are indicative of Malema's growing political ambitions and the lengths to which he would go to achieve them. In June 2000 the sitting president of COSAS, Lebogang Maile, was stepping down from the position. As the provincial chair for Limpopo, Malema had worked on the National Executive Committee (NEC) with Maile, and was supported by him and many other NEC members when he decided to run for the presidency.[18] But another candidate, Kenny Morolong, the chairperson of COSAS in Northwest Province, was the favourite in the race; he had wider support among the branches than Malema did, and was backed

[16] For more on this process – particularly the reintegration of the Bantustans – and the contentious negotiations around it during the CODESA period, see J. Robinson, 'Fragments of the Past: Homeland politics and the South African transition, 1990–2014', *Journal of Southern African Studies*, 41(5) (2015), 953–67.
[17] Forde, *An Inconvenient Youth*, p. 74.
[18] Ibid., p. 76.

by six of the provinces to Malema's three. '"But just a few days before the conference, rape charges mysteriously surfaced out of nowhere," Morolong remembers.'[19] Kenny Morolong was accused of raping Mosa Molale, a member of his Provincial Executive Committee. Charges were never officially brought and Molale denied the allegations, but the rumours were devastating to Morolong's political chances. The COSAS NEC suspended him, effectively banning him from the upcoming conference. When he decided to attend anyway and was denied entrance by security, 'The delegates, whose support he still enjoyed, went wild.'[20] Fiona Forde has described how figures outside COSAS were brought in to try to broker a negotiation: Fikile Mbalula, then secretary-general of the ANCYL, failed to persuade the delegates to accept a negotiated settlement with Morolong as president and Malema as his deputy. Eventually Winnie Madikizela-Mandela was 'called in and briefed about what was going on. She quickly assessed the matter for herself and a short while later disbanded the conference.'[21]

When the conference resumed the following year, Morolong had been effectively driven out of COSAS, and Malema comfortably won election to the presidency. Under his leadership, COSAS renewed a form of confrontational politics that they had not employed since before South Africa's democratic elections. Several months after Malema's election in late 2001, and again in May 2002, thousands of COSAS students turned out in the streets of Johannesburg for two protest marches in support of free education. The marches turned violent and destructive, resulting in looting, theft, and damage to property. In a statement condemning the December 2001 march, Nelson Mandela said, '[The COSAS students] went on a rampage and destroyed property belonging to hawkers. They had no reason to behave like this.'[22] The Gauteng Department of Education threatened to suspend the COSAS leadership, including Malema who was ostensibly studying for his matric in a Soweto school (despite his continued enrolment at Mohlakaneng in Seshego), as a disciplinary measure. But Malema and others in the COSAS executive refused to be cowed. In a press statement he mooted the possibility of calling for a school stay-away, and claimed, 'How can we be held responsible for a

---

[19] Forde, *An Inconvenient Youth*, p. 76.
[20] Ibid., p. 77.
[21] Ibid., p. 77.
[22] 'Mandela hauls COSAS over the coals', *Mail and Guardian*, 1 January 2002 [*Mail and Guardian* archives].

few who misbehaved when there is no proof that those hooligans were even part of our organization? We are being victimised.'[23]

Eventually the situation was resolved without suspending the COSAS leadership from school, but the incident reveals that, under Malema, COSAS was willing to buck the ANC and other party allies, much as the ANC Youth League had been under Mokaba. Malema graduated from COSAS into the ANC Youth League leadership, becoming, as mentioned above, the provincial chairperson for Limpopo in late 2003, and holding that position for several terms, consolidating his base of power in the province, before finally becoming the national ANCYL president in 2008.

The consideration of Malema's early political years at the helm of COSAS, and then as provincial chair for the Limpopo Youth League, provide a fruitful comparison with Mokaba; the two are arguably the province's most famous sons. As I have noted, it is significant that they, and not other activists, continue to be associated with the region. Their shared populism has come to define youth politics in the post-apartheid era, associating Limpopo with radical – and even racist (thanks largely to their use of 'Kill the Boer, Kill the farmer') – politics in the minds of many. In addition, the province is subject to some of South Africa's worst cases of graft, corruption, and in-fighting between political factions. Some of this is not particularly new: in the late 1990s Peter Mokaba 'was at the centre of selecting and setting up an interim leadership to lead the ANC after the formal provincial structures were dissolved due to incessant factional and ethnic battles'.[24] And Limpopo is no stranger to intervention by the central government in dysfunctional provincial affairs: in 2011 five of its eleven provincial departments were brought under national administration by order of then-Finance Minister Pravin Gordhan owing to bankruptcy.[25] Several of the departments at stake were headed by key allies of Malema and his patron in regional politics, then-provincial Premier Cassel Mathale. Press speculation at the time suggested that the removals were a blow to Mathale's personal power in the province[26]; it came at a time when Malema was fending off attacks on the national stage, and was in the midst of suspension hearings from the ANC itself. Politics in Limpopo involves substantial

---

[23] 'Mandela hauls COSAS over the coals', *Mail and Guardian*, 1 January 2002 [*Mail and Guardian* archives].

[24] 'Hold your horses – I'm back in the saddle', *Sunday Times*, 1 July 2001 [GPP].

[25] 'Five Limpopo departments under administration', *City Press*, 5 December 2011. *City Press* Online Archive [http://www.citypress.co.za/news/five-limpopo-departments-under-administration-20111205] Accessed 19 December 2013.

[26] Ibid.

patronage networks, and business success can rely on party and personal connections to access lucrative government tenders. In the later 2000s, Malema in particular came to dominate provincial politics, mixing political power with business dealings. This led to his 2013 indictment on charges of fraud, corruption, money laundering, and racketeering. (The charges were later struck off the roll by the court, owing to trial delays created by the prosecution.)

But in spite of the controversies surrounding both Malema and Mokaba, their appeal is deep among both youth and students alike, thousands of whom rally loyally around Malema, much as the previous generation had with Mokaba. Both men came from poverty, and in spite of having 'made good' – Mokaba as the proprietor of a string of hairdressing salons, and Malema in the murkier world of government tenders – maintained a deep popularity among the poor, especially in their home areas. Both were also political protégés of Winnie Madikizela-Mandela, who adopted Malema much the way she had Mokaba twenty years earlier: supporting him and appearing by his side at political rallies. Through her association with these young men, 'Ma Winnie' became a sort of matriarch for the ANC Youth League – arguably even more than for the main body of the ANC. Often decried as 'buffoons', both Mokaba and Malema were actually keen political strategists, though their formal educations were interrupted by their political involvements: Mokaba adeptly manoeuvred the reconstitution of the ANC Youth League to privilege SAYCO over the ANC Youth Section, and to position himself as its first president. In the COSAS elections of 2000, Malema so thoroughly buried his opponent, Kenny Morolong, in scandal, that the entire conference had to be disbanded and Morolong eventually left COSAS.[27] A combination of political savvy and ruthlessness has attached itself to the reputations of both men.

But their distinctions are important as well: though both Mokaba and Malema rebelled against the ruling party at times, Mokaba was better able to toe the line when absolutely necessary: 'he was disciplined enough to never actually criticise the ANC itself'.[28] In contrast, Malema's feud with President Jacob Zuma eventually resulted in his expulsion from the ANC in 2012.

These two figures, arguably the most high-profile that are associated with Limpopo, can tell us a good deal about the state of politics in the province at the end of apartheid and in the early years of South Africa's

---

[27] Forde, *An Inconvenient Youth*, pp. 77–8.
[28] 'Peter Mokaba, Deputy Minister of Environmental Affairs and Tourism in the Mark Gevisser Profile', c. 1995 [GPP].

democracy. Provincially, youth occupied a powerful political space, able to challenge other political structures, including the UDF in Mokaba's era, and even the ANC itself in Malema's. The dominance of youth politics in the region accelerated the national rise of its youth leaders; none of Limpopo's older politicians experienced comparable rises to Mokaba and Malema, though they also benefited from its lucrative patronage networks. This may be due in part to Limpopo's demographics. It is an uncommonly young, poor, and rural province,[29] and rabble-rousing, harbingers of change like Mokaba and Malema appeal to those apparently left behind by South Africa's transition. They also join a tradition of perhaps less well-known, but similarly radical students at the forefront of the struggle in Limpopo: Onkgopotse Tiro, Ephraim Mogale, and Thabo Makunyane, the young men who founded the Sekhukhune Youth Organisation and other youth congresses like it, all pioneered important shifts in youth politics that changed the trajectory of national movements. Malema and Mokaba joined this tradition, continuing Limpopo's role as being a driver of national youth and student politics.

Polokwane, 2007

In December 2007 Turfloop, which had recently been renamed the University of Limpopo,[30] was back in the national spotlight once more. In contrast to the student protests and boycotts with which it had been associated in the 1970s and 1980s, when it was on the physical margins of life in South Africa, it was now at the very heart of power. The ANC's fourth post-apartheid conference – often referred to simply as 'Polokwane' for the nearby host city – was actually held on campus at the university. It marked a pivotal moment in ANC history, when the

---

[29] Figures from 2010 census, analyzed by StatsSA, note that 33% of Limpopo's population was below the age of 14 [http://tcoe.org.za/areas-of-operation/42-limpopo-province/71-limpopo-province.html], and a PROVIDE Project Background paper on regional demographics notes that in 2005 while 86.8% of inhabitants resided in rural areas, only 12.4% lived in strictly defined agricultural households, suggesting that in most rural households agriculture does not 'present an important source of income for the household'. 'A Profile of Limpopo Province: Demographics, Poverty, Inequality, and Unemployment', August 2005 [http://ageconsearch.umn.edu/bitstream/15607/1/bp050009.pdf] Accessed 23 December 2013. The 2010 census further suggests that two-thirds of Limpopo residents depend on state grants for their livelihood.

[30] The renaming was a result of the 2005 merger of the University of the North (Turfloop) and the Medical University of South Africa (MEDUNSA) outside Pretoria.

party confronted its own image as a 'broad church' holding together a coalition of varied groups and opinions, and nearly tore itself apart.

The Polokwane conference has sometimes been described as a war within the ANC.[31] Two factions came to the party conference at Turfloop that December – one led by incumbent President Thabo Mbeki, and the other by his challenger and former deputy, Jacob Zuma. The Zuma coalition was a mixed bag of delegates, held together by their frustrations with Mbeki and his austere, technocratic approach to governing. It included powerful factions representing trade unions, the ANC Women's League, the Young Communist League and the ANC Youth League. They were bound by populism, a rhetoric of politics for the common man and woman. As one pro-Zuma delegate from KwaZulu-Natal told a reporter at the conference, 'Everything is going to change because Zuma cares about the people.'[32]

Though the group comprised disparate representation from many corners of the ANC and its key allies, COSATU and the South African Communist Party (SACP), a large number of the Zuma supporters had been rallied to the cause and were led by the ANC Youth League, with Julius Malema at their helm.[33] In late 2007 he was the heir-apparent to Youth League president Fikile Mbalula, and had already established himself as one of Zuma's most vocal supporters. In some of his most high-profile national coverage since leading COSAS to protest in the streets of Johannesburg in 2002, Malema had been a visible (and voluble) presence outside the Johannesburg High Court during Zuma's trial for rape in 2006.[34] Eighteen months later, when the party conference was held in his own backyard in 2007, Malema was in his element. He was the provincial president of the Youth League, on the cusp of becoming its national leader, and was one of Mbalula's closest associates. He was also becoming a key player in provincial politics,[35] and had

---

[31] S. Booysens, *The African National Congress and the Regeneration of Political Power* (Johannesburg, 2011), p. 41.

[32] R. Wolmarans and M. Burbidge, 'Zuma is new ANC President', *Mail and Guardian*, 18 December 2007. [http://mg.co.za/article/2007-12-18-zuma-is-new-anc-president] Accessed 24 February 2014.

[33] Booysens, *The African National Congress*, pp. 41–5, 49–51.

[34] Malema and other representatives from the Youth League were criticized by gender equality activists for violent rhetoric about Zuma's accuser, Fezekile Kuzwayo, during the course of the trial. Zuma was acquitted of the charges. K. Maughan, 'Malema in hot water over rape claims', *IOL News*, 26 May 2009. [http://www.iol.co.za/news/politics/malema-in-hot-water-over-rape-claims-1.444435#.UzF3CYePPcs] Accessed 19 February 2014.

[35] Forde, *An Inconvenient Youth*, pp. 182–90.

come to the attention of national figures: he even shared platforms with Zuma himself in the months of campaigning before the conference at Polokwane.[36]

Though the Youth League delegation at Polokwane officially numbered only 68, Clive Glaser has argued that this number belies their influence and importance.[37] One outcome of SAYCO's successful influence in the re-formation of the Youth League was the large overlap between league membership and membership in the ANC itself, due to the age cap of 35. This gave the league outsize influence over party matters, beyond their block vote. In the lead-up to the conference at Polokwane, as factions formed around both Mbeki and Zuma, the Youth League claimed 800,000 members, larger than the ANC itself at the time.[38] Consequently, the Youth League's influence was much greater than its delegation numbers might suggest; at conference it commanded a large degree of support, and succeeded in flexing its muscle from the outset. Youth Leaguers were able to derail the first day's schedule with a heated debate over whether ballots should be counted by computer (as had been pre-arranged by the National Executive Council), arguing that computers were more susceptible to interference and rigging than a manual count.[39] That night the Youth League brought a motion that computer counting be banned, and it passed. In the wake of the 'humiliation' of losing control on the first day, Mbeki's supporters held a rally in the Turfloop sports stadium at lunchtime on the second day of the conference.[40] This 'unprecedented spectacle'[41] was met with defiance as, in response, the Zuma supporters threw an even larger, competing rally on the nearby field, where in 1974 students had confronted police in the aftermath of their Viva-FRELIMO rally. Mbalula addressed the Zuma rally, reinforcing the importance of youth in Zuma's base of support.

---

[36] Glaser, *The ANC Youth League*, p. 135.

[37] Ibid., pp. 129–30.

[38] Ibid., pp. 129–30; it is important to note that the Youth League acts as a recruitment base for the ANC itself; it recruits a younger membership (starting with membership at age 14) and once members turn 18 they automatically become ANC members as well.

[39] R. Wolmarans, 'ANC conference off to shaky start', *Mail and Guardian*, 16 December 2007. [http://mg.co.za/article/2007-12-16-anc-conference-off-to-shaky-start] Accessed 3 March 2014.

[40] M. Rossouw and M. Letsoalo, 'Zuma, Mbeki camps rally in Polokwane', *Mail and Guardian*, 17 December 2007. [http://mg.co.za/article/2007-12-17-zuma-mbeki-camps-rally-in-polokwane] Accessed 3 March 2014.

[41] Ibid.

When all the votes were counted (by hand), Zuma had won comfortably. His candidates for the top six posts in the NEC did the same – with approximately sixty per cent of the vote. It was a remarkable electoral sweep from a challenger for the party presidency, and it presaged change not just in the party but also in government itself. Less than a year after the conference, Mbeki had been removed from the national presidency.

The effects of Polokwane on the ANC and on South African politics more broadly have been discussed widely.[42] But what the conference indicates about Limpopo and the evolution of youth politics in the province has been generally overlooked in favour of national narratives. For this reason, considering the Polokwane conference of 2007 is a useful point on which to conclude this book. It illuminates some of the key issues that have been addressed: questions of marginality and centrality, both of the province and of its young people; of the roles that youth can exercise politically and their use of populism, violence, and rhetoric in that exercise; of the ideologies they deploy and how they mobilize groups; and finally, of the place of Limpopo – and its institutions and actors – in this heady mix.

---

[42] For a discussion of the impact of Polokwane on the end of Mbeki's presidency and his removal from office, see F. Chikane, *Eight Days in September: The removal of Thabo Mbeki* (Johannesburg, 2012); M. Gevisser, *A Legacy of Liberation: Thabo Mbeki and the future of the South African dream* (New York, 2009), especially the Epilogue; and Booysens, *The African National Congress*, pp. 44–9.

Epilogue: Legacies of Limpopo

The introduction to this book opened in the present, on the scenes of student protests at Turfloop in 2016 when the campus joined nation-wide student strikes as part of the FeesMustFall Movement that had been sparked on other campuses. But the body of the text has argued that Turfloop – and Limpopo as a whole – has a much deeper history of student protest, and youth-driven change. In fact, even FeesMustFall had earlier precedents at Turfloop and its fellow former 'bush' colleges; students on these campuses led calls for the institution and improvement of aid schemes like the National Student Financial Aid Scheme (NSFAS) in the 1990s and early 2000s. As one protesting student told researcher Musawenkosi Malabela,

> There were countless protests, countless shut downs and countless efforts but were not given the same space like what you call #FeesMustFall movement, which is given attention by the media. You can't dissociate the fact that there used to be TEFSA [Tertiary Education Fund for South Africa] now there is NSFAS and now you even have the NSFAS saying that final [year] students who have passed their entire course, their loan must be changed into a bursary. These are victories of relentless struggles and violent protests that have been waged by students and generations of student leaders at Turloop and other black universities.[1]

Turfloop, then, has remained an important site of ideological and political formation, even as it has faded from the front pages of South Africa's papers. But as in the 1960s and 1970s, students on this peri-rural campus are raising some of the key political issues of their time, often before their national counterparts do so. I have tried to argue here for its crucial place – and for the place of Limpopo as a whole – in the historiography of South African struggle.

---

[1] Protesting PYA-affiliated student, quoted in M. Malabela, 'We are already enjoying free education: Protests at the University of Limpopo (Turfloop)' in *#Hashtag: An Analysis of the #FeesMustFall Movement at South African Universities*, ed. M. Langa (Center for the Study of Violence and Reconciliation, 2017).

Who is remembered? Associational legacies in Limpopo

This book has chronicled three major periods in the history of student and youth activism in the Northern Transvaal over the latter decades of the twentieth century: from the relatively elite-led, university-oriented ideological protest of the Black Consciousness movement, to the locally rooted regional expansion of protest politics under COSAS and youth congresses, to the congregation of those once-disparate groups under the banner of the unbanned ANC Youth League. In each of these stages I have recalled the work of important political actors who came from or, in some cases went to, the Northern Transvaal and influenced the development of political expression there. Some of these have been remembered, associated, and memorialized as the province's famous sons; some have been remembered, having gone on to greater political fortunes, but have been divorced from their political roots in the region; and some have been broadly forgotten, as history and politics have moved on from their contributions. To conclude this story, it is useful to consider what these associations, and this process of collective memory, indicates about politics in Limpopo.

A host of the people mentioned in these pages have gone on to greater political prominence from their days as student activists: Cyril Ramaphosa, Frank Chikane, Mosiuoa Lekota, and Aubrey Mokoena, all nationally recognized figures today, were Turfloop students during the 1970s. As discussed in Chapters 1 and 2, they contributed to and participated in the increasingly politicized atmosphere on the campus, through the vehicles of the Students' Christian Movement, the South African Students' Organisation, and the Students Representative Council.

Cyril Ramaphosa, after his first period of detention at the Mankweng police station for his involvement in the 1974 Viva-FRELIMO rally, spent much of the late 1970s in and out of detention, and then founded the National Union of Mineworkers (NUM) in 1982.[2] During his involvement with trade unionism, he became involved in the UDF and later the MDM, and was a key negotiator for the ANC during the 1990s, both in navigating the transition to democratic rule and in crafting the 1996 constitution. He was infamously sidelined in favour of Thabo Mbeki for the position of Nelson Mandela's deputy president after the 1994 election,[3] and by the late 1990s his involvement in politics

---

[2] For a complete biography until 2008, see Butler, *Cyril Ramaphosa* (Oxford, 2008).

[3] Ramaphosa's biographer, Butler, suggests that his sidelining was due, in part, to falling afoul of Peter Mokaba and Winnie Mandela, and the populist power they commanded at the time. Butler, *Cyril Ramaphosa*, p. 318.

seemed to be secondary to his successful career as a businessman. But after years in business, he returned to the heart of politics when he was elected ANC deputy president under Jacob Zuma in late 2012. In February 2018 the ANC National Executive Commission (NEC) recalled Jacob Zuma under a cloud of corruption allegations; the next day Cyril Ramaphosa was sworn in as the president of South Africa.[4]

Frank Chikane maintained and deepened his involvement in both Christianity and political activism beyond his involvement in the Students' Christian Movement at Turfloop. After leaving the university in 1975 and tutoring students at Naledi High School, he was ordained as a minister in the Apostolic Faith Mission, but owing to his continued and increasingly vocal opposition to apartheid, he was suspended from the conservative congregation. He went on to become involved in the South African Council of Churches (SACC), first through its Institute of Contextual Theology (ICT) and later as the secretary general of the organization. While at the ICT, Chikane participated in the founding of the UDF, and spoke at its launch in 1983.[5] After South Africa's democratic transition, Chikane concluded his term as secretary general of the SACC and later became a member of the ANC's National Executive Committee. The Apostolic Faith Mission also apologized to him, and reinstated him as the Rev. Frank Chikane. He served as the director general of the presidency under President Thabo Mbeki, and wrote an observational account of Mbeki's ouster from power, *Eight Days in September: The removal of Thabo Mbeki*. When FeesMustFall protests ignited in Johannesburg and Cape Town in October 2015, Chikane made headlines when his son Kgosi was arrested protesting outside parliament. Chikane, now an esteemed elder churchman, was called with other religious leaders to mediate between students and administrators at Wits University, and publicly voiced his support for protesting students.[6]

Mosiuoa 'Terror' Lekota remained involved in student politics and connected to Turfloop even after his expulsion during the Onkgopotse Tiro affair in 1972. He went on to become permanent organizer of SASO after two Turfloop alumni (Tiro and Harry Nengwekhulu)

---

[4] G. Davis, 'Cyril Ramaphosa sworn in as President of RSA', *Eye Witness News*, 15 February 2018. [http://ewn.co.za/2018/02/15/watch-live-ramaphosa-to-be-sworn-in-as-sa-president] Accessed 20 March 2018.

[5] For a more complete biography to the 1980s, see Chikane's autobiography, F. Chikane, *No Life of My Own* (London, 1988).

[6] Redi Thlabi interview with Frank Chikane, 'Rev Frank Chikane says #FeesMustFall must be supported to take SA forward', 23 October 2015. [http://www.702.co.za/articles/5960/rev-frank-chikane-says-feesmustfall-must-be-supported-to-take-sa-forward]

had held the position, and he was instrumental in establishing the off-campus branch of SASO in Mankweng, when university authorities had banned the organization, as discussed in Chapter 2. Later that year he was arrested for his involvement in planning the Viva-FRELIMO rally in Durban, and he became one of the defendants in the trial of the SASO 9, resulting in his imprisonment on Robben Island. After his release from prison in 1983, Lekota, like Chikane and Ramaphosa, abandoned Black Consciousness ideology in favour of the multiracialism of the United Democratic Front. He eventually became a National Executive Committee member for the ANC, and Premier of the Free State after the end of apartheid. In 2008, when President Thabo Mbeki was ousted from office after Zuma's triumph at Polokwane, Lekota, an Mbeki ally, resigned his position as Minister of Defence and founded the Congress of the People (COPE), an ANC splinter party.

Aubrey Mokoena, the president of the Turfloop SRC that had invited Onkgopotse Tiro to speak in 1972, was expelled with Lekota in the aftermath of that event. His time at Turfloop had introduced Mokoena to Black Consciousness, and when he left the university he continued his involvement with the Black Consciousness Movement, first through SASO and then as an organizer for Black Community Programmes. He based himself and his family in Soweto during these years, and was a trusted adult adviser to some key student leaders of the 1976 revolt in schools there, as described in Chapter 4. Eventually in the crackdown against the BCM during 1977, Mokoena was detained and later given a banning order. He was not able to publicly participate in political life again until the early 1980s. In 1984 he joined the Release Mandela Campaign (RMC), a UDF affiliate, finding it more organized and a preferable alternative to AZAPO, despite the fact that the latter had been founded by some of Mokoena's Black Consciousness cohort from Turfloop. The RMC was a pocket of more radical Africanism within the multi-racial umbrella (as discussed in Chapter 6), and Mokoena was eventually the most vocal critic of the supposed 'cabal' of Indian leadership that was accused of dictating UDF decision-making and sidelining African leaders. He was a member of parliament for the ANC until 2014.

These four men followed similar trajectories out of university, from which they were all expelled for their political involvement in SASO, the SRC, and the Students' Christian Movement. With varying speed they left the ideology of Black Consciousness behind in favour of involvement in the United Democratic Front. They all became – and most remain – allied with the ANC at the time of its unbanning. In part this was simply pragmatic; the fate of Black Consciousness organizations had been clear since the failure of AZAPO to compete with the rising tide of Charterism in the 1980s, and subsequent splits in that party doomed it to increasing political irrelevance. When Ramaphosa, Lekota, and Mokoena emerged from periods of imprisonment, detention, and banning, the UDF allowed a broad scope of participation in anti-apartheid politics – through trade unions, churches, and civics – and even some space for questioning the fixity of Charterism. But somehow in jettisoning their ties to Black Consciousness, popular memory has also jettisoned their roots at Turfloop, and instead relates them to their entry into Charterist politics: for Ramaphosa, it is the trade unions, for Chikane, the churches, but for all it is through their roles in the UDF. They each made an ideological shift that, whether by strategy or happenstance, kept them on the right side of shifting political trends in South Africa, and eventually positioned them in relative proximity to national power. These trajectories also served to divorce them from the radical student politics of their youth at Turfloop.

Compatriots of Ramaphosa, Chikane, Lekota, and Mokoena – those from the Turfloop cohort of the 1970s who did not make that critical shift from Black Consciousness to Charterism – have found their legacies less enduring. Those who championed the cause of Black Consciousness beyond its banning in 1977, like Harry Nengwekhulu, and who founded its inheritor, the Azanian People's Organisation (AZAPO), like Lybon Mabasa and Ishmael Mkhabela, are among those who I argue have been broadly forgotten in the national and regional narratives of struggle.

Nengwekhulu remained in exile in Botswana until South Africa's democratic transition in 1994; he worked as an organizer for the Black Consciousness Movement (later the Black Consciousness Movement of South Africa) until the exile structures of the organization deteriorated, as discussed in Chapter 4. He then became an academic at the University of Botswana, withdrawing from political life until his return to South Africa, where he has acted as an education consultant to provincial and national structures.

Lybon Mabasa and Ishmael Mkhabela continued to face aggressive state repression in the late 1970s and early 1980s; they were among Turfloop's student-teacher activists in Soweto schools in 1976, and in the wake of the crackdown on Black Consciousness organizations in 1977 they pioneered the founding of AZAPO. Mkhabela recalls this as an explicit attempt to preserve space for 'citizen's action':

> Just after the 1977 banning of the organizations, the predominant view of the ANC was that the space for civil disobedience and social action, citizens' action, were over. The only option was military struggle. Those

of us who formed AZAPO, we believed there would always be space – a very important space – for citizens' action.[7]

This emphasis on social action is reflected in the turn his political career took; after the expiration of a banning order in the early 1980s Mkhabela became involved in community organizing through the Wilgespruit Fellowship Centre, an ecumenical body founded by the Anglican Church, and he later founded his own community development organization, leaving the world of political parties behind him.

Lybon Mabasa, his co-founder in AZAPO, took a different path. He was also banned for five years after founding AZAPO, but in his own words, 'After five years I had not learned my lesson – I went back to politics, I went back to AZAPO.'[8] He remained with the organization through its transition to a political party and when it contested the first national democratic election in 1994. After a schism in AZAPO in 1995, Mabasa left and formed the Socialist Party of Azania (SoPA), which he still heads.

Juxtaposing these two groups of Turfloop alumni – those who have gone on to political prominence through their connections with the ruling party, and those who have been largely sidelined in struggle narratives owing to their association with other parties and ideologies – is in part a story of political 'winners' and 'losers'. But it is more than that as well; it may shed light on the way that Turfloop itself has been remembered in recent history. The university rocketed to national attention from rural obscurity in the early 1970s for its close associations with Black Consciousness and SASO; it was a hotbed of political activism and a centre for the reinvigoration of Africanist ideas. But by the time Charterism came to the fore of student and national politics in the 1980s, another important shift had taken place, moving the nexus of youth political action in the Northern Transvaal outside the university and into schools and villages. Though Turfloop still played an important role in contributing to the development and work of new organizations like COSAS and youth congresses, it was no longer the epicentre of activism in the province, and its public profile reflected this.

If the shift to Charterism in the 1980s is important for how Turfloop is remembered, it can also expose some clues about the third group of political figures I mentioned above: those who are remembered, and whose legacies, importantly, are associated with Limpopo. As discussed in Chapters 6 and 7, the two most significant political figures to be

[7] Author's interview with Ishmael Mkhabela.
[8] Author's interview with Lybon Mabasa.

associated with Limpopo today are Julius Malema and Peter Mokaba. Both share an array of characteristics, from their similarly impoverished backgrounds to the adept employment of populism and inflammatory rhetoric that they used to galvanize their youth base. They emerged from a multi-racial, Charterist/ANC tradition (though Mokaba was initially conscientized by Black Consciousness thinkers in the wake of 1976), but were able to maintain a great deal of autonomy over their organizations – SAYCO and the ANC Youth League – within the UDF/ANC fold, and even to challenge dominant ideologies. They shared a tendency towards militant politics with their regional counterparts from the 1970s, a legacy that has associated itself with the rhetoric of provincial politics in Limpopo in the post-apartheid era. Many of these traits are also implicitly associated with the politics of youth. It is significant that it was only after Ramaphosa, Chikane, Lekota, and Mokoena ceased to be student political activists and moved into more 'adult' activist arenas that they stopped being associated with the province. Onkgopotse Tiro never lived long enough to make such a transition, and his legacy remains deeply associated with the region, and with Turfloop in particular.

Mokaba and Malema's legacies are deeply rooted in the politics of the Youth League; even Malema's new party, the Economic Freedom Fighters, emerged from this space and has come to lead the SRCs at many of South Africa's universities, including Turfloop. These political formations arguably share some traits with the political culture of Limpopo itself: among them, a tendency to buck authority and to engage in radical and even militant political rhetoric. Limpopo, then, is politically characterized by its youth, making it important to better understand the role of young people have played historically in shaping politics in the province.

Bibliography

Archival Sources

Bodleian Library of African Studies at Rhodes House, Oxford [RHO]
Howard Barrell Papers
Gail Gerhart Private Papers [GPP]
Hugh Macmillan Private Papers [MPP]
Limpopo Provincial Archives – Lebowakgomo [LPAL]
Limpopo Provincial Archives – Giyani [LPAG]
Hudson Ntsan'wisi private correspondence
    Gazankulu Government Publications
National Archives of South Africa, Pretoria [SANA]
BAO X109 (Bureau for State Security Files)
    MJU 727 (Regional Court Records, Durban)
    URU 7083 (Venda Administration Records)
Rhodes University Cory Library, Grahamstown [RUCL]
MS 18 (National Union of South African Students Records) Sixth Interim
    Report of the Commission of Inquiry into Certain Organisations: The
    University Christian Movement (Pretoria, 1975)
South African Historical Archive, Johannesburg [SAHA]
AL2425 (South African Youth Congress Collection)
AL2451 (ANC Youth League Collection)
    AL2457 (SAHA Collection)
University of Fort Hare, NAHECS Liberation Archives, Alice [UFH]
AZA (Azanian People's Organisation / Black Consciousness Movement
    Collection)
University of the Witwatersrand Historical Papers Research Archive [HPRA]
    A835 (Spro-Cas Collection)
    A2176 (SASO Collection)
    A2177 (Black People's Convention Collection)
    A2675 (Karis–Gerhart Collection)
    A2953 (Soweto Riots Collection)
    A2981f (Azanian Youth Unity Collection)
    AC623 (South African Council of Churches Collection)
    AD1126 (University Christian Movement Collection)
    AD1790 (COSAS Collection)

AD1912 (South African Institute of Race Relations)
AD2021 (SASO 9 Transcripts)
AG2635 (AZASO Collection)
AG2735 (TRAC Collection)
AG2843 (Institute for Contextual Theology Collection)
AK2117 (Delmas Treason Trial Collection)

Online Resources

@ULVarsity Twitter
702.co.za
http://sabctrc.saha.org.za
iol.co.za
www.anc.org.za
www.azapo.org.za
www.thedailyvox.co.za
www.disa.org.za
www.enca.com
www.ewn.co.za
www.justice.gov.za
www.mg.co.za
www.statsa.gov.sa
www.thepresidency.gov.za
www.timeslive.co.za
www.witsvuvuzela.com

Interviews with the Author, 2011–13

Collins, Colin. By correspondence, 20 August 2012
Dederen, Godfried. Thohoyandou, 4 September 2012
Hanisch, Edwin. Thohoyandou, 4 September 2012
Lekganyane, Soviet. Frans Mohlala House, Polokwane, 23 August 2012
Mabasa, Tiyani Lybon. Johannesburg, 28 September 2011
Mabunda, Klaas. Bela Bela (Warmbaths), 25 April 2012 (a); Modimolle, 10
    September 2012 (b); and 8 November 2013 (c)
Madikoto, Ian. Seshego, 16 November 2011
Madikoto, Mokanna Dorcas. Westenburg, Polokwane, 20 November 2011
Mathale, Cassel. Frans Mohlala House, Polokwane, 3 September 2012
Matshidze, Pfarelo. Thohoyandou, 4 September 2012
Mkhabela, Ishmael. Parktown, Johannesburg, 21 October 2011
Mokwele, Alfred Percy Phuti. Turfloop, 20 September 2011
Nchabeleng, Maurice. Polokwane, 13 October 2011 (a); and 6 September
    2012 (b)
Nchabeleng, Mpho. Pretoria, 22 October 2011
Nefolovhodwe, Pandelani. Germiston, 27 September 2011

Nengwekhulu, Harry. Pretoria, 19 October 2011 (a); and Pretoria, 21 April 2012 (b)
Moore, Basil. By correspondence, 14 August 2012
Sekonya, Richard. Apel, Sekhukhuneland, 18 November 2011
Seolonyanne, Sydney. Parktown, Johannesburg, 24 November 2011
Seopela, Mandla. Melville, Johannesburg, 17 September 2011

Printed Primary Sources*

Alexander, N., *Robben Island Dossier, 1964–1974* (Cape Town, 1994).
Association of University Teachers (Great Britain), *South Africa's Universities* (London, 1988).
Biko, B.S. *et al.* (eds), *Black Viewpoint* (Durban, 1972).
Biko, S., *I Write What I Like* (Oxford, 1988).
Black, R.C., *Black Renaissance: Papers from the Black Renaissance Convention, December 1974* (Johannesburg, 1975).
Chikane, F., *No Life of My Own: An autobiography* (London, 1988).
Collins, Colin, *Where the River Runs* (self-published, undated (c. 2009)).
Cone, J.H., *Black Theology and Black Power* (Maryknoll, NY, 1997).
Cooper, H.T. (ed.), *Deeds Speak: The views of Professor H.W.E. Ntsan'wisi, Chief Minister of Gazankulu* (Nelspruit, 1987).
Goba, B., *An Agenda for Black Theology: Hermeneutics for social change* (Johannesburg, 1988).
Horrell, M., *The African Homelands of South Africa* (Johannesburg, 1973).
——, *Bantu Education to 1968* (Johannesburg, 1968).
Kairos Theologians (Group), *The Kairos Document: Challenge to the Church; A theological comment on the political crisis in South Africa*, 2nd edn (Johannesburg, 1986).
Kathrada, A., *Memoirs* (Cape Town, 2004).
Kgware, W., 'Education of the Africans in South Africa', *South Africa International*, October 1974.
Maharaj, M. (ed.), *Reflections in Prison* (Cape Town, 2001).
Mandela, N., *Long Walk to Freedom: The autobiography of Nelson Mandela* (London, 1995).
Mashinini, T., 'Behind the Growing Upsurge in South Africa', *Intercontinental Press*, 15 November 1976 [not paginated].
Mphahlele, E., *Down Second Avenue* (London, 1959).
——, *Afrika My Music* (Johannesburg, 1984).
Moore, B., 'Learning from Black Theology', speech given at Rhodes University Graduation, 8 April 2011. [http://www.ru.ac.za/media/rhodesuniversity/

---

* Where necessary, shortened forms of titles have been used for ease of citation in the text and are indicated in brackets following the full citation in the bibliography.

content/ruhome/documents/Basil%2 Moore%20Spe ech%20%20-%20
Black%20Theology.pdf] Accessed 15 August 2012.

Nettleton, C., 'Racial Cleavage on the Student Left' in H.W. Van der Merwe
and D. Welsh (eds), *Student Perspectives on South Africa* (Cape Town,
1972), pp. 125– 37.

Nkondo, G.M. (ed.), *Turfloop Testimony: The dilemma of a Black University
in South Africa* (Johannesburg, 1976). [Turfloop Testimony]

Ralushai, N.V. *et al.*, *Report of the Commission of Inquiry into Witchcraft
Violence and Ritual Murders in the Northern Province of South Africa*
(Pretoria, 1996).

Republic of South Africa, *Report of the Commission on the Separate
University Education Bill* (Pretoria, 1958).

——, *Report of the Commission of Inquiry into the Riots at Soweto and
Elsewhere from the 16th of June to the 28th February 1977*, 2 Vols
(Pretoria, 1980). [Cillié Commission]

Snyman, J.H., *Report of the Commission of Inquiry into Certain Matters
Relating to the University of the North* (Pretoria, 1975). [Snyman
Commission]

Sono, T., *Reflections on the Origins of Black Consciousness in South Africa*
(Pretoria, 1993). [*Origins of Black Consciousness*]

Winter, G., *Inside BOSS: South Africa's Secret Police* (London, 1981).

Wolfson, J.G.E., *Turmoil at Turfloop: A summary of the Reports of the
Snyman and Jackson Commissions of Inquiry into the University of the
North* (Johannesburg, 1976). [*Turmoil at Turfloop*]

Secondary Sources*

Abel, R.L., *Politics by Other Means: Law in the struggle Against Apartheid,
1980–1994* (London, 1995).

Abbink J. and I. van Kessel (eds.), *Vanguard or Vandals: Youth, politics, and
conflict in Africa* (Leiden, 2005).

Ashforth, A., *Witchcraft, Violence, and Democracy in South Africa* (Chicago,
2005).
[*Witchcraft, Violence, and Democracy*]

——, 'On living in a world with witches: everyday epistemology and spiritual
insecurity in a modern African city (Soweto)' in H.L. Moore and T. Sanders
(eds), *Magical Interpretations, Material Realities: Modernity, witchcraft,
and the occult in postcolonial Africa* (London, 2001), pp. 206–25.

Badat, S., *Black Student Politics: Higher education and Apartheid from SASO
to SANSCO, 1968–1990* (Pretoria, 1999). [*Black Student Politics*]

Barkan, J., *An African Dilemma: University students, development and politics
in Ghana, Tanzania, and Uganda* (Oxford, 1976).

* Where necessary, shortened forms of titles have been used for ease of citation in
the text, and are indicated following the full citation in the bibliography

Beinart, W., 'Beyond "Homelands": Some ideas about the history of African rural areas in South Africa', *South African Historical Journal*, 64(1) (2012), 5–21.

——, 'The Mpondo Revolt through the Eyes of Leonard Mdingi and Anderson Ganyile' in T. Kepe and L. Ntsebeza (eds), *Rural Resistance in South Africa: The Mpondo Revolts after fifty years* (Leiden, 2011).

——, *The Political Economy of Pondoland, 1860–1930* (Cambridge, 1982).

Beinart, W. and C. Bundy (eds), *Hidden Struggles in Rural South Africa: Politics & popular movements in the Transkei & Eastern Cape 1890–1930* (Berkeley, CA, 1987).

Booysen, S., *The African National Congress and the Regeneration of Political Power* (Johannesburg, 2011). [*The African National Congress*]

Botiveau, R. 'The ANC Youth League, or the Invention of a South African Youth Political Organization', *Les Nouveaux Cahiers de l'IFAS* (Institut Français d'Afrique du Sud), 2007.

Bozzoli, B., *Theatres of Struggle and the End of Apartheid* (Edinburgh, 2004). [*Theatres of Struggle*]

Brewster, K. and C. Brewster, 'The Mexican Student Movement of 1968: An Olympic perspective', *The International Journal of the History of Sport*, 26(6) (May 2009), 814–39.

Brown, J., An Experiment in Confrontation: The pro-Frelimo rallies of 1974', *Journal of Southern African Studies*, 38(1) (2012), 55–71. ['An Experiment in Confrontation']

——, *The Road to Soweto: Resistance and the Uprising of 16 June 1976* (Oxford, 2016).

Bundy, C., *Govan Mbeki: A Pocket Biography* (Johannesburg, 2013).

——, *The Rise and Fall of the South African Peasantry*, 2nd edn (London, 1988).

——, 'Street Sociology and Pavement Politics: Aspects of youth and student resistance in Cape Town, 1985', *Journal of Southern African Studies*, 13(3) (1987), 303–30. ['Street Sociology']

Burnett, J., *Generations: The time machine in theory and practice* (Farnham, Surrey, 2010).

Butler, A., *Cyril Ramaphosa* (Oxford, 2008).

——, *The Idea of the ANC* (Athens, OH, 2013).

Carmichael, S. and C. Hamilton, *Black Power: The politics of liberation in America: With new afterwords by the authors* (New York, 1992).

Chikane, F. *Eight Days in September: The removal of Thabo Mbeki* (Johannesburg, 2012).

Chisholm, L. 'From a Revolt to a Search for Alternatives', *Work in Progress*, 42 (1986), 14–19.

Cole, J. and D. Durham, 'Introduction: Age, Regeneration, and the Intimate Politics of Globalization' in J. Cole and D. Durham (eds), *Generations and Globalization: Youth, age, and family in the New World economy* (Bloomington, IN, 2007), pp. 1–28.

Cone, J., *Black Theology and Black Power* (Maryknoll, NY, 1997).

Crais, C., *White Supremacy and Black Resistance in Pre-Industrial South Africa: The making of the colonial order in the Eastern Cape, 1770–1865* (Cambridge, 1992).

Cruise O'Brien, D. 'A Lost Generation? Youth identity and state decay in West Africa' in R. Werbner and T. Ranger (eds), *Postcolonial Identities in Africa* (London, 1996), pp. 55–74. ['A Lost Generation?']

Delius, P. *A Lion Amongst the Cattle: Reconstruction and resistance in the Northern Transvaal* (Oxford, 1996). [*A Lion Amongst the Cattle*]

——, 'Migrants, Comrades, and Rural Revolt: Sekhukhuneland 1950–1987', *Transformation*, 13 (1990), 2–26.

——, *The Land Belongs to Us: The Pedi polity, the Boers and the British in the nineteenth-century Transvaal* (London, 1984). [*The Land Belongs to Us*]

——, 'Migrant Labour and the Pedi' in S. Marks and A. Atmore (eds), *Economy and Society in Pre- Industrial South Africa* (London, 1980), pp. 293–312.

Diseko, N., 'The Origins and Development of the South African Students' Movement (SASM): 1968–1976', *Journal of Southern African Studies*, 18(1) (1992), 40–62. ['Origins and Development of SASM']

Dubow, S. *Apartheid, 1948–1994* (Oxford, 2014).

Durham, D. 'Empowering Youth: Making youth citizens in Botswana' in J. Cole and D. Durham (eds), *Generations and Globalization: Youth, age, and family in the New World economy* (Bloomington, IN, 2007), pp. 102–31.

——, 'Youth and the Social Imagination in Africa: Introduction to Parts 1 and 2', *Anthropological Quarterly*, 73(3) (2000), 113–20.

Egan, A., *The Politics of a South African Catholic Student Movement, 1960–1987* (Cape Town, 1991).

Ellis, S., *External Mission: The ANC in exile, 1960–1990* (London, 2012). [*External Mission*]

——,'The Historical Significance of South Africa's Third Force', *Journal of Southern African Studies*, 24:2 (1998), 261–99.

Ellis, S. and T. Sechaba, *Comrades Against Apartheid: The ANC & the South African Communist Party in exile* (Bloomington, IN, 1992).

Everatt, D., 'Non-racialism in South Africa: Status and prospects', *Politikon*, 39(1) (2012), 5–28.

Forde, F., *An Inconvenient Youth: Julius Malema and the 'New' ANC*, rev. edn (London, 2012). [*An Inconvenient Youth*]

Gastrow, S. *Who's Who in South African Politics*, 5th edn (Johannesburg, 1995). [*Who's Who*]

Gerhart, G.M., *Black Power in South Africa: The evolution of an ideology* (Berkeley, CA, 1978). [*Black Power in South Africa*]

Gevisser, M., *A Legacy of Liberation: Thabo Mbeki and the future of the South African dream* (New York, 2009).

Gibbs, T., *Mandela's Kinsmen: Nationalist elites & Apartheid's first Bantustan* (Oxford, 2014). [*Mandela's Kinsmen*]

Glaser, C., *A Jacana Pocket History: The ANC Youth League* (Johannesburg, 2013). [*ANC Youth League*]

——, *Bo-Tsotsi: The youth gangs of Soweto, 1935–1976* (Oxford, 2000). [*Bo-Tsotsi*]

——, '"We must infiltrate the tsotsis": School politics and youth gangs in Soweto, 1968– 1976', *Journal of Southern African Studies*, 24(2) (1998), 301–23. ['We must infiltrate the tsotsis']

de Gruchy, J., *The Church Struggle in South Africa*, 2nd edn (Cape Town: David Philip, 1982).

Hadfield, L.A., *Liberation and Development: Black Consciousness community programs in South Africa* (East Lansing, MI, 2016). [*Liberation and Development*]

Hammond-Tooke, W., *Boundaries and Belief: The structure of a Sotho worldview* (Johannesburg, 1981).

Hanna, W.J. (ed.), *University Students and African Politics* (London, 1975).

Harrison, N., *Winnie Mandela: Mother of a nation* (London, 1985).

Hay, M., 'A Tangled Past: Land settlement, removals, and restitution in Letaba District, 1900–2013', *Journal of Southern African Studies*, 40(4) (2014), 745–60.

Heffernan, A., 'Black Consciousness' Lost Leader: Abraham Tiro, the University of the North and the seeds of South Africa's student movement in the 1970s', *Journal of Southern African Studies*, 41(1) (2015), 173–86.

——, 'Blurred Lines and Ideological Divisions in South African Youth Politics', *African Affairs*, 115(461) (2016), 664–87.

Hirson, B., *Year of Fire, Year of Ash: The Soweto schoolchildren's revolt that shook Apartheid* (London, 2016, originally published 1979). [*Year of Fire, Year of Ash*]

Hooper, C., *Brief Authority* (London, 1960).

Horn, G.R., *Rebellion in Western Europe and North America, 1956–1976* (Oxford, 2007).

Hyslop, J., *The Classroom Struggle: Policy and resistance in South Africa, 1940–1990* (Durban, 1999).

Ivaska, A., 'Movement Youth in a Global Sixties Hub: The everyday lives of transnational activists in postcolonial Dar es Salaam' in R.I. Jobs and D.M. Pomfret (eds), *Transnational Histories of Youth in the Twentieth Century* (Basingstoke, 2015).

Johnson, S., '"The Soldiers of Luthuli": Youth in the politics of resistance in South Africa' in S. Johnson (ed.), *South Africa: No turning back* (Basingstoke, 1988), pp. 94–152.

Junod, H-A., *The Life of a South African Tribe* (New Hyde Park, NY, 1962).

Kane-Berman, J., *Soweto: Black revolt, White reaction* (Johannesburg, 1978).

Kanyane, C., *Turfloop, A Conscious Pariah: How the University of the North brought in the Age of Barack Obama beyond our wildest dreams* (Trafford, 2010).

Keller, E.G., *The Lady: The life and times of Winnie Mandela* (London, 1993). [*The Lady*] van Kessel, I., *Beyond our Wildest Dreams: The United Democratic Front and the transformation of South Africa* (Charlottesville, VA, 2000). [*Beyond our Wildest Dreams*]

Kirkaldy, A., *Capturing the Soul: The Vhavenda and the missionaries* (Pretoria, 2005). [*Capturing the Soul*]

Kirkaldy, A. and L. Kriel, 'Converts and conservatives: Missionary representations of African rulers in the Northern Transvaal, c. 1870–1900', *Le Fait Missionaires*, 18 (2006), 109–44.

Kretzschmar, L., *The Voice of Black Theology in South Africa* (Johannesburg, 1986).

Kriel, L. and A. Kirkaldy, '"Praying is the work of men, not the work of women": The response of Bahananwa and Vhavenda women to conversion in late nineteenth- century Lutheran missionary territories', *South African Historical Journal*, 61(2) (2009), 316–35.

Krige, E.J. and J.D. Krige. *The Realm of a Rain-Queen: A study of the pattern of Lobedu society* (London, 1965).

Lekgoathi, S., 'The United Democratic Front in Lebowa and KwaNdebele during the 1980s' in *SADET, The Road to Democracy in South Africa, Volume 4, Part 1 (1980–1990)* (Pretoria, 2010), pp. 613–67.

——, 'Teacher Militancy and the Rural Northern Transvaal Community of Zebediela, 1986–1994', *South African Historical Journal*, 58(1) (2007), 226–52.

——, 'Chiefs, Migrants, and North Ndebele Ethnicity in the Context of Surrounding Homeland Politics, 1965–1978', *African Studies*, 62(1) (2003), 53–77.

Lim, L., *The People's Republic of Amnesia: Tiananmen revisited* (Oxford, 2014).

Lissoni, A., 'Student Organisations in Lehurutshe and the Impact of Onkgopotse Abram Tiro', in A. Heffernan and N. Nieftagodien (eds), *Students Must Rise: Youth struggle in South Africa before and beyond Soweto '76* (Johannesburg, 2016), pp. 34–44.

Lobban, M., *White Man's Justice: South African political trials in the Black Consciousness era* (Oxford, 1996). [*White Man's Justice*]

Lodge, T., *Mandela: A Critical Life* (Oxford, 2006).

——, *Black Politics in South Africa since 1945* (London, 1983). [*Black Politics in South Africa*]

Maaba, B. and M.V. Mzamane, 'The Azanian People's Organisation, 1977–1990' in *SADET, The Road to Democracy in South Africa, Volume 4, Part 2 (1980–1990)* (Pretoria, 2010), pp. 1306–60. ['The Azanian People's Organisation']

——, 'The Black Consciousness Movement of Azania, 1979–1990' in *SADET, The Road to Democracy in South Africa, Volume 4, Part 2 (1980–1990)* (Pretoria, 2010), pp. 1361–98. ['The Black Consciousness Movement of Azania']

Macmillan, H., *The Lusaka Years: The ANC in exile in Zambia, 1963–1994* (Johannesburg, 2013). [*The Lusaka Years*]

Macneil, F., *AIDS, Politics, and Music in South Africa* (Cambridge, 2011).

Macqueen, I., 'Students, Apartheid and the Ecumenical Movement in South Africa, 1960–1975', *Journal of Southern African Studies*, 39(2) (2013), 447–63.

Magaziner, D., *The Law and the Prophets: Black Consciousness in South Africa, 1968– 1977* (Athens, OH, 2010). [*The Law and the Prophets*]

Malabela, M., 'We are already enjoying free education: Protests at the University of Limpopo (Turfloop)' in M. Langa (ed.), *#Hashtag: An Analysis of the #FeesMustFall Movement at South African Universities* (Centre for the Study of Violence and Reconciliation, 2017).

Mangcu, X., *Biko: A Life* (Johannesburg, 2013).

Mannheim, K., 'The Sociological Problem of Generations' in *Essays on the Sociology of Knowledge* (London, 1952).

Marks, M., '"We are fighting for the liberation of our people": Justifications of youth violence by activist youth in Diepkloof, Soweto', *Temps Modernes*, 585 (1995), 133–58.

Marx, A.W., *Lessons of Struggle: South African internal opposition, 1960– 1990* (Oxford, 1992). [*Lessons of Struggle*]

Massey, D., *Under Protest: The rise of student resistance at the University of Fort Hare* (Pretoria, 2010). [*Under Protest*]

Mathabatha, S., 'Missionary Schools, Student Uprisings in Lebowa and the Sekhukhuneland Students' Revolts, 1983–1986', *African Studies*, 64(2) (2005), 263–84.

Mazrui, A., *Political Values and the Educational Class in Africa* (London, 1978).

Mkhabela, S., *Open Earth and Black Roses: Remembering 16 June 1976* (Johannesburg, 2001).

Mngxitama, A. *et al.* (eds.), *Biko Lives!: Contesting the legacies of Steve Biko* (Basingstoke, 2008).

Moloi, T., *Place of Thorns: Black political protest in Kroonstad since 1976* (Johannesburg, 2015).

Moore, H.L. and T. Sanders, 'Magical Interpretations and Material Realities: An introduction' in H.L. Moore and T. Sanders (eds), *Magical Interpretations, Material Realities: Modernity, witchcraft, and the occult in postcolonial Africa* (London, 2001), pp. 1–27.

Mzamane, M.V., B. Maaba, and N. Biko, 'The Black Consciousness Movement' in SADET, *The Road to Democracy in South Africa, Volume 2, 1970–1980* (Pretoria, 2006).

Ndlovu, S.M., *The Soweto Uprisings: Counter-memories of June 1976* (Johannesburg, 1998).

Niehaus, I., *Witchcraft and a Life in the New South Africa* (Cambridge, 2013). [*Witchcraft and a Life*]

——, *Witchcraft, Power and Politics: Exploring the occult in the South African Lowveld* (London, 2001). [*Witchcraft, Power and Politics*]

——, 'Witchcraft in the New South Africa: From colonial superstition to postcolonial reality?' in Moore, H.L. and T. Sanders (eds), *Magical*

Interpretations, Material Realities: Modernity, witchcraft, and the occult in postcolonial Africa (London, 2001), pp. 184–205. ['Witchcraft in the New South Africa']

Nkomo, M. *et al.* (eds), *Within the Realm of Possibility: From disadvantage to development at the University of Fort Hare and the University of the North* (Cape Town, 2006). [*Within the Realm of Possibility*]

Oomen, B., *Chiefs in South Africa: Law, power and culture in the post-apartheid era* (Oxford, 2005).

Peires, J., *The Dead Will Arise: Nongqawuse and the great Xhosa cattle-killing movement of 1856–7* (Johannesburg, 1989).

——, 'Ethnicity and Pseudo-ethnicity in the Ciskei' in W. Beinart and S. Dubow (eds), *Segregation and Apartheid in Twentieth-Century South Africa* (Abingdon, 1995).

Posel, D., 'The ANC Youth League and the Politicization of Race', *Thesis Eleven,* 115(58) (2013), 58–76.

Ranger, T., *Peasant Consciousness and Guerrilla War in Zimbabwe* (Oxford, 1985).

Reynolds, C., *Memories of May '68: France's convenient consensus* (Cardiff, 2011).

Robinson, J., 'Fragments of the Past: Homeland politics and the South African transition, 1990–2014', *Journal of Southern African Studies,* 41(5) (2015), 953–67.

Ross, K., *May '68 and Its Afterlives* (Chicago, 2002).

Rueedi, F., 'Siyayinyova! Patterns of violence in the African townships of the Vaal Triangle, South Africa, 1980–86', *Africa,* 85(3) (2015), 395–416.

Schuster, L., *A Burning Hunger: One family's struggle against Apartheid* (London, 2004). [*A Burning Hunger*]

Seekings, J., *The UDF: A history of the United Democratic Front in South Africa, 1983- 1991* (Cape Town, 2000). [*The UDF*]

——, *Heroes or Villains? Youth Politics in the 1980s* (Johannesburg, 1993). [*Heroes or Villains?*]

Seidman, M., *The Imaginary Revolution: Parisian students and workers in 1968* (New York, 2004).

Tafira, H.K., *Black Nationalist Thought in South Africa: The persistence of an idea of liberation* (Basingstoke, 2016).

White, C., *From Despair to Hope: The Turfloop experience* (Sovenga, South Africa, 1997). [*From Despair to Hope*]

Woods, D., *Biko*, 3rd edn (New York, 1991).

van Wyk, C. (ed.), *We Write What We Like* (Johannesburg 2007).

Zewde, B., *The Quest for Socialist Utopia: The Ethiopian student movement, c. 1960- 1974* (Oxford, 2014).

Zuern, E., *The Politics of Necessity: Community organizing and democracy in South Africa* (Madison, WI, 2011).

Unpublished Papers and Theses*

Asheeke, T., 'Arming Black Consciousness: The turn to armed struggle and the formation of the Bokwe Group/Azanian Peoples' Liberation Front (APLF), April 1972–September 1976', under review with the *Journal of Southern African Studies* (2018).

——, 'Silenced Fronts of Africa's Liberation Struggle: Black power, Black Consciousness, and South Africa's armed struggle, 1967–1993' (State University of New York – Binghamton, PhD, 2018).

Botiveau, R., 'Les Avatars de l'African National Congress Youth League: ou l'invention d'une organisation politique de jeunesse sud-africaine' (Université Paris Panthéon-Sorbonne, Le Master de Science politique, 2005).

Bridger, E., 'South Africa's Female Comrades: Gender, identity, and student resistance to Apartheid in Soweto, 1984–1994' (University of Exeter, PhD, 2016).

Brown, J., 'Public Protest and Violence in South Africa, 1948–1976 (University of Oxford, DPhil, 2009). ['Public Protest and Violence']

Gibbs, T., 'Transkei's Notables, African Nationalism and the Transformation of the Bantustans, c.1954–1994' (University of Oxford, DPhil, 2010). ['Transkei's Notables']

Glaser, C., 'Youth Culture and Politics in Soweto, 1958–1976' (University of Cambridge, PhD, 1994).

Heffernan, A., 'The Ralushai Commission and a South African Witch-hunt in Legal and Historical Perspective' (University of Oxford, MSc, 2008). ['The Ralushai Commission']

McKay, C., 'A History of the National Union of South African Students (NUSAS), 1956–1970' (University of South Africa (UNISA), PhD, 2015).

Macqueen, I., 'Re-Imagining South Africa: Black Consciousness, radical Christianity and the New Left, 1967–1977' (University of Sussex, PhD, 2011).

Maftashe, I., 'Gender Politics and Activism: A comparative study of African National Congress Youth League branches in Seshego (Limpopo)' (University of the Witwatersrand, MA Thesis, 2015).

Matona, T., 'Student Organisation and Political Resistance in South Africa: An analysis of the Congress of South African Students, 1979–1985' (University of Cape Town, Honours Thesis, 1992). ['Student Organisation and Political Resistance']

Murphy, O., 'Race, Violence, and Nation: African nationalism and popular politics in South Africa, 1948–1970' (University of Oxford, DPhil, 2013). ['Race, Violence, and Nation']

---

* Where necessary, shortened forms of titles have been used for ease of citation in the text, and are indicated following the full citation in the bibliography.

Rueedi, F., 'Political Mobilisation, Violence and Control in the Townships of the Vaal Triangle, South Africa, c.1976–1986' (University of Oxford, DPhil, 2013).
Stokes, S., 'Paris and Mexico City: 1968 student activism' (University of Oxford, DPhil, 2011).

Index